The foundations for building a successful family

Jacquelin Xavier

THE FOUNDATIONS FOR BUILDING A SUCCESSFUL FAMILY

Read me, your marriage life will be magnificent, prosper, delicious and full of success!

Index

Preface 9

Love at first sight 12

The stage of the election 25

The love of adventure 41

Pre- in love 53

Discipline in communication before the choice 57

The act of falling in love 76

The emotion 91

Thought and spirit 99

The couple's behavior at the dating stage 109

Love without compromise 122

The uneven yoke 131

The compromise covenant 140

The marriage vow Part 1 145

The marriage vow Part 2 150

The husband's papers at home 162

The wife's papers at home 173

The profession and the finance of the couple 185

The couple's economy in married life	195
The expenses of the two at home	205
Growths within the home	220
You and I	224
The first temptation in the Garden of Eden	235
Children in marriage	242
The discipline and correction of children	262
Spiritual discipline at home	276
The true worship of the Creator	282
The church's worship and worship department	295
Vices in the home	312
The homosexuality	323
Assaults and abuse in the home	336
The couple's separation and divorce	346
The role of grandparents in the discipline and correction of grandchildren	365
The children's thanks to the parents	373
About me	384

"But we all, with open face beholding as in a glass the glory of the Lord, are changed into the same image from glory to glory, even as by the Spirit of the Lord": [2 Corinthians 3: 18].

This is how our homes are when Jesus is the center of them.

A good family education is the best subject that can lead our children to success from generation to generation. Well-bred sons are like plants grown in their youth, our daughters are like carved corners like those of a palace.

The main requirement for having a successful family is "fear of Jehovah." If you fear Jehovah, you will let Jesus be the center of your home, because there is no success or happiness in any home without Jesus.

This book is written in favor of all those who want to have their happy homes with Christ, and who also want to see a world without gender and family violence; where the home becomes a nest of love or a spring in which all those who inhabit it, can satisfy their thirst for love. The home should be like a dove's nest where the young receive good training for a better tomorrow.

This book is dedicated to all present and future married people, as well as all those people who have a lot of time in that beautiful school called marriage, which is the source of love. If we read very carefully, it can serve as the guide that will lead us to the final victory.

Hopefully it will help them obtain the greatest benefits in married life, as well as in the education and training of children.

I hope these tips can help you have Jesus as the center of the home; even if there are contrary winds, we will never sink. There will be no separation or divorce, because with Jesus we will be more than conquerors.

AMEN.

Preface

There are many books dedicated to the topic of family formation, but not all have completely covered the problems of families, or have put the Bible's advice first, before human wisdom. Science does not consider God the creator of the family; she devises secular theories to remove God from the family. But you can never have a united family without the presence of God.

All married people, young people, singles, should read this book to discover all the great secrets that are written within it; his advice to have an exemplary and different family. This book will prepare us for the practical realities of home life: your opportunities, your responsibilities, your defeats, and your professional, financial, and moral successes. How you cope with those experiences, whether you are to succeed or be a victim of circumstances, will largely depend on your preparedness to deal with them.

True education has been defined as the harmonious development of all faculties, or failure for a lifetime. The preparation that is received during the first years at home and during the subsequent years in the school where you have studied, is essential for success in life, because they are two educations that can allow you to be successful in family and professional life.

So a good father should not put his children in any school, they should be in schools where teachers are fearful of Jehovah.

Why is education essential in the development of the individual's mind and the formation of his character?

This book comes to answer that question. And is that if we make the wrong choice, all members of the family will fail from generation to generation. All people who want to have a successful family should avoid unequal relationships and unequal yokes, because they are two great dangers that can destroy any home: if one goes to the left and the other goes to the right, the relationship will never work. .

A person who does not abide by the rules of the Bible, it is very difficult to have a successful family. There are three things a person needs to have a successful family: God first; second, a good family education or training; third, a good profession. The three always walk together.

No one is responsible for the success or failure of others, only the parents. You must also have a good training and mental development. It is very clear and true, and all the clarity of a good family and professional education that tends to develop the mental faculties, to give skill to the hands in useful tasks, etc.

A family and professional education guided by the hand of God, is the source of all wisdom and understanding. When the individual is God-fearing, he can never do wrong to have money; your family will prosper with God's blessing; all the things that he or she is going to do, they will do it consulting God first.

The theme of family formation and education are capital in the life of each individual in order to be a good citizen, a good Christian, where they have been prepared very well from the bosom of their parents, which translates into good conduct towards their parents and their children, with good morals, professional and economic development and, above all, God-fearing.

With immaculate personalities and hearts faithful to principles, because Solomon said: "The fear of Jehovah is the beginning of wisdom, because nobody can have wisdom if they do not fear Jehovah."

All people who have received good family education are distinguished by their values, as are those who have been forged with negative values. Its fruits are made known in society. Some healthy, others rotten.

As the world is shaped by bad teachings, it spins to the rhythm of that tares. How will this world be after 2030, if Jesus has not returned? Well, I see every day that good family education is losing value. Now it is cartoons, violence movies, witchcraft movies, soap operas transmitting obsessive and selfish love, reggaeton, denbow, drug traffickers idealized as heroes... those who are educating children.

Every mother and father should ask themselves that question: how will my children be in 20 to 30 years? Every father and mother needs time to educate their children well so that they can make a difference.

No one can give and teach good education to their children if they do not fear Jehovah, because it is the Holy Spirit who is going to teach us how we should educate our children. There are two types of education: that taught by the Holy Spirit supervised by God, and that of the enemy through vices and all the things that can lead us to perdition.

Each father and mother must know which is between the two, the one they will choose to educate their children.

The decision is in your hands, and with it the future of your children, society and humanity in general.

Chapter 1

Love at first sight

Human beings do not have the same techniques or the same ways of falling in love or speaking for the first time with those they like.

Each individual has his own way of approaching and speaking to the person who attracts him; nor can you not have a single strategy of approaching the guy who thinks he can be part of his love life for life. It is a process that has many steps to follow until you reach your final destination.

Conquering a girl for the first time is not so easy, on the contrary, the person who does not have very good strategies to seduce her heart with good contagious expressions of love, not for a temporary taste, will fail. It must be a feeling emanating from beyond the heart. Because falling in love is something that is so sweet and special everyone should take it as seriously as possible.

The conqueror must have different ways or techniques to approach his admired, never forget that each individual has their own way of approaching, nor can the same expressions be used with all women; everyone has their own way of falling in love. As a conqueror you should look for the propitious moments where she herself indicates how you should approach her and express your wishes.

All your expressions have to be very calculated, without mistakes, never speak to speak; you have to avoid not infecting it with the emotion of the moment; You have to master body language very well, with good vocabularies and a very pleasant tone of voice, because it is the first impression that will define who you are, what you are looking for, what type of relationship you want to have with her.

If you fail at the first impression, it will be very difficult to recover again, and if she has discovered your mistakes on the first attempt, you will never be able to conquer the throne of her heart, no matter how hard you try. Because all those in a hurry will never reach their final destination.

The signs that she is in love

As everyone has their own taste, it is not an obligation for her to choose you as her future partner, although all the ladies fall in love with those who listen, they are free to make their own decisions, whether good or bad. When making her decision, she must take into account these considerations:

1.- Accept the conqueror immediately, either for love or for some interest.

2.- A deep friendship relationship, where there are some qualities in common, or some interests that merit time to discover and analyze if it is something that can be followed up or not.

3.- A simple friendship without any love interest, sometimes over time automatically becomes a courtship, for the deals and time; because love is a mystery and nobody can understand it.

4.- Total rejection. All men should try to avoid that stage because it is a total failure. For that reason, man must take all necessary precautions not to fall on this level.

Ladies and gentlemen, never forget: a good romantic relationship must start with a good friendship, when love manifests itself between the two individuals with all the chemistry. Thus, even if many opposing winds come, they can never knock it down, because it has very solid bases.

Friendship is the key that opens all doors; it is the guide that can lead you to total success. You can never have a good friendship without sensitivity, or a good human heart, true friendship does not seek its own, nor take advantage of the moment, it is a total surrender with all the heart, body and spirit.

Friendship is so vast it never ceases to exist in any relationship. It is the main base that can lead you to all kinds of successes.

When the man wants to have a relationship beyond a simple friendship with a beautiful lady, he must use some expressions where she does not confuse the loving friendship with a normal friendship. The expressions to be used in this case are: "What beautiful eyes you have!"; "What pretty lips you have!"; "You have a beautiful voice!"; "What a beautiful mouth you have!"...

They are expressions that make her understand you are looking for more than a simple friendship; that allow the prince to strike her most sentimental nerve. Automatically you can see the change it causes, and if you should continue or not.

Second, you must find something in her that you like, such as pants, skirt, blouse, dress, shoes, clothes, watch. All ladies feel good when a gentleman is talking to her that way. The good gentleman always talks to her at all times with great respect and simplicity, he can never face her at any time; you should always treat her like a queen.

If you want to touch her, never do it without her permission, you must use all your courtesy to ask permission; And if she gives the reason or permission, you should not touch her where it is not allowed.

Because by emotion she can accept, and by emotion she can make another decision against you. You must know is in the knowledge stage.

No one has the right yet. There are also many women who are very wise, they can let themselves be touched where you have no right, to discover who you are, what you are really looking for with her, for any nonsense you can lose a good opportunity. What place especially should the knight ask his conqueror where he can touch himself? His leg if they are both sitting, his back, his hand, etc...

When there is visual and physical contact, there are more possibilities to start connecting with each other. You must control your emotions at all times. All those people who cannot dominate and control their emotional state are doomed to failure.

There are many people who when they have gotten what they were looking for, the friendship ends. It is a great mistake on their part. Friendship must not end in no relationship for any reason, only the death can end that relationship.

It is the friendship that will allow one of them to vent the good and bad moments that have happened during the day. Friendship is an expression of trust to express good wishes towards your partner, who is your refuge and protection. Your best friend after God.

All people, both Christians or not, should use friendship in their homes. It must be the essential or primary part of all relationships, no one should share the secrets or life of their partner with others. They must be private bone secrets for both of you. Therefore, each individual must take enough time to know and understand if the guy they are courting is their ideal partner.

Given this great decision, if there are still doubts, it is not the time to take the necessary step. You must be very confident in all the decisions you are going to make, because all the bad decisions you have made in the beginning will affect your future. Everyone has been wrong, because nobody is perfect, but everything possible must be done not to fall.

What is friendship?

It is a beautiful relationship of affection, sympathy and trust that is established between two people who are family or not, in order to give pleasure to their infinite friendship. Also two lovers can be two good friends, two husbands must be very good friends, because friendship has no limit or social rank or race or color, it is universal.

In the first impression until the time of trust, if you do not give any sign that you want more than a friendship, when you establish the friendly relationship it will make it much more difficult to express your true feelings. Well, automatically, she will feel cheated and without any confidence in you; she will be closed little by little until the end of this relationship.

How can you conquer a young Christian girl?

You cannot use the same technique or the same expressions to seduce a Christian young girl than a non-Christian one. Each one has its audience, its customs, its rule, its principles and its vocabulary.

Now, if a man wants to avoid the unequal yoke, he should not fall in love with any Christian woman, the same for the Christian boy, because it is a mortal danger for all those falling in love outside their context, because each one has his culture and his way of life. Live different from the other.

Falling in love with someone who does not share the same Christian faith with you, is putting yourself in the enemy's net.

Now, if it is strategic, you must use the language of her and her world, to get to conquer her or win her completely. Now, if you are going to use your own versions, you should know that the Christian will be much more difficult to conquer or attract than the world. And this is much more risky for the Christian boy who is in love.

If he uses Christian expression and language with her, she will mock and exploit financially and if he uses her expression, it is a danger to his Christian faith, for that reason there are more Christian girls who have had romantic relationships with the unconfessed than the boys, because she is the recipient.

The true Christian never makes any decision without first consulting God. Jesus as a good shepherd always enlightens and guides all those who seek him with faith through constant prayer. The true Christian never disconnects for a second with his God, for them God is their only true and faithful friend. They are very difficult to conquer if you want to win them you have to win their God first, otherwise you work in vain.

The Christian girl always lets the Holy Spirit guide her life; she knows there is no romantic relationship with a Christian and a wordly. If there is conquest it is in vain: the suitor will never reach his goal. And if by some mistake she gives some signs of love — and since nobody is perfect — God will act quickly in her favor, and although she is very much in love, she will never reject divine intervention by any man.

If there have been many Christians who have had romantic relationships with worldlings, it is because they never invited God before making any decision. Sometimes God makes his intervention for them who never reject it. They say they have free will to choose the people they like. There is another group that accepts the intervention from above with two modalities:

1.- In their prayers they ask God for the kind of person and the qualities they must have. They put the choice in their hands.

2.- They look for the guy and they want God to accept it by force. All people who have that mentality never have a stable relationship, because God never does anything without first using the prophets. It is we who need God, no God to us.

God has never reacted like humans. He always sees the person from the inside. All those who want God to intervene in their relationships must do things according to the Bible.

How to conquer a shy girl?

You cannot use the same method of approaching a shy girl as an open one, each one has its language and its expressions different from the other: the shy one can say bad expressions, bad words to get away or discourage her.

The man in charge of this situation should not be discouraged or answer in the same way, not because she doesn't appreciate you, it's because she can't control or handle her nerves. What should the conqueror do in this situation? Leave her alone for a moment until she calms down; the gentleman must change the conversation to a level where she can have nerve control again, so that the two of them can reach their goals.

The shy one speaks little. He is the man who has to make her talk, otherwise she will never say anything.

How can you find out when a girl is nervous?

People when we are nervous, we look for unconscious ways to calm ourselves. There are various gestures of body language that we can observe in a person to detect that they are nervous. The gesture of nervousness par excellence is biting. There are those who bite the inside of the mouth, the tongue, the hands, the nails or a pencil, etc. [According to Sandra Burgos].

Everyone goes through this situation, when you are doing something in public for the first time, you feel that the sky is falling apart on you, regardless of rank or social class, everyone lives this moment of insecurity; that proof of self-control.

Therefore, no one should underestimate the person who is in such an uncontrollable situation, the only solution to recover, is the support of the public.

From childhood, they must put them to develop their talents in public, so when they are older they will never be afraid or nervous at all, because they have already got used to being in front of the public.

The shy girl does not express herself in the same way as the uncluttered one; They also do not give the same signs of love to the man they like, they are two totally different people in everything, if the man has seen the signs of love in her, he has to go a little slower so as not to intimidate her, because the nerve can change all the good wishes that she had for you. Also, everyone has started with a first time.

When the man has gained her trust, she will start to express herself without nerves, you will automatically get to the point you want with her.

The shy one is much more romantic than the open one, because the latter experiences the practice much more than the theory, although the two have their places in a relationship. As she feels insecure in herself, the lover must open all doors so that she can feel confident and express her personality, feelings and concerns without prejudice.

How the poor-spirited feels insecure by nature, the lover must have a lot of patience, he needs a third time, even a sixth time, so that she can be in confidence, otherwise all opportunities to be with her can be lost.

How does a shy girl behave when she is in love with someone?

There are two categories of shy girls:

1.- As she feels insecure, she will never show any sign of love, even if a melted strawberry ice cream is made, she could use her best friend as an intermediary to transmit her interests to the boy.

If she knows the boy has received the messages, the nerves will put her in extreme trouble, if the man does not know how to handle that type of situation, all the opportunity may be lost, even if she is the one interested.

The man must control his emotions to start a very simple conversation with her, until she is in the right frame of mind, where their common interests can meet.

2.- she falls in love like all the ladies, but she keeps herself or stays silent and says nothing, nor comments anything, neither to her best friend nor to anyone, her tool is: transmit some body signals with all shyness and shame towards the knight.

She can also send some requests through social networks, because as she is very shy and careful, she doesn't want anyone to know if she's interested in this guy.

When the guy has received those signals, he cannot go with despair before her, he must start a friendship until all the common desires are in tune. Because despair is the source of failure, you can never take things in a hurry. Everything in time.

There are three great primordial signs that can indicate that the shy girl is interested in you, and they are:

1.- She looks you straight in the eyes and with a contagious smile and, at the same time, with fear, because she still doesn't know how you are going to react.

2.- Expressing their intention to be by your side although with fear and nerves, with actions that could generate negative or positive responses.

3.- In body language, if she is white, her face blushes, her gaze at every moment reveals the hormonal convulsion of her body. If she is close to you, drop some objects with clumsy movements, etc.

How should the conqueror treat her?

If there is common interest, you should find a way to respond positively to her concerns as a gentleman, if she answers negatively never react in the same way. You must find a way that she feels good and safe with your behavior.

If there is no common interest it is not an obligation to accept it, you have your right to choose the person you like, but she as a human has the right to fall in love with any guy as well. Now, it is you who must know if she suits you or not, the good gentleman is not an opportunist, he is someone who has morals and awareness, who knows how to choose between good and evil.

When man is faced with this situation, he must put two things into action according to his conscience:

1.- You must answer the conqueror with positive signs and acceptance, never forget, although it was she who had the initiative, you should always follow all stages of falling in love, to see if you are making a worthy choice. If man is a Christian, he must go before God first to see if it is his will, because no Christian should choose anyone without God's approval first.

Now, if the two are not Christians, the man must follow her direction to approach it, without any despair or rush, when you spend time on something you like, you can taste all its flavor and fragrance: that flavor will always remain on your lips.

2.- If there is no common interest, you should not make her feel bad, nor be rude. There are two ways you can respond to her:

1.- You can answer his signals in a very correct way, like a good gentleman, without approaching danger, you must control your emotional state at all times. If you approach danger to take advantage of its weakness without anything seriously, you become an abuser, because nobody can play with the feeling of others.

2.- You can behave as if you have not seen anything, after a few minutes, you can leave this place, because the good knight must flee from temptation.

All the gentlemen who are making this beautiful decision are supporting pro-family; They are participating in a better world where love and prosperity reign; where all children can be born and raised in the love nests built by their parents.

There are many gentlemen who never say no, they always like to take advantage of all the opportunities or the innocence of the ladies, to abuse them sexually and economically, although they know that they will not be with them or form homes. All men must have the character to say no, even if it costs them a lot.

How should you answer a person who is totally in love?

Try not to take advantage of his feeling, his weakness, his sincerity... As a good gentleman, you have to know how to handle this situation with great care and delicacy. If there is no common interest, or qualities, don't try to give false hope in vain. Love must be mutual, whether Christian or not, it must be a realization, a life project. The change must begin with yourself.

If Martin Luther King thinks the same way you do, we could never have a world with less racism. No black could marry or be in the same place with whites. Every human must be a Martin Luther King, if we want a better world tomorrow.

Martin Luther King delivered his famous speech that went down in history with the name "I have a dream," turning the Southern movement into a declaration on civil rights across the United States.

Martin Luther King thought that we are all responsible for the well-being of everyone, "anything that affects one directly, affects everyone indirectly", so "injustice anywhere is a threat to justice everywhere. We are caught in an inescapable network of solidarity.

Also Martin Luther made his own decision in such a critical era to make the reform on religion, although all decisions were very difficult for him, he never thought negatively. He always saw victory and reform in his mind. Each individual must become a Martin Luther King, a Martin Luther, to make a difference.

Before giving a false hope to a lady, you must think the same as Martin Luther King, we are all responsible for the destruction of this world, each man and woman must cooperate in the recovery of a better world without suffering or pain or tears, where the true love can reign over all the earth; where all children can receive a decent home to develop in all kinds of growth.

Martin Luther King saw things differently from all men of that time. In the 21st century, all men must practice the thinking of those two great men: Luther and Luther.

No one should fall in love to fall in love, it must be a feeling without any ephemeral interest, but in the long term. Those of little faith say love does not exist, of course, for them, but for God and those who take refuge in his light.

True love will last forever!

Chapter 2

The stage of the election

Choosing a partner for life is not something as easy as many think: there are many steps, rules, disciplines, that each individual must follow if he wants to achieve his destiny.

No one has been born to be rejected or failed at any time; Each individual has been specially created to be blessed with many prosperities but, due to the oversights of the rules, there are many people who have failed in their choices: this for violating all the rules of how to choose an adorable couple for life.

Not only has humanity violated all the rules of infatuation, the choice falls completely into despair, preventing them from having enough time to get to know each other a little better before creating definitive ties. It is very complex that no one should take lightly.

Lovers should take a maximum of time to get to know each other even 25%. There are many secrets hidden among people, with little time to know each other they will not be able to discover them.

It is true there is no school or university that teaches individuals to fall in love, but with the discoveries and analysis, they can very likely discover a little of that guy they want to choose as their lifelong partner.

Humanity's great problem is haste, and haste equals failure. If you need to have a relationship with a lot of growth; You must take the time to find it.

What should you take into account to choose a correct person?

The crush is the first look. Try not to woo for emotion, or for something outside that can destroy, it must be for something natural, which was born only between the two; it must be because of the chemistry between the two; you must avoid all kinds of temporary emotions and adventure; You must identify if there is a real feeling or if for some interests.

How can you find out? Through signs and reactions, although love has no limit, race or color, the two must have different qualities in common. Each must correspond to the other, the two must be the same.

If there is inferiority or superiority between the two, the same hierarchical relationship will exist in that relationship. All those people who want to sink into your love life, must learn to make a good choice.

All people who fall in love out of interest, or for what they have seen, or for some objects, will end in failure or total defeat, because there is love even when the objects are working. If there are any breaks or losses, love automatically ends too. If you want to be successful in your relationships, you must woo for feelings, not for material desires that can be broken by being made of mud and not of gold.

What should you do to make sure if your woo is totally in love with you?

You have to let him talk and analyze his expressions, check his mood very well, if he is in love with emotion or feeling. If he is in love with emotion or with some objects, lies a lot, never remembers anything, speaks like a parrot; sometimes his words are not well organized. If you want to know if he's lying, let him talk and ask him the first question in a week. He will answer you something else because he will never remember the previous ones.

Liars or deceivers are much more than good people. They are everywhere, they are like salmonella that reproduce every second. The vast majority are difficult to discover, you need a microscope to see them. Among the tools to use to discover them, is the lie detector, the holy bible, a good discovery and a deep analysis.

You have to ask them wise questions, very calculated, because in the time of discovery what he wants from you will be manifested: if something formal or temporary, if for a definite or indefinite time; because there are many bad men in the world whose plans are to destroy all the young girls. They are in the streets like lions roaring looking for the one who devours, who are their prey?

They are all studious young women who are looking for a better life through professional preparation, but their purpose is to plunge them into poverty with two or three children aimlessly and direction. They must be oriented to take care of the birds of prey that fly over each Garden of Eden.

Cannibals have no compassion for any prey, although their stomachs are full of food, their mentality and nature are to hunt with or without motives. They are very bloody. The most dangerous man-eaters in the world are difficult to identify, because they are dressed like sheep, sometimes they speak and react like lamb, they are meek like them.

However, they are more bloodthirsty than cannibals who look like such; They will never be able to change their nature by their own strength, they have the behavior of sheep, the bodies of lambs, but their hearts are of lions. Yes, they are very difficult to discover.

No maiden can give her heart to a stranger without discovery and deep analysis. Parents must assume their role and teach them to discover the deadly cannibals that are in all parts of the world. No maiden can resist their strength and power. They are psychologically and mentally well prepared to catch their prey. The only solution that can save any maiden is to flee from temptation.

A young girl who is in front of a very dangerous and very deadly wild animal will be devoured. Everyone knows that the admirer is a very ferocious cannibal, but since she does not take any advice, neither from parents nor from neighbors, everyone is seeing the danger except her, because she is so contaminated with its poison, the only solution is to drop her because nobody can save her only God.

Tips are very important before making any decisions. But all those who do not take advice are totally doomed to failure for life. The only supreme being who needs no advice is Deity. So everyone needs advice before making any decisions.

The wise ask for advice before acting, but fools think they know everything, they never ask for advice before doing anything, so their destiny is to burn, both in life and in death.

A wise man who has advised never puts has reacted at the same moment, he analyzes all at the end he draws his own conclusión. That is why no one should act in the moment of emotion, they must remain calm, only after understanding the designs of God towards him/her, they must act.

How should you behave in the time of falling in love?

Everything must begin at that stage, the time to know each other is essential in any relationship: friendship as sentimental. You cannot ask the same questions when interest is at stake, nor can you ask question on question.

You can never ask another question if you are not satisfied with the first question; the exhibitor must never interrupt his presentation, without the termination he will never be able to understand the subject, he must wait for the conclusion to give the subjection.

If you have any questions you should write it down, if it is very urgent you should ask permission before boarding, when you are in front of a wise exhibitor, never interrupting it unnecessarily. He can fully read your thoughts and mind, no receiver should let his mind and thought read under any concept, if you want to reach the heights of success.

You should never leave any gaps open, you should close everything, so you can get to what you are looking for. There are many people who transmit or give all the information to the adversary without realizing it. Never forget at the moment of the conversation your future is at stake or in danger, you must defend it with all integrity.

All the girls must know that the lovers have nothing to lose, it is only them, so they must take all precautions to be victorious. If Eve had taken the necessary precautions to flee from that great adversary, the world would never have been filled with so much evil.

All maidens must be very careful with cannibals who use a beautiful and romantic verb, a fine net so that they can fall; they know no girl can resist with the verbs of love. That is why many authors say ladies fall in love by sweetening their ears. Not only do they have the theory, they also have the practice. Fortunately, cannibals' skills last for a short time.

How can you identify when a cut girl is in love?

There are many men who cannot distinguish family education and the courtesy of a young girl with falling in love, are two different things.

It cannot be confused, although the two almost have the same fruits, they are not the same, the simplicity and the smile of her does not mean that she is in love, it is because she has received a good formation before which everyone is equal and each one You must have the same humane treatment.

What is the difference between kindness and infatuation?

They are two very different things, there is nothing in common between the two, a kind person, is someone who has received a good training in etiquette and protocol, someone who thinks everyone is the same, the rich as the poor, professionals as the illiterate, the whites and the blacks, all deserve the same treatment.

Someone who does not have the meaning of guy, who shows affection to everyone. The person who has received a good family formation, applies these principles to all the people around her.

Everyone notices the quality of all those Christians who are following Christ, because God has no love, "He is love." If God is love, all followers must have love for all people. Falling in love is feeling and saying how you feel about the other guy. There are two steps to follow when you are in love:

1.- emit signals of love towards the other person, if it is reciprocal, she will be caught in the network of the other's signals.

2.- It has to be mutual, because nobody falls in love alone. When a man confuses kindness with love, he will never be able to conquer the throne of her heart, because she did not feel the same. Her answer will be "no thanks".

Nobody falls in love for falling in love, they have to be very sure of what you are going to grow, nobody wants to work in vain. So you must make very sure of what you are going to do, if you are going to be successful or not.

If you want to meet a person you have to talk. Extracting the right words, you can get what you are looking for, when you finish knowing her and want a definitive reaction in her, you ask the closed question, where she can say yes or no. Sure, what suits you best in this situation is yes.

There are also girls who are very open, very friendly, so their simplicity, their kindness, can be confused with infatuation. Before expressing your feelings towards her, you have to be very sure that you have discovered some love in her, otherwise failure awaits you.

Distinguishing the whim from the true intention of friendship are two very similar things, but they are not the same. Therefore, man must identify very well what state she is in tune with.

Before expressing your feelings to a lady, you should see or find some signs that may reveal her intention, otherwise it is pure failure. You must know the man cannot and must not be mistaken in the conquest. So signs are weapons and tools that can help you discover her intention for you, you have to make sure that there is some quality in common; the signs are guides that can open all roads to her throne.

Who between the two must conquer the other's heart first?

In Latin American countries, it is not very common to see a lady seduce a man, because they teach us ma.chismo from birth.

If that happens, we consider her a prostitute, or that she is useless, obviously, the lady is equal to the man and has feelings and sensations the same as men, therefore, she has her right to express like any man.

In Europe and the USA, the lady conquers the man like any man, she expresses her feelings without fear like any gentleman, not because she does not serve, it is because the two are equal in love. If that happens with any male she is not criticized, on the contrary, she considers herself as a brave lady.

A woman who has conquered her beloved will never be unfaithful to him, nor will she mistreat him, or let him suffer under any circumstances, she will treat him like a king, like a prince. The man must also reciprocate in the same way, because where love is sown, the same love is reaped in abundance.

When a lady seduces a gentleman, either with words or signs, It is because she is very much in love with all her heart. No man should miss that great opportunity. But historically, they are the gentlemen who have seduced the ladies, and this with direct, conquering signs. Since they are by nature an issuing agent.

What should the gentleman do when he is falling in love with a doll for the first time?

The great mistake of most gentlemen, is that they do not know how they should fall in love with a flower, there are many who fall in love with wealth, the vehicle or something temporary. But that is not the correct way in which they must conquer a queen; they must send the signals first before approaching to her. They are the signals that go as the intermediary between the gentleman and the lady.

The signs will depend on where and how you found her: if it is a person you have seen for the first time, or if it is someone you are used to talking to. This last option is the best, because we are already known. If it is the first time, the signs are mandatory.

What should you do in this situation?

The only recourse you can use in this case are signals through body language. How should you transmit the signals? You have to be in a place not far away where she can see the transformations, staring into her eyes with a cute contagious smile. When you are sure your transmissions are past, you have to look elsewhere. You have to do that several times: transmit attractive signals, not words.

The importance of body language in falling in love

It is a way of studying someone through their body movement, expressive, appellate or communicative meaning of learned or somagenetic gestures, not oral; of visual, auditory or tactile perceptions in relation to the linguistic and paralinguistic structure and, of course, with the situation.

Love at first sight is made or demonstrated with gestures, where the interested party can transmit it with good eye contact, a look, with a very contagious smile, where the interested party can express their love for the first time to their admirer his/her answer can mean two things: acceptance or curiosity, if it is acceptance he/she is in a position where the conqueror can approach without any fear.

However, most express themselves out of curiosity, because they want to know what is behind those signs. All ladies are curious by nature, so their reaction should not be confused with signs of infatuation. Many men have failed in this way, because their despair does not allow them to see exactly what they want to convey through their responses. There are many ladies who have answered positively in three ways:

1.- I also like you, I give you the privilege of conquering my heart.

2.- I give you the entrance only for a simple friendship.

3.- I let you get your hopes up, just to hurt yourself and then completely reject you.

At the same time that you are expressing yourself or knowing her, you must know and discover who she really is. If she is a reliable girl, where you can have all the confidence or not, because little by little she is going to say you who is she and what she wants from you, through body language. Is the same for both sexes; that is why the time of mutual knowledge and discovery is essential in all kinds of relationships.

Her attitude is going to tell what kind of relationship she can bring you. It is worse for a man when he is at the level of rejection. No girl can reject a boy at the same time for his misunderstanding. Rejection means she does not want to have any relationship or communication with you for any condition. For that reason, you must control your mood and your emotion when you are talking to her.

The woman has many ways to feign a man, the most common trap in most of the ladies is: she can open any romantic conversation with you to see your reaction. If the man wants to conquer and win her heart, he must not fall into this trap, he must automatically change the conversation. The exhibitor must find a way to guide his topic to the field of his domain.

If you fall into her trap under the blindness of enthusiasm, she will inadvertently treat you for what you are not, you must keep your emotion at check, nor let yourself be provoked at any time. The expression of provoke can destroy all the good wishes and feelings you have towards others. Before answering a question, you should think of four things:

1.- why the question.

2.- the cause of the question.

3.- How should you answer it.

4.- the reason for the question.

Never answer yes or no, because all questions have their consequences at the end. What is a question really? A question can be a linguistic expression used to make a request for information, or the request itself made by that expression. The requested information can be provided through a response. The question has two phases:

1.- I just discovered something in you, I want to confirm it through a question.

2.- I want to make you fall into my trap, I am going to ask you a question, but I want you to answer in the way that I want.

In order for someone to manipulate other people, they must ask questions, So everyone must think and analyze each question before answering it. All lovers must fall in love with people of their level to avoid manipulation.

There are three very essential places where lovers can meet each other the first time: in church, at work, and at university. There are many more places where they can be found but those three are more common. There are other frequent places to look for infatuation are: social networks.

There are all kinds of people who are connected through the networks, but for me it is not an ideal place for people to seek a relationship to form. There are many cases that have passed through the networks that put a good relationship at risk.

They can have friends on the networks, but they should not fall in love with them, because they do not really know who they are talking to. They must have "face-to-face" visual contacts to see if one is lying, because body language is a detector of all lies.

There are many people who have found good partners on social networks, if a person wants to have a good choice and a successful relationship, the two must meet and talk in person, face to face before...

The boy's maneuvers when he's in love

At work: if they work in the same department, the man must help her finish her job as quickly as possible, so that the two can go out to eat together. Along the way, he must talk about what she likes, more often about work, he always has to congratulate her on everything so that she feels good about you.

Never speak in vain speech so that she does not get bored with you, if she is bored with your expressions, she will never want to talk to you more, and thus lose all opportunities to conquer her. Must have a lot of laughs or a smile in your conversations. When they are talking, you cannot change a journalist, of course you can ask questions, but when it is necessary.

Try not to transform into a clown; Your expressions must be very calculated and fun. When you arrive at the restaurant, you must help her select the varieties, you have to choose the same menu with her, at lunchtime you must be her waiter, so she will see that you are a good gentleman. Possibly she can let you conquer her heart.

At the university: if they are in the same course or not. You have to ask her if she has understood everything. If not, you should help her understand the class as clearly as possible, so you can have more confidence to conquer her heart.

You have to ask her precise and contextualized questions: What motivated you to choose that university? What motivated you to choose this career? Any response, you have to congratulate her on her good choice. At recess time you have to invite her in the cafeteria, because all women like detail men.

If you have a vehicle, you have to take her home every day and equally go to look for her until, little by little, you penetrate the field of love, so the two of you will be gaining confidence. Because without trust it is impossible to reach her heart. All conquerors must learn that as a lesson, sloths cannot search for girlfriends because a relationship is costly in terms of time and energy.

It is highly recommended to have entry before looking for brides, without money they will never be able to cover the expenses, if they do not have cars they must have even a motorcycle, because efficiency and freedom of movement is paramount.

In the church: you must be in all the activities that she is, so that you can speak. To know a person a little better you should ask. In the same vein, there are questions you can't ask if she doesn't give you permission. The questions you can ask her are: Have you been born in this religion? How long have you been a Christian?

How long have you been a member of that group? Etc... At the end of the meetings or services, you should accompany her to his house, but you cannot enter without her will or permission.

The young Christian woman reviews everything. You could miss the opportunity you are looking for due to a slip.

If she does not have a vehicle, on the day of worship or activities you can come and look for her. Never move things forward, you still can't think that she belongs to you without a pact between the two. And to have that pact, she has to give the reason or the permission, just as the conviction and agreement of both are necessary.

Surely, there were many men to whom she gave permission to talk, who thought they owned her, but it was not so, everything has its time.

Things that should not happen to one person when seducing another

The defects that should not pass to the conqueror at the point of infatuation are: bad smell, bad breath, lack of general hygiene, vain speeches, conversations or meaningless expressions, rudeness, etc... These are things that can make them lose all opportunities to be with her.

Before conquering it you must practice in front of a mirror first, to see all your defects before presenting yourself in front of her. If possible, record your voice on the cell phone to see how they come out.

Before leaving the house you should check your whole body very well; You should not have a very strong perfume but a pleasant smell. If there is careless bad breath, fix it with chewing gum, to disinfect your mouth.

Not only before the ladies, nobody wants to approach or speak to someone who is going through this situation. Bad breath problem occurs from very hot air stream or from juice or very cold water, or a hole in the tooth can also cause it. Mark Wolff, DDS, PHD, Director of Restorative Dentistry at the State University of New York at Stony Brooks. It states that approximately 75 percent of bad breath, or "halitosis," is caused by the mouth itself, he said:

"Other causes include gastric problems, sinus infections, or severe gum disease," he adds. Bad breath can be caused by:

External Actors: foods such as onion and garlic, drinks like coffee and alcohol, and smoking. Poor oral hygiene, where plaque and food residue are left on the teeth. Diseases such as gingivitis and periodental.

Dentures; There may be plaque formation and food residue on dentures, which should be cleaned daily. Tonsils: Cryptic areas (grooves) in the tonsils can allow food debris to lodge in this area. Respiratory tract infections; throat, sinus, and lung infections.

Dr. Mark goes on to say: dry mouth (xerostomia) can be caused by salivary gland problems, medications, mouth breathing, radiation therapy, and chemotherapy. Systemic diseases such as diabetes, liver, kidney, lung and sinus diseases, as well as gastrointestinal disorders.

When we feel that we have one of the symptoms, we should visit a specialist before going to conquer a person. You have to be very clean, with a lot of hygiene in every way before approaching an admirer, otherwise they will be very embarrassed.

There are many girls and ladies who have some elements in their bodies as well, not only gentlemen, both sexes can lose all the good opportunities to get partners due to one of those defects. It is not only harmful to the conquerors: in society no one wants to talk to the bearers of those stains.

Everyone must take care of their body, maintain good hygiene at all times, if you want to be social, if you want to have a good partner or friendship too; no one should neglect your body in any way.

Remember, our body is the temple of the Holy Spirit, we must not only take care of it for society and our partner, but also for the Holy Spirit who does not feel comfortable in dirty homes.

Chapter 3

The love of adventure

Many people say or show that they are madly in love. If we analyze deeply, they are bluster they use to harm others. Because of them, that original fragrance, that candy is losing a favor every day, how should we get it back again? Through reading this book.

So we see what it is about. It is undefined, which is above the flesh. There are many people because of their bad choices they distrust the opposite sex, in this case a woman. Who is right in this case them or the Author? The creator of love is never wrong, love will last forever and ever. The problem is that when they make their choice, they are guided by emotion or interest.

The Author says how we should use it, everything on earth has its own rules; even nature has its rules before acting. Love is so sweet, so pleasant, so special, so powerful, that it breaks all human rules and all the traditions that man invents.

Has love lost its fragrance in this century?

In no way will he last forever and ever, the world will end, but that sweetness will remain forever, where that pleasant fragrance cannot be any root of hatred, indifference, racism or any social class; it is the light that illuminates all people who want to have a successful family according to Jehovah's requests.

There is no life without it, nor happiness, each person who wants to have a better tomorrow must first be perfumed with the fragrance of love, the world is as it is now, it is because we lost its smell, due to the most dangerous hatred. Nor is there prosperity in any way without that beautiful scent flavoring in our lives.

What is love; how can we define it?

It is a total surrender, without conviction, without interest, or anything in exchange, everyone should have it; you have to let it germinate in your heart. No one can have it with their own strength, there has to be a connection between you and God.

If you meet all the requirements day by day, people will see the big difference between your past and your present. Loving is an action verb that gives growth to each individual who is looking for it.

We should never confuse it with emotion, they are two different things, each one has its function, although they manifest themselves in a similar way. Remember that even if there is a manifestation of love, you have to see if it suits you, because you can feel love for a lazy guy, a criminal, a brat, a drug addict, a depraved. If so, you can not let that love grow, because it is really a malignant tumor.

Neither can love be confused with desire, they are two very different things that have nothing in common: one remains forever, the other for a time. All those people who want to be successful in their relationships must sow true love, and they must follow the requirements. They can never burn their fruits. These are rules that can bring our relationships to a successful conclusion.

Without the covenant there is no courtship. Love is in the air, for any mistake she can change her thinking, even if they are dating, you do not have all the right to her. Dating is a big commitment, no one should take it lightly. They must know each other very well before reaching this stage.

What does human wisdom say about love?

The psychologist Diana Obrante Morales says the following: «When love is in the air, it shows. It is inevitable to demonstrate what we feel, because as much as we try to hide the feelings, our body is in charge of giving clear signs that the ground is moving just by looking at that special person».

Here are 10 clues that, according to the cited author, indicate that a man is in love. If you have more than 5, there are clear feelings towards you, but if you reached 10... You can be sure that he loves you!

1.- He can see you from miles away, whether you are in the middle of a crowd or walking alone, he will realize that you are there. As you get closer, you will notice how he makes eye contact with you, and even hints at a smile.

2.- He looks at you with a smile, he may have had the worst day of his life, but he sees you and his face changes completely. Perhaps his smile is not effusive, but with the gesture of his eyes you will notice his happiness.

3.- Share your interests, it does not mean that he likes the same as you but that our real interest in the things that you are passionate about and seeks to share them with you.

4. He cares about you, your health, food, study, etc... He is always aware of what happens in your life and, if you need help, he will give you his support in less than what a rooster crows.

5.- Highlight your virtues, although he recognizes that you have defects, he always focuses more on the virtues that characterize you. He specializes in changing the negative.

6.- It makes you feel the center of the universe, no matter how many are around you, their attention is always towards you, they will listen to you carefully and look you in the eye, every time they talk.

7.- He is happy with your happiness, "if you are happy, me too". Although your happiness means its unhappiness, it will support you and encourage you to keep going until you achieve your goal.

8.- His eyes shine every time he looks at you, his gaze lights up, he smiles with his eyes and he cannot stop looking at you with attention.

9.- He does not lie to you, no matter how painful the truth may be, he will always be able to tell you, looking straight at you, since the most important thing is you.

10.- It always has time for you, and if it does not, it will manufacture it, Although only a few minutes, it will be able to give you the priority you need.

The psychologist Octavio Jiménez, specialized in Cognitive Behavioral Therapy, online courses, published on July 16, 2018 [at www.psyciencia.com], saying the following: "The theme of love is embedded in our culture and consequently in our psyche, we see it everywhere: in movies, songs, books, magazines, videos and, recently, in conferences and scientific studies."

Still, people suffer to sustain a real love experience that eludes them. Ann Swidler (2001), tries to understand how culture determines our expectations about love, and how we actually achieve something else. The problem with this is that people don't live on a single culture, but a diverse one with multiple perspectives.

There is a paradox that, on the one hand, culture suggests that love is something perfect and instantaneous; But at the same time, it promotes a constant need to improve love relationships.

"Psychology of love", article written by María Ángeles on her page [depsicologia.com 06/07/2017], reads as follows: «Love is the engine of life, of human relationships, of feeling of the senses. And with so many things, love is still a mystery to many today, understanding love or how love has to be, if everything is chemistry or illusion, how it makes a couple work».

All people understand love in a way, in the end they all reach the same result, there is nothing more beautiful than when two people are in love, they are given to each other.

Love has seven great expressions that everyone must have if there is love between them: God, the economy, the passion, the trust, the freedom, the time and happiness, all those who want to have a successful family, must have those ingredients.

How many types of love exist in the world according to psychologists?

Each one gives a different amount according to their imaginations, their intellects or their research: Irene Solaz Velázquez commented [on March 5, 2018], in Psychology Online about the seven different types of love according to Stemberg, she puts it this way:

In love, not everything is black and white, because it is not just about wanting or not wanting. There are different ways of loving. Our feelings towards that special person can include passion, can motivate us to feel committed to her and can create a bond that unites us to her. Or perhaps our feelings only include some of these characteristics, or none at all.

Our understanding of love changed in 1986 with the publication of the psychologist Robert Sternberg in the journal Psychological Review. In the magazine he explained his triangular theory of love, which would completely change our knowledge of one of the most studied feelings.

According to the psychologist, there are different types of love relationships that determine our feelings towards our "better half" and our connection to it. In that article in Online Psychology, the seven different types of love are shown according to Sternberg. You may also be interested in: «Types of love for couples and relationships».

Sternberg's triangular theory of love: What does it mean?

The first characteristic that determines our type of love relationship is intimacy. When we are intimate with our partner, we have attachment in our relationship and we feel a special connection, which leads us to feel close to our partner. Our bond is affective, because we feel affection towards the person.

Intimacy is the characteristic responsible for wanting to give our partner what they love most at Christmas. It is the characteristic responsible for surprising you with your favorite dish, telling you our secrets and fears, and wanting to discover what makes you happy. According to Sternberg, some love relationships are intimate but other couples, on the other hand, do not have that affective bond.

The second characteristic that determines our type of love relationship with our partner is passion. This intensity is usually present during the beginning of a relationship, but it decreases over time. Other couples, on the other hand, never feel passion.

The third and last characteristic that will determine what type of love relationship we have with our partner is commitment. Engaged couples are aware of how much they love each other, and they don't want love to ever end. They make decisions that will affect them in the long term as a couple, and these promises are kept even when the couple is going through bad times. Like the other two characteristics, for Sternberg commitment is not present in all relationships.

What is the triangular theory of love, according to the psychologist Stemberg?

According to Stemberg: the relationship we have with our partner can change over time. You can start with a lot of passion and yet lose this intensity after a few months. The couple may not feel committed during the beginning of the relationship, but the decisions that will affect them in the long term could be made later, when they get to know each other better and when they become more intimate.

For the psychologist, relationships can have a combination of these three characteristics (or they could have all three). However, it is not very likely that the love of a couple that only has one of the three characteristics is forever. By playing with the different combinations of characteristics, we discover what the seven types of love are.

The seven types of love according to Stemberg.

1.- Honey

This relationship is typical of two people who only feel friendship, because the only characteristic they will have is intimacy. They love each other, but they don't feel passion and they don't make decisions that will unite them in the long term. Many relationships begin in this way, because during the beginning they are only friends.

2.- Infatuation

This type of relationship has only one characteristic: passion. They do not have intimacy, so they do not really know each other or share their fears and joys, nor do they have long-term plans. Many couples start a relationship that, for them, has been "love at first sight."

3.- Empty love

In this type of relationship there is only commitment, because the couple does not have confidence or passion. This relationship is common when a marriage of convenience is formed, or when two people who have been together for many years still intend to continue together, but feel nothing more.

4.- Romantic love

Stemberg describes these relationships as a combination of passion and intimacy. They love each other and share everything, but they do not plan for the future.

5.- Sociable love

This type of relationship includes the characteristics of intimacy and commitment. The missing feature is passion, which could have disappeared over the years of relationship.

6.- Fatuous love

It is the combination of passion and commitment. Intimacy is lacking as they are not open and do not feel a strong bond or connection.

7.- Consummate love

It is the type of relationship that all couples seek, as it combines intimacy, passion and commitment. According to the psychologist, the difficult thing is not to reach this stage, but to stay in it, because over the years it is common for couples to lose the passion they once felt.

Such is the opinion of human wisdom, without consultation of the owner, according to his thoughts, or his imaginations. Now we are going to see what THE GREAT I AM says about love. The most important thing in Stemberg's illustration is: each individual must take time to do a very deep analysis and detect what kind of love the lover has for you.

There are many ways in which a person can detect if the lover wants to have something seriously or if it is just pleasure. The most correct way to detect the mentality of the individual in auto visual, because 60% of cases are reflected in their eyes and face.

For whom was love created?

Love was created especially by humanity, each individual must cultivate that beautiful fragrance called "love", he must be everywhere: offices, schools, universities, in churches, where there are two people, he should be, the birds and the children teaches us how we should love each other. God has created three types of love, so that man can live happily in all circumstances.

The hero: that beautiful and pleasant fragrance manifests itself between a man and a woman.

The filial: it is manifested between the father, the mother and the children, each individual must love his creatures as himself, we must protect them, guide them and educate them in the right ways.

The brotherly: that love should be manifested in all hearts, because no one can live happily without it. According to an article published in psicologiadeamor.blogspot.com, where Freud is quoted: brotherly love is the love of all human beings; It is characterized by its lack of exclusivity. If I have developed the capacity to love, I cannot stop loving my brothers.

Brotherly love is based on the experience that we are all one. In Freud's words: «Love is love between equals: but, without a doubt, even as equals we are not always equal; insofar as we are human, we all need help».

I agree with Freud, because if we do not consult God, we will never be able to understand or succeed in any relationship that we want to form. But no one wants to put and consult God before taking or making any kind of romantic relationship as friends, even those who claim to be followers of Christ.

What does God say about brotherly love in his holy word?

Is brotherly love for people who have the same father or mother? To whom can this love be fervent? There are many people who say they are their families, what does the Bible say about this great confusion?

The great architect of the universe has clearly said how we should use it. He put it this way: «You shall not kill, you shall not commit adultery, you shall not steal, you shall not give false testimony against your neighbor. You shall not covet your neighbor's house, you shall not covet your neighbor's wife, nor his male or female servant, hiso x or donkey, or anything that belongs to your neighbor»: [Exodus 20: 14-17].

Every person in the world must put that love into practice, because there is no better joy in the world than serving people who are not blood relatives. There is no indifference between you and me, although we do not have the same social rank, we do not share the same, we are all brothers in Christ Jesus; we were molded by the Creator himself, if we practice that love for all human beings, we would have another world.

THE GREAT CREATOR OF THE UNIVERSE created us especially to love each other, if we love each other we must serve each other without any conditions, because the difference between you and your neighbor is the breath of life. A race, the economy, they are all passengers, plus love will last.

The apostle John said: «Beloved, let us love one another; for love is of God; and every one that loveeth is born of God, and knowweth God because love is from God. Everyone who loves is born of God and knows God. He that loveth not God; for God is love: [1 John 4: 7-8].

All those people who love their neighbor have been born of God, but those who do not love do not know the King, they have been born of the enemy, because it is he who puts all these differences between us, sows hatred among us; That hate makes us kill each other, swapping the sweet love for sour and toxic hatred.

To all those who want to live life with such happiness and prosperity, they must exchange their hatreds for love. God can make you be reborn again, a new dawn in his life, because it is never too late to change.

Agape love: that fragrance is sweeter than honey, it is the only one over the whole universe, it is the one that has created the world, nobody can have it, only the Deity.

Who created love?

No one can know the origin of love if he does not know God. He has created it, that is why he is above all things. John said: «He who does not love, has not known God; because God is love»: [1John 4: 8].

So the quality and personality of God is love, because that is why the world cannot explain or understand very well that sweet smell. Lovers do not seek to understand what love is, how it manifests itself. They want to choose a partner for life, they want to have success in their relationships, but they should seek God first. Without him you will never be successful in your relationships; God is the only ingredient that a human being needs to give good flavor in their relationship.

Because he said, "Seek first the kingdom of God and his righteousness, and all these things will be added to you."

That ingredient is above all knowledge and human sciences, because if the world is degenerate, it is because we want to interpret love with our knowledge, our human wisdom, we reject the author, we change love for hate; we have to know that where there is hate, love cannot be, and where love is, the essence of hate and satan cannot be.

God is love, the enemy is hatred, God's followers sow and reap love, plus Satan's followers sow and reap hatred, pride, racism, and indifference. God is calling every human to return to the source of the love that is Jesus Christ, if we want ultimate success in our relationship.

You are very much in love, you think you have already obtained your prince charming. Have you found all the ingredients in it? Are you sure that man loves you as he says? If you are aware and sure that he is complying with all the requirements, the rules, etc..., you have known enough.

So, it is time to move to another more advanced stage which is the pre-lover.

Chapter 4

Pre- in love

The process of choosing a person for life is very complicated. In a world where there is so much evil, nobody should be wrong in this decision. Between both sexes, 80% of lovers have made bad decisions.

Millions of people have fallen into one of the different types of love that the psychologist Stemberg mentions, although there is no school where people are taught to fall in love, or how to make love. It is something that is born only in each individual. When you fall in love there are two guiding spirits: good and evil.

Each has its own fruits, if we listen to good, we will make a good choice, but there is no good choice without a good conscience. If we incline to the opposite pole, its fruits are of total destruction.

The evil spirit is so popular in the world 90% of human beings are in its favor. They prefer to be with whom they feel good, although good comes from God. He is so fair and good, he created us with free will, we are responsible for our own actions, we have the right to make our own decisions, to choose the people we love.

But if we want to carry our elections to the final victory, we must first verify the decision beforehand, and we must listen when he speaks, because he has always answered all requests.

Why have voters so failed in the election?

For two main reasons:

1.- We do not take enough time to meet the prospect, nor do we make a study or a deep discovery about that guy, because It is impossible to choose someone like your partner shortly after meeting him, for this to happen you must spend time together in communication.

2.- We do not consult the Creator before the election, we decide on our own, when we react in that way, we will pay for our mistakes in the future, because all bad choices have their consequences.

We can never achieve final success with our decisions, because man's decisions lead to failure, but the one who consults and hopes in Jehovah will be like a tree planted next to streams, which bears fruit in its time and its leaf does not fall; and everything he does will prosper, because Jehovah will always be attentive and ready to lead him from victory to victory.

No one pays without making a mistake. If you could not wait to take enough time to get to know your lover, perhaps out of despair, or criticism from friends, or poverty, but sooner or later you will pay the consequence.

What is the behavior of the man with the girl when he is in love?

All women are always in love with the facts, and those who are listening to them, the good expressions, must come out natural, nobody should invent anything to conquer a lady, if you invent something in a short time she will be discovered, you try not to lie to her for any circumstance. All women hate lies, the worst moment a woman can go through is when she has discovered the lie of a lover.

Radishes never have lasting relationships, they refuse to invest. But spending something on a girlfriend is profit, it is not the amount that is worth, it is the intention.

Almost all women are crazy with flowers, the man must conquer her girlfriend with flowers, songs, romantic poems; You must be very detailed with her, invite her to the movies frequently, and to romantic dinners as necessary; never show her anything negative or malicious if you want to win her for life.

You have to show concern for all her issues, you have to pay close attention when she is expressing herself, never interrupt her when she is talking to you, because a person who does not listen will never be able to understand and answer any question correctly, whether positive or negative. Be a good gentleman at all times.

There are many men who share themselves as a good knight only at the time of the conquest, but when they are together they demonstrate another guy, with different characters. They are rams in the time to conquer, carnivores in coexistence. All men and women must have one face if they want to be successful in their married life.

How does a lady fall in love?

Not all women fall in love in the same way, each one has their personality, it is the man who has to discover it in her: there are women who fall in love at first sight like men, who give or send different forms of signals. No man should be against the character or custom of any woman; if you want to win her, you must get used to it and get to the heart.

The lover's behavior

The man must have a good presence, with good body language that can attract the attention of the opposite sex. You can never leave a smile behind. Because the smile is the key that can open all hearts, regardless of whether they are made of iron or stone, a good smile is the most important thing that the lover must use to reach the heart of the lover.

The smile is the most contaminating virus in the world. It positively affects sad, despicable, dejected, bitter hearts. A visual contact with a cute smile transmits something very special to lovers, although they are in the valley of death or bitterness, it can revive them in a state of joy, peace and love in a second.

The smile is the antidote that heals all fallen hearts. The smile transmits common interest between two people, it is something so contagious, nobody on earth can resist in their presence. But there are many people who confuse courtesy with infatuation.

What conditions must a man have to fall in love with a lady?

The man must have a professional and economic preparation to be able to correspond to the demand of that great responsibility that is falling in love or dating, because within that relationship many things can happen.

To avoid "yes, I knew", the conqueror must have two great things: first he must not fall in love with the wrong guy. Second, you need to have financial security. Otherwise, they will only find stumbling blocks.

Before choosing that person as your partner, you must find four great things that can change your life forever: God; true love without malice and deception; good conscience; and morale. Without all three it is impossible to have a successful family.

Chapter 5

Discipline in communication before the choice

Lovers must have discipline when they are talking to their future partners, that discipline is not only important for lovers, but also for all human beings. What is communication? It is a set of rules or norms whose compliance constantly lead to a certain result.

Where should the individual acquire this training? Only inside the first school, which is called the home of his parents. Children can learn two formations, the good or the bad.

Which one of the two have you learned at home? No one can live without one of the two, there are never bad students without bad teachers, if you want to choose a guy for your life, you must find a good discipline in him or her before the election.

Discipline, order and respect are three elements in the accumulation of values where the school, the family and the community must have the greatest influence, in order to achieve not only the educated child or young guy, but also fully formed in service to society. And the own subsidiary ties that are the basis of a solid future.

People lacking discipline or orders, foolish who never go in the right direction or say anything of value, their own expressions condemn them. They are their own destruction, their own enemies, their failures. Having order is not a small thing, nor a small matter.

It is one of the most precious virtues for the good balance of individual life and for the good harmony of common life. Order is a means of developing in our children self-control and, in a certain sense, the spirit of sacrifice, forcing them to fight abandonment and neglect. .

What is communication?

There are many homes that have been destroyed for lack of that nutrition called communication, that expression that is most important of all the interactions that exist in the world. What is communication? It is the union of two people or it is the process by which information is transmitted from one point to another. It is something that has a lot of value, especially between two future boyfriends.

When you are conversing with a person who loves or wants to have something, you should pay much more attention, you cannot use the cell phone much to avoid getting disconcentrated, he/she has much more value than the people who are chatting, because you can lose all the opportunities if you give more value to the network tan your applicant.

There are two important moments in the life of lovers: the day of the first agreement of acceptance with a wet kiss, and the day of the marriage agreement. Two times that are never forgotten even when one reaches old age.

What is the difference between a leader and a boss?

The difference between leader and boss is that a boss is an imposed authority that uses his power to command others, but instead a leader is one who leads and motivates a team of people without imposing his own ideas. Leadership is a capacity that not everyone has, so not everyone can be a leader.

Bertrand Regader [Barcelona 1989]. Educational psychologist in Barcelona and Director of ORGANIZATIONS, HUMAN RESOURCES AND MARKETING, on the page Psychology and

Mind, commented on the 10 differences between a boss and a leader.

Leaders and bosses have very different management styles: "In a previous article we talked about the 10 personality traits that every leader should have, today is the time to record the 10 differences between a boss and a leader."

He begins with a question: Boss or Leader?

Let's first define both concepts. "Boss" is defined as the person who has authority or power over a group to direct their work or activities. Instead "Leader" is the person who heads and directs a group or social, political, religious movement, etc. In principle, the difference is clear. But in the day to day, there are many attitudes that can make a person enter the profile of leader or boss.

We propose to point out the ten most important factors within organizations, since if you occupy a relevant position in decision-making and lead a human group, it is convenient for you to adopt a leadership position, in order to motivate and join forces in your organization.

The 10 differences between a boss and a leader:

1.- The perception of your authority

For a boss the use of authority is a privilege granted by his command post. Instead, for a good leader, authority is a privilege only if it is a useful tool for the organization. The chief endorses the maxim of "I am the one who commands here"; while the leader finds his inspiration in the phrase "I can be useful here". The boss spurs the group and the good leader stays in front, guides them and commits himself day by day.

2. -To impose vs convince

The boss bases his influence on the authority that comes from the position he holds. The leader earns the sympathy and will of those around him. The boss enforces his position within the hierarchy, while the leader cultivates and cares for his leadership on a daily basis.

The boss feels the need to impose his criteria, using long arguments; the leader convinces and exemplifies, his arguments do not seek to banish others, but to build knowledge and a plan of action.

3.- Fear vs confidence

The boss instills fear, fear, often threatens and his team is suspicious of him, they put on a good face when he is close but they criticize him harshly when he is not present. The leader is a source of trust, empowers people, generates enthusiasm when working, stimulates the group recognizing the good work and effort of its members.

The boss needs blind obedience, the leader wants motivation to permeate everyone. If you are afraid of your superior, he is an ordinary boss; If instead you value and appreciate it, your superior is a leader.

4.- The management of problems

The boss wants to point out who made the mistake; implants the belief of looking for culprits. In this way, he honors, punishes and shouts if something does not go well, to warn the culprit and the rest of the people. The leader knows how to understand mistakes and calmly redirects the situation.

It is not in charge of pointing out the mistakes of others or accusing anyone, but rather seeks to solve the problem and helps those who have committed it to get up.

5.- Technical organization vs creative organization

The boss distributes the tasks and orders, and remains supervising if their orders are being strictly followed. The leader encourages, provides example, works side by side with his collaborators, is consistent with what he thinks, with what he says and with what he does.

The boss makes the tasks an obligation, but the leader knows how to look for motivation in each new project. The leader transmits the desire to live and to progress.

6.- Orders vs pedagogy

The boss knows how everything works, the leader knows how to teach each task, he knows how to teach. The first is suspicious of his secret that has led him to success, the second decisively protects people so that they can develop and even overcome him. The boss organizes the production, but the leader prepares them to reach their full potential.

7.- The degree of personal closeness

The boss relates to his team in a depersonalized way, like chips on a board. The leader personally knows all his collaborators, genuinely cares about their lives, does not use or objectify them. He is respectful of the personality of each one, defends people regardless of their position in the hierarchy.

8.- Closed schemes vs open schemes and in constant development

The boss says "do this", the leader says "let's do this". The boss pursues stability, the leader promotes his collaborators through group work and the training of other leaders. The leader is capable of integrating the sincere commitment of those around him, designs plans with clear and shared ends, infects others with his hope and determination.

9.- Comply vs lead

The boss arrives on time, but the leader always arrives first. The boss waits for the collaborators sitting in his chair, the leader comes out to welcome them. The leader wants to always maintain his presence as a group guide and inspires commitment, friendliness and loyalty.

The boss is satisfied with an acceptable performance of its members, the leader wants to see further and wants his group to stand out.

10.- Power vs inspiration

The chief defends tooth and nail his position of authority; the leader makes normal people feel extraordinary. The boss craves reverence, but the leader manages to engage his team on a mission that allows them to excel and transcend. The boss wants to keep his privileges; the leader gives meaning and inspiration to his work, his life and that of those around him.

There are many men who have confused the leader with the head of the household, from before the right to fall in love, they make all their decisions to be her boss. According to the psychologist Regader this is not the case, they still have no right to be her boss, because they have not yet decided.

Women before making any decision, you must see or know who is his the guy, if he is a disciplined man or not, if someone worthwhile or not, if he is a boss or a leader, if it is a boss, you cannot expect any good communication in this relationship because all the heads of households are ma.chismo.

If the lover has the three negative aspects, he cannot give him any priority of being his companion, because his life will be hell, he must know that man very well before letting him conquer the throne of your heart. Who between the two of you can choose as the blue prince of your heart, the leader or the boss? Although the boss is a professional, he will never be able to live without any confrontation because he is his character.

Nor should a man choose a young woman or lady who has one of these criteria, otherwise his life will be equal to an earthly hell. Although there is love and chemistry between the two.

What the man must do to get the attention of the lover

The first thing the conqueror must do is: listen to his admirer with great attention every time she expresses herself, he must find something good in his favor.

When the man behaves like this, it does not mean that the man is inferior to her or that she is the dominant one, only when you listen well before speaking, can you give a good answer in her concern, or what she wanted to know, both affirmatively and negatively.

No one should seek to be dominant in any relationship, although each has its different role, it does not mean that one is superior to the other, the two are equal. There are many receivers who never want to let exhibitors express themselves, they are willing to interrupt them at any time.

Are those people who have no family training or any discipline, they can cause two big problems for that mistake: completely forget all the good points of the conversation and the topic they are trying.

When a man listens to a lady with a lot of attention and with good eye contact, she feels his concerns and his information are making their way, and she feels happy. She can have more confidence in the man to be part of her love life, because he is paying close attention to her request, she also feels secure.

The thing that most bothers a lady is when the recipient doesn't want to let her freely express her concerns or her idea. When two people are talking, or explaining something, you cannot speak until the other has finished, if the receiver wants to clarify something, he must ask permission before interrupting. Two major bad decisions are caused in the interruption:

1.- You'll never be able to give a good answer, because you have not heard the whole conversation.

2.- Because of how uncomfortable he is inside her heart against the bad behavior of that man is: to stay away forever, they lost all good wishes for a nonsense that is bad education.

Every human being has two eyes to watch, two ears to listen, a single mouth to speak when it is necessary, the fools speak all who come into their mouths without any restriction. The wise are always silent, when their time comes, they always speak with bases and arguments.

There are people who say 50 thousand words in an hour and none of them makes sense, nor is it worth it. Each individual should speak less and listen more carefully.

When his turn comes, he must do it with great care, the sage analyzes each iota within his heart before being public, when they are expressed they are done with bases and foundations. When you are thickening you should not leave any gap open, because there are many people are their own words that condemn them.

Each individual should speak less and listen more carefully. When his turn comes, he must do it carefully, no person should leave any gap open when he is expressing, he must speak with base and argument, all his words must be very calculated before...

For all these reasons, the future lover must be on her level so that the two can understand each other; the two must be equal, one must not be superior to the other. The man was created to be the priest of the home, as a leader he must be equal to or slightly superior.

The man should not be inferior to the girlfriend at first they may not be able to see the difference, but in living together the difference will cause a problem for both of them. When a person wants to buy a new outfit or shoes, in a mall or a store, he starts different actions:

1.- Search for money, because without money it is impossible to acquire it.

2.- He has to go to the store, nobody can do it for him; each one has his own taste.

3.- Among thousands there is a decision to choose.

4.- You have to like it first. Among all, the brand is very important.

5.- You have to test it to see if it is your size, nobody can buy something smaller or bigger than your foot.

6.- Finally, you must pay it at the ATM.

It is the same for the guy who is making a choice for life, you must find all those ingredients in the other. If there are people who are going through a lot of difficulties in their relationships, It is because they were not looking for those ingredients that are very important before the choice.

They are guided by emotion, they make bad decisions to choose someone who is much superior or inferior to them, if they want to enjoy their taste with all the flavor, there must be no superiority and inferiority.

What will happen when a person chooses shoes that are bigger or smaller than their foot? Possibly you can find three things that, extrapolated to the life of a couple, will affect you for the rest of your life:

1.- It is a total loss, because you will not be able to use it.

2.- Wasted time in the election, could have invested in something else. Lost time is never recovered.

3.- If you try to use it, it will cause you a lot of pain and suffering and, possibly, it may have a permanent scar on your body or soul.

There are two big problems that can influence a human being to make a decision like this: emotion and poverty. When a person is going through difficult times, he can do anything to survive, he can get together with the wrong people. So parents are responsible for all their children's mistakes.

Why is there so much pain and suffering in the world?

For three main reasons:

1.- For lack of a good family formation.

2.- For lack of good orientation in childhood.

3.- For the wrong choice.

Young people! Although life is more complicated, never make any decision for the emotion, try to see if this guy suits you, if he is someone worthwhile. They must not see "the present" or the good presence only, they must see beyond that "the future".

What will your future be like with this guy who is trying to fall in love, because all bad decisions are paid with pain and great suffering, nobody has been born to be suffered in this world... but ourselves: I say to the conduct of those who have been chosen.

How can a guy make a good choice?

Choosing a partner is the same as someone who wants to buy footwear, who makes the decision to visit a store, who has to do a few things before choosing:

1.- Among all footwear, you have to like one.

2.- You must also like the brand.

3.- You must ask for the price to see if the money is enough.

4.- Before preserving it, see if it suits you.

5.- You have to measure it first to see if it is your size, nobody can wear any shoe that is not your size. If it is smaller, it will leave a scar for his whole life, if it is bigger, he will never feel good. But possibly it has to be a little bit bigger to be much more comfortable.

No woman should choose a man who is inferior to her, nor superior, she must be equal, or that the man is a little superior than her so that the relationship can work well. There are many women who are speaking ill of men, they say they are very bad.

But they do not realize, or want to admit, that they are paying for their mistakes in choosing sizes that were not their measure. They must learn to choose the appropriate measure, so as not to regret it. Never forget mistakes are paid for in pain, and recidivism in them is a sin.

Perhaps at first they will not see the difference, nor feel pain, because love is blind, when there is no more strength to endure more, they have to make new decisions to ease their lives. By nature, the human being never recognizes his mistake, he always likes to find a culprit.

All people who are going through that situation must know their guilt first, if they want to recover, because there is no improvement without recognition, they are two things that go together in recovery. God also cannot forgive anyone who does not know their guilt.

You have fallen into one mistake; you must do a self study, a very deep analysis in your life, to see where you failed. Because "the cat that has fallen into the hot water always takes care of all the waters"; he is never neglected again, because he always remembers the pain and suffering of hot water.

There is a man who likes to make the person who is superior to him fall in love, because in his mind, he thinks with false promises he will live for his assets. He is making a serious mistake. She will never be able to live happily, she will always feel something that does not work well, the moment she has found her own size, she will break that relationship forever.

Everyone should live on their own with what they have, not look at the assets of others because they are not theirs. If a guy wants to have a better tomorrow, he must try hard, with a good preparation he can go as far as the impossible.

Here is the list of the 10 signs of a woman when she likes a man:

1.- Good humor is spontaneous

Mischievous, natural smile, nervous giggles... a woman laughs openly when she enjoys the company, she feels happy and pleased. To keep him comfortable, the man should not be in a hurry.

2.- It touches him "unintentionally"

When a woman tries to approach the man she likes, she accidentally touches him: he brushes her arm, his shirt or even his leg... Men should not miss this moment, but try to differentiate the accidental touches of the intended.

3.- There are too many coincidences

There are so many coincidences that it seems that the woman reads the man's mind and guesses what she is going to do. There are many encounters that seem fortuitous.

4.- Launch intermittent glances

Researchers advise men to learn to analyze such glances, which discard a man with just a glance.

5.- Play with the hair

Although women are always always adjusting their hair, there are times that they only do it to attract men, it is a more deliberate gesture, a more thorough movement than normal. Maintain eye contact.

6.- Cross the legs

The woman puts the leg furthest from the man over the other leg to show the calf. In that position, the leg muscles are smoother and more provocative.

7.- Direct the chin and face towards the man

The woman slightly turns the chin towards the man. It is a gesture that reveals that you are interested in what your partner says. Women like to talk head-on.

8.- The feet are a little apart

When the woman is standing, the dynamism with which she maintains her balance tells us the emotion she feels. If both legs are straight and expressionless there is no passion. If they are slightly open or playing with the ankles, she is nervous.

9.- Remember details of previous conversations

A woman, however distracted, does not forget the small details that a man says when he is interested. It may be that the man has forgotten them, but she has not, look at those details.

10.- She does not feel intimidated by the proximity of the man

If she really likes the man, she does not mind that he approaches her, but it must be at the right time, without haste. How do you know? An easy way to approach a woman without threatening her space, is to direct your attention away from the man: look for something that can attract attention (another couple, a sculpture...), point it with your eyes, while approaching her. If he gestures backwards it is a bad sign.

Mariel Reimann says: «Most women develop a maternal sense from a very young age and showing love for everything and everyone, generally it is not a problem. By its nature, it is sometimes difficult to know what a woman truly feels about a man. If you are in love, there are 8 things you will only do with him.

If you are a man and you wonder if she really loves you, or if you are a woman and you are not sure if you are really in love, keep reading and discover the answer».

1.- She feels comfortable when she is with you

This is perhaps one of the great signs that a woman has crossed the line of just wanting to love him deeply. Women put a lot of barriers when they first meet a man avoiding suffering. They only download them when the heart has made the decision to fall in love.

2.- His face lights up every time he is with you or thinks of you

Women are one of the most expressive creatures in creation. A woman's face says it all, and there are two emotional states in women that she will unfailingly be able to hide: falling in love and motherhood. A woman's face never shines more than when she is in love or expecting a baby. If her face radiates that peace and feeling of eternal happiness when you are with her, chances are she loves you.

3.- Has attentions with you

The social and coexistence rules somehow establish that men are the ones who will have the attention with women in the process of conquest. When a woman takes the initiative to give you gifts, or to take care of you, do not hesitate, that woman loves you.

4.- She listens to you and your life has become part of hers

What happens to you and what stops you from happening is as or more important than your own life. Women in love stop seeing the line that separates them from your life. You worry him; what makes you happy also makes her happy.

5.- Sacrifice what would make her happy for your happiness

Women do not have many barriers when it comes to sacrificing themselves for the happiness of others; They do it for their friends and family all the time. When a woman falls in love, she tends to do this all the time. And beware, value it as gold and do not abuse those sacrifices: she does it because she really loves you, but you must be something mutual.

6.- He reveals his worst fears

Women try not to expose what scares them to avoid being vulnerable and therefore suffer, when a woman decides to share her fears and weaknesses with a man, it is because her heart has decided that she is safe with you and that she can do it for you open.

7.- It does not always prove you right

When a woman is not in love, she doesn't care what you say or let say, and to keep the party in peace, she will often agree with you (the reason for the fool, as my grandmother used to say). However, when a woman loves someone, she will make sure you know her views and there will be discussions, but only because she cares enough about you as a middle ground between the two.

8.- The idea of losing you paralyzes your heart

Imagining her life without you leaves her breathless. You are part of everything that dreams, projects, and longs for. If you're with someone who loves you like this, don't waste it. Millions of human beings walk the earth without having had the opportunity to be loved like this, according to Mariel Reimann.

Now, although you are very much in love with this lover, you have to see if he is also in you. No one can fall in love alone, it has to be mutual. Sometimes there are women who fall in love with emotion, when a person falls in love with emotion, many mistakes can be made, because the love for emotion never lasts for a long time. It has to be natural, even if you're crazy about that man.

Many people have thought, after their future lovers have received the signals, that they are already dating and have access to everything. They too have confused these three elements:

love, friendship and knowing are three different things. Knowing is the first step that can lead to friendship and infatuation. They both need those three elements in order to continue.

Before reaching the verbal infatuation step, they have to leave the knowledge step to take them to that step without despair, no one can fall in love with a guy without knowing them for at least 25 to 35%.

To get to know her, they must spend time together, sharing together to fully discover who that person is who wants to make a home with you. Falling in love is a process, when someone is falling in love with another person, he is saying I am almost ready for marriage.

No one can seek to make another person fall in love without knowing who he is, where he lives, his offspring, if it is true that this man does not have a woman in the house, or if he is not committed to another guy, if he is lazy or not, if he is someone who has vices or not, if he is someone who, if something happens, has something to take responsibility with, how is his family.

You have to know everything about him; you have to got some friends in his neighborhood who can transmit you all information about him/her.

There are also women who are engaged to a husband at home or in another country, who have double or triple lives, looking for other lovers just like men. That is why the knowledge stage is very important to discover who is in front of you, what he/her is looking for with you, something formal or adventure.

Everyone should know that it is a mortal danger to be with the wrong guy, or married. No one should have the confidence to be with someone without a very deep analysis.

The person who thinks that he will never deceive you because of his way of being, expressing or living, in the end turns out to be your worst enemy. The prophet Jeremiah expressed about men who likes to trust another, he said: "Thus saith the Lord: Cursed be the man that trusteth in man, and maketh flesh by his arm, and whose heart departeth from the Lord": [Jeremiah 17:5].

After the investigation you will react according to what you have found. God has created each person with his own decision to choose the guy that suits you. Some Christians seek divine intervention, or a sign from God before making any decision, but it is not an obligation to do so, so each person is responsible for their own resolution.

But it is impossible to forge a relationship contrary to the holy word God. All those who want to start a successful family are based on it.

Why are there so many children suffering in the world?

It is because there are many young men who have girlfriends at immature ages and who reach sexual relations earlier than time, without any preparation (job or business), because they are teenagers.

Their ages do not allow them to work; They are immature and therefore do not think about their economic incompetence. Her wishes are to take advantage of the emotion of sexual nature. Then come the consequences: unwanted pregnancy; problems for parents who had no ability to educate them, no resources.

They are going to make two decisions, they leave the children abandoned due to lack of income or responsibility. They will steal to keep them. Young people aged 12 to 19 should not have "courtship" in their minds at all. It is something that is the enemy of your future. There are two things that allow young people to have children very early, without any preparation: «poverty and education».

At what maximum age should a young guy have a relationship?

It is when he is doing a thesis at university, or has a profitable job, a business where he can correspond to any obstacle at the time of dating, it can be at the age of 22 to 28 years. When young guy are 16 to 22 years old, they think only of adventure, uncontrolled pleasure, enjoying their youth; most of them don't want to take any responsibility. And why do it?, if they have the world ahead.

At the age of 28 to 33 years, they are mature, they want to form a home, they want to take their own responsibilities, they don't want to depend on their parents anymore; they want to have their own homes like their parents. Likewise, since we are all human, we are condemned to make mistakes. So you can also find many who continue to do the same when they were 18 years old.

After all the discoveries, the analyzes, the infestations, if everyone tests positive, you can give that boy the opportunity to fall in love verbally, "eye, you never stopped knowing him. You should also not stop discovering and analyzing him.

Chapter 6

The act of falling in love

Falling in love with someone is something so sweet and special that, no one should take it lightly, if you discover that the suitor is qualified, you can open your heart to him/her where you can receive from all expressions of love, romantic songs, in summary, everything that has to do with love and good feelings towards you.

He/she havs an 80% chance of being your boyfriend/girlfriend, because you know that he/she is qualified to obtain this position. Even if you are sure that it is the right guy, you still cannot give the wet kiss that has been waiting for a long time.

The lover cannot question her about that kiss, it must happen with her conviction, nothing forced works. You have to follow the step and the rules of falling in love before the first pact that is acceptance.

After the pact romance, you can give him/her all kinds of kisses, because everyone already has the right. Before… you have to continue talking with all kinds of loving expressions, without limits or fear, because now there is much more trust between the two.

They can talk at all hours through the chat according to their interests, because lovers always have something to say, they never finish their words, they always want to be next to each other, although there are winds and storms, they always want to be together. But although there is a lot of love between the two, each one must respect the rules of the house, because the true priest has an exact time to accept visits in his home. No priest of the home should lose his leadership for any reason.

True parents always take complete care of their nests. They can never go to bed without closing their door, if they are Christians they have an exact time to have the family worship before going to sleep, all the maids must be together to celebrate the family worship. So the visit of the bride and groom must have a limit.

Christians have another way of falling in love. They humanly converse while seeking the presence of God through prayer to see if God agrees with that future relationship. If they are not Christians, a more liberal and much easier measure than the Christian one is used.

The norms of lovers

The lovers they must love each other with love poems, sweet words that can take them to the clouds in a second, they must bring flowers, because they are the weaknesses of all the ladies, in the time of infatuation they can go to the movies, dinners romantic with candles, the lovers must be very detailed with them, they have to bring them as queens, because they are queens of their own hearts, they must feel good about their lovers. So employment is paramount in all relationships.

There are many men who conquer women with vanities, offering them money, a vehicle, a house, the payment of the university, their expenses, etc... This is not called love, because love is not sold or bought, it is a manifestation, it is a feeling, a total surrender. The ladies must pay close attention to these offers, no one gives a damn, they have to pay for that offer sometimes with an incurable disease, deaths, unhappiness, anguish, etc...

There are also women in the world who come to the man with a list of problems for the man to put on their shoulders, as if they were couples already. That is not love either, it is a total deception, deceitful "a slap" or "chapiadora", as they say vulgarly.

"Chapeo" this is a Vulgar term used in the Dominican Republic and that refers contemptuously to the woman who receives goods (expensive gifts) and/or money for having a romantic relationship (simply sexual in many cases) with a wealthy person, generally a man old enough to be your father or grandfather. No only the woman can do that, the men too. There are religious women who are "chapiadoras" too.

In infatuation, a man cannot become a hummingbird. You must to have only one partner, you must not despair because you are closer than yesterday and tomorrow will be another day. When two guys are in love, even if the light goes out, they will go to bed chatting almost every night, because there is common interest between the two.

They never speak negative things, they are always laughing, they are happy and content because they are in their world.

What do scholars say about falling in love?

OMSK RUSSIA, commenting on a Wikipedia entry, opined: "Falling in love is an emotional state product of joy, in which one person is powerfully attracted to another, which gives the satisfaction of someone who can understand and share as many things as life brings.

From a biochemical point of view, it is a process that begins in the cerebral cortex, passes to the endocrine system, and is transformed into physiological responses and chemical changes caused in the hypothalamus through the segregation of dopamine. Infatuation is based on gestures, and emotional, motor, sexual, intellectual and instinctive communication, and they are carried out by moving, looking, caressing and speaking.

According to Yela [2002], unlike the widespread belief that infatuation is an unpredictable and random phenomenon, an increasing number of social scientists have constructed different theoretical models that describe and explain infatuation. The main characteristics of infatuation are symptomatic, which, according to most authors, are:

1.- Desire for intimacy and physical union with the individual, touching him, hugging him, kissing him and even sexual relations. Desire of reciprocity (that the individual also falls in love with the subject).

2.- Fear of rejection.

3.- Frequent thoughts about the individual that interfere with the normal activity of the pure subject.

4.- Loss of concentration.

5.- Strong physiological activation (nervousness, cardiac acceleration, etc.) in the presence (real or imagined) of the individual.

6.- Sensitivity to the wishes and needs of the other.

7.- Attention focused on the individual.

8.- Idealization of the individual, perceiving only positive characteristics, according to the subject, and mitigating or justifying the negative characteristics.

All people do not see reality in the same way, each interprets infatuation according to their understanding and belief. I respect everyone's belief, because even if we do not share the same ideology, it allows me to see things differently, from the other shore, I see infatuation with another criterion.

There are two categories of infatuation and culture, the true and the false. From my point of view falling in love is a feeling, it is something that has been born only in the mind of each individual, and that you want to execute with good purpose with someone special.

It is something that is beyond human knowledge; which is above human science. Wanting to enjoy someone without having a formal relationship with her is not true love.

Falling in love and feeling pleasure are two different things. No one should use one for the other, each has its fruits, millions of people have confused one for the other, even professionals. No one can fall in love with someone without knowing even 20%.

But to feel pleasure is to want to do something without commitment, it is to want to enjoy him/her for a time or a moment, it is something that has no basis, something fleeting. Love is not a game, it is a feeling, no one should play with the feelings of others, should not say what he does not have and feel, even nature is against deceivers.

For this reason, the receiver must analyze the exhibitor very well to discover if he or she is speaking the truth or lying, and although there are people who are professionals in the "lie", it is not difficult to discover him/her, because with a good silence and analysis you can discover the hidden secrets.

When a guy is in the infatuation stage, they cannot put "sexual intercourse" on their mind, even when they are already dating. Sex should be after marriage. It is the last step to give yourself completely to him or her. Human beings are not "instincts", they cannot react like animals, we are human, we are "right", we are slightly inferior to angels, but superior to all terrestrial animals.

There are two reasons that warn of not having sex in the time of infatuation, you still do not know if you will be together, although there is chemistry and many signs of love, before making that decision you have to be very sure that it is not a fraudulent decision.

Because there are people who get excited and fall madly in love with each other when they are in the act, so the two must be sure if there is something in common. There are two sensations that prevent lovers from making love in the infatuation stage.

1.- The doubt

You do not know if it is true that this lover is in love with you as he said, all the men who have discovered the nakedness of a lady before time, they think she is very easy, she can do the same with other guy, they will never stay with her, nor will they form any home, they will never take that relationship seriously, when a lady is more conserved, they love her more.

Ladies, never give up for any reason if you want to earn respect, you must respect yourself first.

2.- Your future is in danger

Sex is done after marriage, if you want to have good sex, to have a better future tomorrow, it is very easy. If your boyfriend or lover wants to have sex with you, you can tell him, so if you love me as you say, then marry me. At once he will find another excuse because his mentality is to enjoy you sexually without any commitment or responsibility. Because all the things that have been made easy go in the same way.

Women, remember that men have nothing to lose, it is you who have to take care of yourself. The laws of motherhood will prevent them from abandoning their children as easily as men do.

Falling in love, commonly confused with love, refers to a state in which one person magnifies the positive qualities of another, and which usually takes place at the beginning of a love relationship. But it is not an adventure relationship.

During that stage, in which we know very few aspects of the other's personality, we tend to force ourselves to ensure that we have found the perfect person, although nobody is perfect, or the love of our lives; someone who has the desire and the ability to understand, to reward affection and care, and to share day-to-day with you. That said, it is understandable that joy and a state of constant enchantment often go hand in hand with infatuation.

For biochemistry, it is a process that originates in the cerebral cortex, continues in the endocrine system, and results in physiological responses. This procedure involves the intervention of multiple elements. By meeting someone and experiencing attraction, a series of chemical and psychological transformations begin in humans.

This phenomenon is practically immediate and certainly involuntary, and can be clearly distinguished from intentional seduction, a process generally more extensive and sometimes associated with cultural and social issues.

Physical attraction and infatuation have that quality of unconscious and inexplicable in common, but only in the eyes of those who live it. Precisely, a series of sensory signals, mainly olfactory, but also visual, are responsible for that individual who, minutes ago, was a stranger, becomes as if by magic at the center of our lives. But it certainly is not.

Falling in love is knowing the guy to see if they can go to the dating stage, if they are qualified for that stage, because there are many people who think that falling in love is synonymous with being a husband and wife. But you still have no right, of course if you can kiss on the cheek, not on the lips.

In the infatuation stage, the male can ask permission to touch her leg, to establish more trust between the two. You cannot ask for wet kisses or caress yourself. If they arrive at that stage it is because they are already dating. Otherwise you have to wait for the moment where she will decide with all her conviction to give you a positive answer.

On time depends the delay of her discovery, she need to have her time without rushing to give an answer according to her conscience and her understanding. If there is pressure, she will never be able to make a good decision that is right between the two of you.

Because of the pressure from the man with despair, there are few women in the world who have gotten married, the few who have gotten divorced within ten years. This serious problem causes many children to breed without the presence of a father or mother.

Disunity causes much suffering, bitterness in the children's world. That bad life allows women to have four children with four different fathers. In the end they are left alone for life. The little ones are receiving bad formations, when they grow up, they will follow the same steps as their parents, because that is what they have learned.

Children are possibly worse than their parents. Because nobody can give what they don't have. There are never bad students if there are no bad teachers.

Is it that God's plan is to have so much suffering in the world? The answer is no. God wants everyone to live happy with a lot of peace and love. God is also sad for all the sufferings in this world, because "He is love." Despite this, he cannot decide for anyone, nor can he tell us what we should do if we do not seek him. Each person is responsible for their own mistake, no one is paying for the fault of another.

If we want to have a different generation and prosper in everything, we must start from scratch, because it is never too late to learn. We have to start making the change from today, always the change brings new things.

When two lovers reach the act of intimacy, many things can happen. The first time is difficult, then they will have a second time, a third, the fourth leads to custom. When they open their eyes, they already have two or three children; the university well thank you, and throw all your dreams in the trash; They begin to spend work to be able to support the creatures, because of a bad decision that caused all those disasters.

That is why each young guy must think very carefully about the decisions they are going to make, whether they will affect their future or not.

There are those who say they are not lucky to meet a good partner, but they never remember the bad decisions they have made in the past, they can never have a good future if they have not corrected the mistakes of the past, and these are tools that can be taken to the future successful. Because of those bad choices, there are so many abortions in the world, so many incurable diseases that are destroying almost the entire human race.

Young man, if you want to have a successful future, never make a decision out of emotion or without thinking, without deep analysis and discovery. Although they say young people don't think, you can make a difference. Fight so that no one can break your dream, if you do not have a good family formation, seek help from the professionals, you have to make a difference. You must be the difference.

Although you are very much in love, you cannot overlook the steps that can lead you to your final destination, you have to control your emotion, passion and desires very well, because you have hormones like all human beings. Everything under control.

You cannot demonstrate your weaknesses to anyone, you have to be stronger than ever, if you want to win the fight. You have to be like a boxer even if the opponent's blows hurt a part of your body, never give up; Your perseverance will win you by knock out.

The life of every human being is a struggle, nobody is exempt from that war. Sometimes we do not know who our enemies are: there are two categories of fight, one with the people we have met, and those who never think if they are our enemies, sometimes your worst enemy is yourself. Also the people that we think are our best friends, after all, are our worst enemies. Deep knowledge and alert to everything.

Many people think that selecting the future partner is very easy. If it were, no one would fail in their relationship, that's why every future married person must search if that guy who is in love with you is your friend or your enemy. What does this guy look for in you!

The infatuation stage is a strong and dangerous stage at the same time, because it is a stage of choice, where nobody can be wrong. It is a very strong fight where the adversary is bombarded with all kinds of arguments, to achieve what he is looking for. In that fight there can be no winner or loser, but a mutual triumph between the two.

The feelings

There are two groups of people in this world: one with a positive mindset, the other negative. The positive leads to a more beneficial behavior, who knows how to make others feel good, who likes to give good advice, who does not seek his interests, someone who sees things beyond, who has a sweet charisma with many natural affections, someone that speaks with base.

When she expresses herself, everyone wants to hear her, a kind and well-educated person, everyone wants to be by her side.

Who has a happy and joyful mood, someone who is always looking for an easier way to solve the situation, someone who sees the solution before the problem, is never sad. He is a being whose object is to turn waste into new products, who has the pleasant sensation of always speaking with a sincere heart. It would seem that we are talking about Christ, but no: there are ordinary humans with these qualities.

Characteristic of the guy who has the positive feeling, his reaction or state produces the good news in all circumstances. Your body can manifest itself in recent events as well as in something that has been revived through memory-activated memories, both intellectually and spiritually; someone who does not give up in any situation. And again: we are not talking about spider man.

A person who is totally optimistic, who knows how to reach others, is a leader who never thinks of a second chance, never thinks of failure, is never afraid to face life, someone who has a feeling of gratitude, who loves everyone equally, someone who does not have a double face, who has a lot of passion, honesty, a good human being.

It can be done, even if it looks too good to be true.

Negative feeling

The negative feeling has many ingredients to make a home unhappy for life. When we analyze, we can discover that most human beings produce some of them. At the same time that we are reading them we must compare each of them with our lives daily. How many do we have? We cannot compare them with other people's lives, because each home is unique in its history.

The situations that produce negative feelings in people are:

Anxiety: it is a person who is worried about any problem and who is afraid to look for the solution, many extras are produced; someone who thinks things will come without looking for her.

Depression: it is a mental illness that is characterized by deep sadness, which allows the individual to be without spirit, with low esteem. If the thing does not come as expected, he/ser gives up.

Hate: it is a serious disease that nests in the minds of all those who have feelings of repulsion towards their neighbor, which can produce desires to harm others. They reveal themselves to discover it with the look and the expression. That person will never be able to live happily for a second. If you want to keep a young spirit and last longer on earth, we must exchange hatred for love.

Sadness: it is a symptom that produces the unhappiness and the affliction in the individual's moral and emotional life, if you do not look for a quick solution, you can produce fatal depression.

Anger: the feeling of anger is very powerful and violent. He reigns within all those who are influenced by hatred in their hearts. It bears blows, physical, moral and emotional abuse.

Rabies: it is a deadly and very poisonous virus that is transmitted in the spit of the individual who has negative feelings, which occurs especially in the hateful person who, when expressed, secretes more poison than a black mamba.

Grudge: It is a feeling of hostility towards a person because of an offense, someone who has no judgment or forgiveness, who never forgets the wrong done by the other guy.

Guilt: someone who never feels their mistakes, as long as they can blame others for their failures, someone who thinks they are always right.

Anger: It is someone who is angry for any reason, or for the lack of another person, who produces anger, bad blood. A human who has that behavior will never feel happiness.

Envy: It is a feeling of sadness experienced in the person who lacks something compared to the person who has it. Someone who likes to possess what does not belong to him, that feeling produces the feeling of theft in the heart of that individual.

Selfishness: It is an attitude or behavior typical of people who do not think of others. If you can't do one thing, you don't want someone else to do it either.

Superiority: It is a quality or a situation that one allows oneself when one feels superior to the other because of the amount of money he has, because of the importance he has in society and because of his rank. There are people who do not boast with words, but with the way of being.

Revenge: Action with which a person takes revenge on others; which uses the "tooth for tooth" principle.

The bad temper: It is an evil that afflicts many people. It can be caused by external reasons, as well as by circumstances that affect you internally. Those who live with the bad temper regularly can lose their temper for things that could be fixed by staying calm.

The discomfort: It is the feeling of discomfort from external causes, especially from another human being. It can make us an antisocial.

Fury: It is a very violent anger that manifests itself with screams and agitated gestures.

Impatience: It is someone who has no patience even for himself. It is unthinkable for him to maintain patience; hates waiting.

The irritation: It is a very big anger both outside and inside the individual.

Violence: Use of force to achieve an end, especially to dominate someone or impose something.

According to Dr. Martha: Everyone has been through some of those negative elements in life, because we are all human and sinful. Sometimes you can have a very positive mind, the enemy has sent some people - your boss for example - to make you negative, even if we fall victim to these feelings, we have to emerge victorious from them.

We must do everything possible to find the first love we had. Because they are networks of the enemy so that we cannot overcome or succeed. So he has sent someone to distract us and put us in the critical state where he wants us to be. The negative fruits cut our relationship with God.

But there is hope and recovery for all those who are going through those processes. If we know our shortcomings, our guilt, there will be improvement, because Jesus tells us in his holy word: "Come unto me, all ye that labour and are heavy laden, and i will give you rest": [Matthew 11:28].

Sometimes we seek professional help that end up making things worse. Christ is the universal panacea. If you are in the stage of the election and you suffer some of those evils, and there is no change, expel it like a devil, because tomorrow others will possess you and it will be worse.

You can break 50,000 pre-dating but not a dating relationship, because you were trying to see if you could have something formal with this guy. But if you have found some of those fruits in the chosen one, you must stop that relationship. Because they are very clear signs that God sends you to demonstrate that you are taking a bad path.

Chapter 7

The emotion

What is emotion?

Emotions are psychophysiological reactions that represent ways of adapting to certain stimuli of the individual when he perceives an important object, person, place, event or memory.

I can say it is a feeling that produces joy or sadness stimulated by an idea, a memory, etc. When a person is dominated by emotion, he cannot make any good decision, because the spirit of normality is not going to be able to do any work in his heart.

You will never be able to see or imagine the dangers that lie in wait. With emotion, he will never be able to return to normal. And when the emotion dissipates, comes the guilt that if I had known, it is now too late.

What do psychologists say about emotion?

A group of psychologists in Madrid [psicoadapta.es] described the emotion as follows: «An emotion is a feeling that arises when the person reacts subjectively to the environment, thus generating an affective state that is going accompanied by physical changes since emotions can cause physiological reactions».

These somatic reactions caused by emotions are controlled by the autonomic nervous system and the hypothalamus, therefore they are considered involuntary (sweating, fast heart rate, etc.). However, we can also say that an emotion can generate more or less controllable observable behaviors such as gestures, non-verbal language, facial expressions, etc.

Despite the fact that in colloquial language it is easy to talk about emotions and emotional state as if it were the same thing, we must know that an emotion has a shorter duration and a greater intensity than a state of mind.

It is considered that there are a series of universal basic emotions that all people, regardless of their culture, experience and that we possess from birth; However, others are conditioned by past experiences and by the learning that is acquired throughout life.

There is no consensus on which are the primary emotions, the most basic, and which are the secondary ones. The latest theories, and especially the most popular, speak of the fact that at least four to eight basic emotions seem to exist. They are those that appear regularly in many listings, and that we consider as the most defining.

Classification of emotions

Primary emotions. They have great speed. They originate in the amygdala and are innate.

Wrath: generates anger, irritability.

Joy: euphoria, gratification, happiness, desire to feel these kinds of situations again.

Sadness: loneliness, grief.

Fear: prepares us for a threat, anticipates it and produces nervousness, insecurity or anxiety, among other states.

Aversion: tendency to move away from what we reject, that disgusts us, etc.

Surprise: the subject feels startled, misplaced, amazed and with some bewilderment.

As we see, there are positive emotions that we must implement in the couple's life. When a person is positive, everyone wants to be by his side, because he will find positive things to feed his being. The fruits of negative emotion are the same psychologist group in Madrid: Shame, Pride, Excitement, Anxiety, Insecurity, Hope, etc.

Well-formed and educated people should not have one of those fruits that produce negative emotion, nobody wants to be with or share with a guy who has these bad qualities.

In short, it is difficult to establish an exact number of the existing emotions, but what can be affirmed is that the basic emotions serve as the basis for the other emotions, which are more complex and numerous than these. In fact, in 1980, Robert Plutchik defined "the wheel of emotions", in which you could see how the different emotions combined with each other to create more complex ones.

Finally, we conclude by exposing that the knowledge and understanding of our emotions allows us, not only to know ourselves and to know how we feel, but it is a great and valuable resource to use to be able to interact with the rest of the world and with oneself in a more healthy, adequate and optimal.

Being able to interact, controlling and managing our emotions, as well as being able to express them, brings great benefits to the subject.

Daniel Goleman, journalist and writer psychologist, and who developed the concept of emotional intelligence, tells us: «Emotional intelligence is the set of skills that serve to express and control feelings in the most appropriate way; motivations, perseverance, empathy or mental agility». Just the qualities that make up a character with good social adoption.

The positive guy never takes advantage of the feelings of others to make them suffer with false promises. If you do not like this guy, that is if you do not feel anything in common for him or her, do not find any method or excuse to cheat him/her, either sexually or financially.

Because in the end he will leave a wound without healing in his heart, nobody should say to his neighbor I love you as a false promise. We must be honest in all circumstances even if the truth hurts.

As conquerors have the right to conquer any person, just as the convincing woman has the right not to accept the invitation, the offer or the promise, also as an educated guy she has to find a way to say no, without the offense or the rejection. If you have discovered his intention from the beginning, you have to put a stop.

Because no one should make a choice without their feelings. No father should choose for his children; they have their rights to make choices based on their feelings.

When a father makes the choice for his son, he will never be able to live happily; he will live a tragedy for the rest of his life. When a person is eating their favorite food, they take all their time to enjoy the taste, just as they have taken their own responsibility to choose the person they like.

The guy who is in love with all his heart, shows it with good behavior and habits. You want to be with your favorite guy every day, you care about each other, you never get tired of seeing him/her for any reason. There are people who cannot discover when someone is in love, but with the knowledge of these concepts, everyone will be able to distinguish wheat from tares.

Because each one has its own fruits, sometimes they are very similar, but they are not the same, by the fruits the individual can identify the tree, without the fruits it is impossible to discover them because the secret is in the fruits.

Have you known who your partner is? Have you discovered the fruits of your lover/spouse before accepting him/her? Do you make a good choice? Is he the ideal person in your life? A person who knows the direction of his bed even though it is dark, goes straight to it.

The person who has a stable relationship is not by magic or luck or destiny, he only takes all his time to discover who that person is, what kind of love he has, what kind of relationship he is looking for; he is someone who would not be dominated by emotion or despair; is someone who has discovered true love in their partner before…

Someone who has been guided by God, who seeks the presence of God before the election, as God never fails, as God is perfect, all his decisions are perfect, because He is never wrong for a second. All who have let God choose their futures will never fail.

The wise guy does a self-analysis of his exposition to discover if he/she is true or false, if it is an emotional or natural feeling. Also the chemistry between the two is very important to discover true love. You should know that there are two categories of chemicals: "emotional and natural." The emotional is dangerous. It represents energy expenditure and bad decisions.

Emotion and feeling

According to the opinion of specialists in health psychology of the Barcelona Psychology Center «Psicoemocionat», [psicoemocionat.com], the answer to this question begins with others: Do you know what is the difference between emotion and feeling? Can they really be differentiated or are they synonymous? Keeping our affective vocabulary updated is important to continue feeding our emotional growth.

Feeling and emotion may seem like the same concept but they are actually two different words and states. We are going to discover what nuances these two words have so that we can use them in our daily life. In both cases we feel, but the condition is different if I am referring to an emotion or a feeling.

What is emotion?

For specialists at this center, an emotion is a complex reaction of the brain to an external stimulus (something I see or hear) or an internal stimulus (thought, memory, internal image). Emotion comes from the Latin emovere, which means to move to or from. Contrary to popular belief, emotions are something transitory, not permanent, that takes us out of our habitual state for a period of time.

Emotions are energies that move through our body and only stagnate if we repress them. Emotions therefore drive us to action, they are more intense and last less time than feelings.

You just bought a car is the second day you use it and when you start it it does not start. You may feel angry. You just found out that you have been awarded a scholarship to study, you may feel joy. They tell you that they have robbed your building, maybe you feel fear.

What is the feeling according to the biologist Humberto Maturana?

Feeling is the sum of emotion + thought. It is the subjective experience of our emotional experience. According to biologist Huberto Maturana, an emotion is transformed into a feeling as one becomes aware of it. In other words, in addition to physiological reaction, a cognitive and subjective component intervenes in feeling. A feeling therefore occurs when we label the emotion and make a judgment about it.

It is when we interpret the feeling that we are having consciously and explicitly. Feelings usually last longer than emotions. The latter will last as long as we think of them. Feelings come after emotions. There is no feeling without emotion.

Some examples of feelings are love, jealousy, suffering or pain, rancor, happiness, compassion. Developing empathy will also allow us to understand the feelings of other people. As we have already mentioned, feelings are generally quite long in duration.

To continue with the previous example, your partner has just left you, and for example, you realize that you feel sad. Sadness turns into feeling when you bring awareness and thought. Another example: you just got fired from work, you can feel the emotion of anger.

And then other emotions come to you when you think about it that end up becoming feelings, for example, sadness, fear of not finding another job, joy for feeling liberated from not listening to your boss ever again, etc.

Chemistry in the individual

The chemistry and power of attraction between two people. Trying to explain and put into words what the attraction between two people is about is extremely exciting. Why a guy is attracted to a certain person and not to another is often inexplicable.

These are some of the interpretations that professionals offer about emotion, feeling and chemistry. Although all three are similar, but each of them has its role in the person.

From my point of view, they are three different things - although at the same time, similar - because each one has its own function in the individual. Chemistry must manifest itself among people naturally.

It is a signal that the individual must put into practice if he wants to know or find the right guy for life. There are many divorces in the world because they have confused the emotion of the moment with natural chemistry. The real chemistry unites two pieces of apple, you will never be able to combine a lemon with an apple: they are two different fruits.

The biggest problem in infatuation: it's haste and despair. Maybe due to age, that is, all my friends have boyfriends, or are married, not me. In this case, despair will bring the false decision, because in my mind I want to be equal to my friends. Total failure.

We are living in a world in a hurry, all the things we are doing is in a hurry and despair for society. We never calculate what will happen in the future with those mistakes. At the same time there are people who have let go of many good opportunities for not knowing how to discern the bad from the good. They must take advantage of all the good opportunities if they want to have a successful future.

At the end of your investigations and discovery you have to give the final verdict for or against. Your decision must be fair without discrimination of any.

Chapter 8

Thought and spirit

Moses said: "And the Lord God formed man of the dust of the ground, and breathed into his nostrils the breath of life; and man became a living soul ": [Genesis 2: 7].

What is man?

The Creator took all his time, and all his intelligence, to design that creature called man. God has created all animals with his lips, but when it was his turn to create man, He not only used his mind and lips, but his hands as well, the only created being that is similar to God is man. Man has different components, the three great parts of man are: dust + water + breath of God = to the living being: a divine equation.

The only being created by God who carries his breath is man. So, God dwells within man in his spirit which is the breath of life. That is why the man, just by knowing God, has control of his life.

Man can bathe fifty times a day and will always find dust in him, because the body produces dust, we are from the dust of birth, but we must avoid degenerating into permanent mud. King Solomon said: All go unto one place; all are of the dust, and all turn to dust again, nobody can avoid that place.

We will all return in the same place where we come from, which is the dust of the earth, the rich as well as the por.

All the things we have achieved here will stay in the same place, nobody can carry anything the only one we will carry is a coffin, if posible. You can have all the university degrees that exist in the world, you can have all the money in the world, all the fame, the hugs of the world, you can never avoid the land where you left.

No human can control that breath that is in you, nor any created spirit, only God, if he wants, he can extinguish it at any time. So no one can see or understand it because it comes directly from God. God dwells in man through his spirit.

What is the human spirit?

The human being has divided into three main parts: mental emotional, biological physical and spiritual being, all dominate and guide by the spirit that is the breath that is within man.

What do the great scholars say about the human spirit?

They say: It is a philosophical, psychological, emotional component, understanding, awareness. Judgment, memory, reasonable. A wind that God blew into man's nose, allowing him to speak and move. It is a gift from God.

Only He has control of that spirit, if that wind is not in him it automatically becomes a corpse. That spiritual energy is not given by evolution, it is not animal, it comes directly from God, believe it or not.

God has control of his spirit, he can remove it whenever he wants, he is the owner, only he can listen and understand all the things that you have said in your mind, because your spirit comes from him. We are not evolution's fruits, we are God's fruits living.

When God finished creating the universe, in his infinite love and wisdom, he decided to form a steward to care for all the things that he had created. So he took the dust from the earth and created a doll called man, to dominate over all the things he created. No one comes to this world by chance, comes for a well-determined reason to fulfill a very special mandate.

That is why each person has a gift, in the end he has to give an account to the Creator if he has wasted it or not. The Apostle Paul said: For we must all appear before the judgment seat of Christ; that every one may receive the things done in his body, according to that he hath done, whether it be good or bad: [2 Corinthians 5:10].

For we must all appear before the judgment seat of Christ; that every one may receive the things done in his body, according to that he hath done, whether it be good or bad.

What is the breath of God?

It is his own strength, in Hebrew which is nefesh = life, power, wind, breath, air, and spirit: it is God himself in the Spirit within man. If he is within man, then he knows of all that man thinks within his heart. Then the whole earth must worship him, because he deserves all the glory and honor for ever and ever.

Where have you got that power you have to create all those things that you have created? It is the divine force that is within you that illuminated your mind and spirit to do or become what you are, if that force a dead dog has more value than you.

Have you taken a few minutes to reflect on where that force that is within you comes from? Have you taken a little time to thank the King of the universe for what you are and what you have done? We must be very grateful, because without him, you could never have done everything you have done.

Your power and your strength have limits, but God's is unlimited, you can never compare yours with God's, because you are a created being. God created himself.

What is thought?

Thought is the activity and creation of the mind. It is said of everything that is brought into existence through the activity of the intellect, the imagination: everything that is mental in nature is considered thought, whether these are abstract, rational, creative, artistic.

Coordination of the creative work of multiple individuals with a unified perspective in the context of an institution is also considered thinking.

God's thinking is unlimited, but man's is limited, with this gift he gave to man, he can create even wonders before the eyes of humanity: a machine flies with 400 people from east to west; a machine runs on the water with 2000 passengers; with his wisdom and intelligence, man has created a technology that from your country allows you to communicate with people from all over the world at the same time.

Although you are exercising your gift, never think that you are better than the Creator, because at any moment he can extinguish that force or that power that is within you; he allows everything to do his works on earth.

The spirit works and guides the whole body through thought, the eyes gave the spirit to capture the external world and memory to create the archive of the mind. It is a group of elements that work together, although each one has its function in the body of the individual.

The spirit is the abstract entity traditionally considered the immaterial part that, together with the body or material part, constitutes the human being; the ability to feel and think is attributed to it.

The hand can never commit any action if the spirit does not allow it, so each individual must take care of his spirit, if he wants to be happy or succeed in all the things he wants to do. So if the spirit goes out in man, it automatically becomes a corpse.

Animals have no spirit, they have instinct, they are not equal to or superior to man, man was created especially to dominate or manage them with the reason, conscience, morality, feeling, thought and spirit that is within him.

The man talks, they don't, the man works and learns a profession, they don't. They are two different created beings in every way; man was created in the image of God the animals, no. When a guy compares a human being to an animal, he is saying or thinking God is a liar and Satan is right. Reflects that he/she is willing to degrade himself/herself to that level.

For this reason, we can not have the same behavior as them, sometimes pets seem to be smarter than man, but they will always be animals. The human being wants to give them feelings, but that will never happen. It is a satanic and animalistic weakness. No created being can change sex, although Satan and science compare us, we will never make them equal because we are two totally different creatures.

Who is your enemy, how can you define him?

Our great enemy is Satan, even if you are a Christian or not, we are in that great battle, although each one has his own cross, because the enemy has no compassion even for his servants, his mentality is evil. Satan is at war with all mankind, rich, poor, black, white, yellow, ability as incapacity, we are all at the forefront of that war, although you are the servant of Satan himself, he is at war with you too.

Satan will not come before you like an ugly devil as painters portray it in his paintings. Satan is not an ugly angel. He was called an angel of light when he was on the mountain of Jehovah.

In this new century, Satan is using people of letters, the great intellectuals, people of great prestige, the famous, people of great values to end your life. As he knows there is no happiness without matronius, his plan is to destroy that institution completely, he enjoys himself very much when we are suffering, therefore, you must know his future location although 30% before the election.

Apostle John said: «And there was war in heaven: Michael and his angels fought against the dragon; and the dragon fought and his angels, and prevailed not; neither was their place found any more in heaven. And the great dragon was cast out, that old serpent, called the Devil, and Satan, which deceiveth the whole world: he was cast out into the earth, and his angels were cast out with him.

Therefore rejoice, ye heavens, and ye that dwell in them. Woe to the inhabiters of the earth and of the sea! for the devil is come down unto you, having great wrath, because he knoweth that he hath but a short time»: [Revelation 12: 7, 8,9, 12].

Why is Satan at war against the church of God?

Because he was on the mountain of God, he knows what he lost, the opportunities he had on the holy mountain of God. He said in his thought: If I have lost everything, I will do my best so that no one can have part in heaven.

Because he knows that it is the followers of Christ who are going to replace him on the mount of God. Every human being must know why he is at the forefront of this war.

Every human being must know who his true enemy is, and with whom he is fighting daily, whether you are a Christian or not, you are at the forefront of this war. Since when have you been at the forefront of this war? Since before your birth, that's why before birth Satan looks for a way to claim his life.

Automatically he has control over your life, he changes your status and your name for animal (horse). Jesus calls his Christian followers, Satan also calls his animal followers; the followers of Christ are very similar to him, the followers of Satan are animals with reasons.

According to him, he has many followers who are making blurb for him in universities and science, because of the way the enemy treats humanity, demonstrates racism, discrimination, hatred comes from him. All the people who have embodied those principles are part of his flock.

He in the minds of the rulers, the kings of the earth, to change the moral and civic matter in all the schools, because he knows that it is the new generation that will lead the world, if they have no morals, they will never to be able to discover the work that he is doing with them.

We are going to do a very simple analysis. If it is true that humanity comes from animals or descendants of animals, why do animals not speak or have consciousness or thought? what a difference between instinct and morality?

Animals react instinctively, they have no thoughts or morals; no matter how hard science strives to make them think, speak, and even give self-help talks, they are divinely inferior beings. The moral person is right, thought and understanding, each individual has spirit but animals do not. The spirit comes from God, because God is the source of all spirits.

The Bible and science, which of the two has the truth about the creation or existence of man? Which of the two should we believe? First, we must define what the Bible is: it is a set of books that are the word of God.

God speaks to His people through the Holy Bible. Because God never does anything without saying it first in his holy word.

Science is a branch of human knowledge made up of the set of objective and verifiable knowledge on a given subject, which is obtained through observation and experimentation, the explanation of its principles and causes, and the formulation and verification of hypotheses.

It is also characterized by the use of an appropriate methodology for the object of study and the systematization of knowledge. Generic name of the different branches of human knowledge, especially those that have the natural or physical world or technology as subjects of study.

They are two very different things, which have no comparison, but each individual has his right to listen to one between the two, although he cannot serve both at the same time. Because each one has its fruits and its own author.

What do scientists say about the existence of humanity?

Charles Robert Darwin has said that man comes from the ape or the gorilla. Is it true that Darwin has said that?

Who WAS CHARLES ROBERT DARWIN? WHAT DOES CHARLES ROBERT DARWIN REALLY SAY? DID HE BELIEVE IN GOD?

Charles Darwin believed in God in his own way, as a naturist. He understood things differently, after all, all archbishops believe in their existence as God, even if they don't do what God says. Darwin had a racist mentality, he thought he was superior than the others. Darwin never said that humanity descended from the monkey.

Philosophers and scientists are misinterpreting Darwin's words, they say what Darwin did not say. What Charles Darwin really said was, "Blacks and Australian Aborigines are equal to gorillas." He then inferred that they, over time, should be "pushed aside" by civilized races.

Darwin also considered white Europeans as more advanced than other human races. Darwin was discriminating other races in front of the European whites, he thought that his race was smarter, more capable of doing things better than the others.

Due to Darwin's racist expression, the vast majority of whites think they are superior to the black race. Pure mistake, no one is greater than anyone, we all mold by the same God.

Darwin was saying that blacks and Australian Aborigines are animals. Because gorillas have no reason, no morals, no thoughts. God never said we have to be superior to others, if whites can develop their minds to do wonders, blacks can also, because God is just, He never limits the knowledge that he has given to a single race or people.

We must prepare our children to do bigger things too, we are all equal in the eyes of God, there are neither white nor yellow, nor black, we are all equal in the eyes of God, we limit ourselves by how conformist we are, but it is not God who limits us. Jay Gould in "Ever since Darwin" comments that children of many African races are little or no less intelligent than European children.

It is normal because the Africans were in the slavery of the whites, their descendants could not leave good foundations or good examples for them, to this day the blacks are in the modern slavery of the whites, they do not allow us to evolve.

They don't want blacks to enter the realm of knowledge, because that would mean emancipation. When their children were in large universities studying and preparing, blacks and their children were doing hard labor with chains on their feet. Therefore, it is normal for them to say that black children are less or not at all intelligent than white children.

We broke the chains of our feet, we can never break the spiritual, in addition the whites close all doors so that no black can grow in any way, the time has come when we should all be free because we are the same people. We must eliminate racism worldwide, because in this new century, no one should suffer racism or rejection, whatever the conditions.

Charles Darwin was not only a great scientist, he was a great racist as well. Darwin had the great privilege of being born and educated in a professional family, and studying at the best university of that time, because his father was a great doctor, it is normal that he has become a person of great favor in the world, but if a black would must had the same privilege as Darwin, that black could have been bigger than Darwin at that time.

Because there is a difference between you and me if we are the same people, because the indifference between you and me if in the end we go in the same place, if you are free help me break that chain and that great mountain that does not want to let me see the wind of the Hope.

If you really love me, we will form a single cycle where whites, yellows and blacks can be one in the spirit of love, because the same guys.

Chapter 9

The couple's behavior at the dating stage

There are many people who have confused dating with marriage, they have a life as husband and wife, they travel together, they sleep in the same bed, they enjoy a lot in the sexual relationship, until they even have children together. They have an animal mentality, they met today and are currently having sex.

We are not animals, animals have no morals, they do everything on top of everyone; the human being, no, we have moral and reasonable mentality, we have to do everything within a pact. If a guy wants to get into a sexual relationship with a girl, he has to be prepared first, then he can have all the rights to do it already in the marriage.

What is dating?

Dating is the condition of the couple, that is, a loving relationship maintained between two people with the possible intention of marriage, it is a process by which two people develop an intimate association beyond friendship.

In the courtship, their names are changed to dear darling, love, my love, my life, my king, my heaven, my dear, my heart, my pretty flower, my little angel, my prince, my princess very often in diminutive accompanying the possessive.

They are two people who are getting to know each other, who have a chance to get married, but they are not yet, they still cannot enjoy the sweetness that all the bride and groom hope to enjoy after the marriage covenant. Respectful people prepare first before enjoying those sweet moments.

There are two authors of love in the world "God and Satan", each one has his followers. God has his discipline of how his followers should enjoy that beautiful wonder that is love.

The enemy makes things very easy for his followers, because of that facility there are many followers of Christ who are listening more to the voice of the adversary than that of God, who promised that all human beings can enjoy that love without any concern.

Today even friends have sex without any commitment, not for love, only for pleasure. No one has a rule or discipline, anything goes for them, without knowing the dangers they are waiting for. When God forbids something, it is in favor of humanity, because he does not want anyone to suffer, he wants all human beings to enjoy sex in marriage, not outside of it.

But the faithful followers of Jesus do not hear the voice of the enemy, they wait for the time of marriage to enjoy that sweetness that is the dream of all future married couples. Never forget the economy is essential in all relationships. If you want to enjoy your partner sexually, you have to ask the marriage first, otherwise it is impossible for them because everything is not valid for those who are in Christ.

Your upper body is not a good tasting cake that everyone wants to try, it is something that everyone should enjoy only in marriage.

What is a love relationship?

Okairy Zúñiga, a law graduate from the Latin American Technological Institute [November 6, 2018], commented on her Better Health page, she said: "There are four types of love relationship according to Zúñiga. Each love relationship is different and depends a lot on the characters of the couple members and how they are able to carry out the different stages of it".

Love relationships are often full of incredible moments and others that are not so much. Similarly, each relationship is different from any other. In the end, it all depends entirely on who makes up the couple. Throughout your life you will have love relationships of different types.

That will depend on how old you are and the person who shares your path. Furthermore, each circumstance is completely different.

1.- The dramatic couple

This is not the perfect definition of a good partner. Dramatic couples spend less time together than others and experience many ups and downs. This type of couples represents the highest percentage within all types of love relationships. According to studies carried out in this regard, after a period of nine months, said couples are more likely to face a breakup.

The enormous emotional intensity is one of the factors that determines this type of couples. Those who are involved are not aware of each other's needs. Simply, both allow themselves to be carried away by their instincts and take the relationship to a level of lack of control that cannot be endured for long. The result is constant conflict in his desperate attempt to free himself from that level of passion.

Many times it is painful when you realize everything you give in this kind of relationship. However, they simply don't bear the fruit you expect. You're always on the lookout for the next drama, because it's what brings interest to the relationship. Loving relationships without any level of drama tend to make couples happier and find excitement and passion in their relationship.

2.- The conflictive couple

These types of love relationships are the ones that fight the most but this does not mean that they will end quickly. This type of relationship is known as an erotic relationship, not only because of its strong sexual intensity, but because, in some way, it involves suffering, intensity, passion, the need for fusion and constant ecstasy.

Therefore, it is impossible to maintain over time. In the end, these types of relationships involve pain and wear. The fundamental problem is that as long as you don't realize that need for control or to feel love as you expect, you will keep repeating the pattern.

3.- The couple socially involved

This couple is the one that provides more stability and satisfaction. They are heavily influenced by social media, but are still interested and committed to themselves. Social media has changed the ways couples interact, so arguably there are considerations for members after a breakup.

Social media is known for causing ups and downs in a relationship. Couples who use Facebook a lot are more likely to have conflicts related to the network itself in their relationships. This, in turn, can cause negative results on the relationship, due to infidelities that lead to the breakup and divorce.

But the good news is that not everything is bad when social media engages in love relationships. Sharing photos of the couple on Facebook has been shown to often lead to greater relationship satisfaction. The network and other social media allow couples to instantly connect with each other. This gives them an opportunity to promote a certain level of positivity in their relationship.

4.- The couple focused on their relationship

This is the couple most likely to marry. That is not a surprising finding either. After all, spending time with your partner is one of the keys to successful love relationships. Couples who spend time together often remember the beauty of their relationship. Even in a world where people are constantly busy and rarely have time to take a break.

You must remember that your partner is the person who decides to spend the rest of his life with you. It may be the same person who brightens your day and helps you through the difficulties that arise. Spending time with your partner is quite simple when you make it a priority.

The good news is that spending small moments together is simple and very positive. This is what really matters to maintain a strong and healthy relationship.

Love relationships are often complicated and can have good and bad stages. Once you identify the type of partner you have, you should analyze if it is the best option and if it is really doing you good. As you can see, some of these relationships are not the best alternative.

Although you can always work on them, you must pay attention and put an end to it when the damage it does to you is greater. There can be love in all of them, but there will always be one that marks you more than the others or that is more lasting.

From my point of view, the love relationship is the sweet moment that lovers begin to enjoy from the first day of dating until real life within marriage; where the unforgettable moments are happening; where one cannot live without the other, but it is not a moment of sexuality between the two, because we have not yet signed any paper or pact that stipulates that they are free to enjoy each other in sexuality, without reservation.

It is a sweet moment and everyone should pass by, when two lovers are together, they never want the time to end, although they have eight hours together, for them it is never enough, they always have something to say to each other. Because everyone's heart claims their presence, all their hormones are active, not to have sex, but to be in each other's arms. When they are kissing those who are devouring a honeycomb.

What is the discipline the individual must have to guide their relationship to total success? There are two essential things the couple must have to reach their goal: Jesus and love without condition and without end. With those two characteristics they are ready for their final goal.

The couple are two trustworthy people, they are two good friends, two lovers, where each one has the key to the other's heart, they always want to be next to each other; they know each other's secrets. They will never discredit each other with friends, one always keeps the secret for the other, they hang out together at all times, they are everywhere together, they never tire of being together.

Each one is always taking care of the other, they are pending if the other eats, if one is well... The life of the married couple is wonderful, they are happy at all times, much laughter. It is incomparable and inexplicable, they never forget the first kiss or the date of commitment.

The dating stage is getting to know each other deeper, their families, their cultures, their customs and their characters, they are two different sexes that do not have the same biological functions. No one can seek to change another, because that will never happen, but adapt to the other with all its criteria.

Dating is the reflection of marriage, if the relationship cannot work in the dating stage, how it will work in reality time; if the life of the courtship was a disaster, the marriage will be hell for both of them; if they fight the sweetness that will happen in the coexistence. So the two sweetheart must have adult thoughts if they want to have a successful family.

How many years should a dating relationship last?

From my point of view, the ideal time that a love relationship should last is two years maximum, which is the right time to know the habits of another. They must also both be mature enough to bring that relationship into a zone of permanent comfort.

There are some elements those involved must have to be successful in the relationship:

1.- Old enough, where the two can know clearly what they have and where they want to go.

2.- You must have a professional career or your own business.

3.- Enough morality to guide that relationship to a good position.

4.- Sufficient economy to respond to the demands of material life.

There are women who, after having time with a engagement, fall into great despair, because her boyfriend hesitates to take the step that is most important to her: commitment or marriage. Every time she sees the friends are getting married, the situation worsens. The family and society press, asking how long that relationship will last.

For all these reasons, both must have a solid preparation, because neither man can allow his partner to despair because of him or due to lack of professional preparation and financial guarantee.

The ages that are best for them to maintain a good dating relationship: they are from 24 to 33 years old, where they are emotionally, sentimentally, professionally, morally and financially prepared; their maturity can sustain any romantic relationship.

Preparation is the most essential point for all those who want to form a home, although happiness is not only the economy, but no couple can be happy without that element. Do you want to form a home?: GET READY! Because when you are married you form your own home, and although your parents are rich, you're already independent. You have with what to respond to all the demands of this relationship.

If you cannot respond to your partner's needs at the dating stage, how you think you will respond in marriage. It is totally impossible, because the dating life is the reflection of marriage. For all these reasons, time is mandatory before making any decision, time will tell if your choice is correct or not, everyone marries to be better than their father's house, not to be worse.

Before you marry someone, you still need to find 40% of those questions. What will your future be like tomorrow with this guy you have chosen as your partner? Are you sure he/she loves you? Are you sure there is a future there? If the answers are yes, you can move forward without fear.

What did God say about love hero

God has not sent an angel to give this good news to man, but with all his love he expressed to him: «And the Lord God said, It is not good that the man should be alone; I will make him an help meet for him»: [Genesis 2:18].

Because there are many needs, the guy cannot do himself. He need a companion, a suitable one, a fit for life, because nobody can be happy being single.

What is suitable help?

A woman who capable of fulfilling her tasks as God has asked, is not a being inferior to her husband; they are two equal people in deals with different positions within the home. An empowered woman is a good human being who knows how to meet the needs of her partner.

She is an incomparable lady, a woman who has that virtue is an intelligent woman and knew that she is guided by the path of the good Teacher, she is not a anyone is a special and unique person. So she needs to be loved, protected and pleased at all times for her husband.

All those who have a single life are not complete, there are many things that you will not be able to do to please yourself. Each human being needs a helper or a companion to be complete, that choice cannot be made without preparation, nor before time, each thing has its time; someone who can face life with you until death, someone who feels the same way about you, that feeling has to be mutual.

All men and women have been created to be part of that great family of husbands and wives where they can always live a life full of harmony and mutual respect until old age.

Why should a man love his wife with all his heart?

The architect Moses said: "And the Lord God caused a deep sleep to fall upon Adam, and he slept: and he took one of his ribs, and closed up the flesh instead thereof; and the rib, which the Lord God had taken from man, made he a woman, and brought her unto the man": [Genesis 2:21, 22].

The great architect of the universe has taken all his time to design a beautiful flower, a precious pearl, an incomparable one, an admirer, a natural beauty, someone who can correspond to man's taste according to his need. That beauty is called a woman. God has not created a slave, nor a servant for man, but an earthly companion for all life.

What did Adam say when God presented him with his ideal?

Then Adam said: "And Adam said, This is now bone of my bones, and flesh of my flesh: she shall be called Woman, because she was taken out of Man.Therefore shall a man leave his father and his mother, and shall cleave unto his wife: and they shall be one flesh": [Genesis 2: 23-24].

Not only did Adam admire the work of art that God had made, he left an example to all future husbands, where they must do like him. Due to that great love Adam felt for his beloved wife, he agreed to lose paradise to be with her in good and bad times, although she screw up, he loved her at all times, good exemple for all. Is a good example for all married people of this century.

All future husbands must make the same Adam decision to love their beloved wives as themselves, because the two formed a single flesh for life in the bosom of marriage. Adam never divorced his beloved wife, nor did he use deceit or dishonest words against her.

Why did they have a good relationship until death?

Because they let God make the choice, all the things that God has made are perfect, lasting, although we are imperfect people, God will be the central part of our home, although many contrary winds come, hurricanes, we are like palm because Christ is in the middle.

Why is there no stability in your home?

Because you have never allowed God to make any choice for you, you have chosen the person according to your liking, you never invited Jesus into your home, without the presence of Jesus any wind can devastate that home because you have built it on the sands, not on the stone that is Jesus Christ.

Why are there so many divisions and stability problems within Christian homes?

Because nobody wants to let Christ become the center of their home. Jesus said in his holy word: "No man can serve two masters: for either he will hate the one, and love the other; or else he will hold to the one, and despise the other. Ye cannot serve God and mammon": [Matthew 6:24].

Many women within the church of God prefer wolves for unhealthy, unhealthy riches, for envy. God's presence cannot be in this place, because he had given all the rules on how his followers should have partners. If you do the opposite it is your problem, not of God.

All those who want to have wealth without sweating, will become their own slave, the apostle Paul gave a good answer to all Christians who join the world for their riches, he said: "For the love of money is the root of all evil: which while some coveted after, they have erred from the faith, and pierced themselves through with many sorrows": [1 Timothy 6:10].

Who should a Christian marry?

God said in his holy word: «Beloved, let us love one another: for love is of God; and every one that loveth is born of God, and knoweth God": [1 John 4: 7].

All those who have known God must form their homes with someone who has shared the same faith. What is the value of the wealth you are looking for without sweating, if in the end you will not be able to enjoy it? Since your partner does not know God or does his will, he will never love you as God has asked.

There are Christian women who say that worldly men are better than Christian men, it is a lie of the devil, with this mentality they say that God is a liar and Satan is absolutely right, with that nonsense his presence cannot be. All households that did not receive the presence of God received the enemy.

No home without Christ can have peace or happiness, all those who have married the wrong people are putting themselves in the enemy's network, because no sheep can feel happiness with a wolf. In the prince everything will be rosy, with time the wolf will show its true face.

God never said, you have to marry a lazy, nor with someone you do not love, because he does not want any suffering son, you have to let him make the choice because he knows what is best for you. The great problem that we Christians have, is that we are very selfish, and we want God to choose to our liking, not based on his infinite wisdom.

Why are animals and birds okay at all times?

It is because they do not have any discrimination, the ugly, unpleasant, poor expressions, races, colors, nationalities... do not exist for them. They treat others as themselves. Humanity has heard the voice of the enemy more than that of the Creator; they have followed the deceiver who is called Satan, the devil, more than God. So the world is going through those bad situations.

In this new century no one knows who belongs to Christ or Satan, they are all alike. The people who are doing the will of God as he has asked, are very few. God has not created humanity to be in this situation, the members of the church of God are more corrupted than the majority who are outside.

Moses said: «And it repented the Lord that he had made man on the earth, and it grieved him at his heart. And the Lord said, I will destroy man whom I have created from the face of the earth; both man, and beast, and the creeping thing, and the fowls of the air; for it repenteth me that I have made them»: [Genesis 6: 6-7].

Why has God not exterminated the world long ago?

The apostle John agreed, said: «And after these things I saw four angels standing on the four corners of the earth, holding the four winds of the earth, that the wind should not blow on the earth, nor on the sea, nor on any tree.

And I saw another angel ascending from the east, having the seal of the living God: and he cried with a loud voice to the four angels, to whom it was given to hurt the earth and the sea, Saying, Hurt not the earth, neither the sea, nor the trees, till we have sealed the servants of our God in their foreheads»: [Revelation 7: 1: 3].

The angels want to exterminate the earth for our acts and rebellions, because they cannot look at the many bad things that we are doing before the eyes of Jehovah.

Their great leader, who is Christ Jesus, said to them: have a little more patience to see if you will not change your bad behavior, Jesus is always at the door of your heart calling you, if you do not want to come or repent of your evil ways He will have to let the destroying angels touch you with their bitter cups.

Most Christians are lost within the church. Because they have the temple of God as a place of fun, they lose all reverence, fear and respect for the holy place of God. Although you have two Christian and worldly characters, it is not too late to soften beans and change your behavior, identity and your character to that of Jesus.

Chapter 10

Love without compromise

Everyone has forgotten the true love for the false, it seems that the author of the false has more followers than the true, because even in the temple of God people do not want to follow the rules to have the qualities of truth. Everyone likes to follow the false because it is liberal and more vain... Because it is a tiguere, said in good popular slang.

Dominicans use the word "tiguere" to describe a very cunning or deceptive person, someone who is an expert in manipulation or who gets what he wants through deception and fraud.

Little by little, those who claim to be Christians are leaving God's norms to follow Satan to the letter. True love almost does not exist anymore, both Christian and pagan, although the thing is very complicated at this time, there is always a small group that is fearful of God, who are fulfilling God's commands as he has said.

Marriage only for the economy

This kind of love is found more in people with less resources, who have been raised in poor family members, think of only one way to recover: through what comes from others. They agree to live or marry for interest, although there is no love or chemistry, they are exchanging their bodies for the economy.

All the things you are doing without the real one will never last long, one of you will either become a victim, or be deceived. It is a terrible thing to live with someone who does not love each other, feels disgust, they will never please each other as they should be. Because the flavor that can season the relationship, which is love, will always be missing.

That great mistake is happening in all countries, especially in the most vulnerable families that cause this crime, are the parents, who did not have a good entrance before starting the relationship.

Their daily income is not enough to satisfy the needs of the family, sometimes the vices do not allow it either. So in order for children to survive, they must marry someone they don't love, but who have money.

There are many wicked who are so abusive, that they are taking advantage of those bad occasions to have sex, without going any further. Parents are responsible and governments too.

What do scholars say about love of interest?

POSTED BY: GLOBAL VERLY [NOVEMBER 8, 2017]: «Relationship of couple for economic interest, in this sense they usually have a couple that solves economic needs and not for love. There are couples with severe problems, both toxic and dependent, but do nothing about it out of attachment to an economic interest.

Since many of the cases when a part of the couple does not work and only depends on the economy, they usually spend their lives in complaint and hardship, but they will not do anything about it. Many people, women or men, when they have an interest in another person, do not want to leave their comfort zone.

For others, cynicism reigns in exploiting the couple, not caring about anything. Economic dependence occurs in both women and men, without distinction. In many of the cases, there are women who get pregnant on purpose to keep the couple tied.

Furthermore, if the other person has financial solvency, they are usually tied up giving birth to a boy. Although this attempt often fails, the child pays the consequences.

The couple that is supported by interest ends their life frustrated, even having what they dreamed of: MONEY. Since it has remained with a person who does not love, but who also fails to be fully happy. You can detect when a couple stays with you for financial interest.

Generally the person concerned is self-centered and selfish. He wants all the privileges and economic benefits, he wants a life of fairy tales.

They want to be in social centers just to make a perfect life, trying to compete with their friends. This person does not tend to share, but only receive and ask the couple for money. Using emotional blackmail, because she is never satisfied with what is given to her.

When an error is pointed out to him, he tends to apologize, but with manipulation and emotional blackmail. It is difficult for them to accept their mistakes since it reigns in him/her, selfishness and immaturity. It has too much ability in people's emotions to make them feel guilty and thus be able to demand.

How can a person discover when someone is in love for financial interest?

There are many ways to find out:

a. By the way of being, because the two do not have the same flavor, nor the same taste, each one has its own fruits.

b. He always has problems, expenses, debts, he thinks that you are the solution to his problems.

c. For their expressions of despair.

d. By the way of looking.

e. Never stop asking.

Some signs that can detect if someone is in love out of interest are:

1.- It is only available when you need or want something

He will never look for you if he doesn't need you, if you look for him, he always has an excuse, the reason that can move him is the need for something; always has a problem; he is always complaining about his situations. If he has some money, it is never enough, he will only look for you to solve his problems, if you call on the phone, he is always busy.

2.- Never stop complaining

It is a way of saying that you have to pay your debts if you want to continue the relationship, if you do not speak in their favor, they will ask you for a loan. You are always blaming your ex or your current situation.

3.- Your tastes are very expensive

He never chooses anything that is not expensive, because he wants to take advantage of the moment.

4.- You always want to change your vehicle every year

The dining room, the fridge, the kitchen, bed, tv, radio, every year. He wants to live a luxurious life with you; the one that has never lived before.

5.- He never meets or works

You are always unemployed, if you work you never last long on the job, because you know where you will get the most out of.

6.- He offers you to move or marry you with a few months of knowing each other

There are many people who are very old, who do not like their generations, they are looking for the new generations to recover the dead cells that they have lost due to old age. Those kinds of relationships are uneven. That relationship always works with love out of interest, nor does one work without another.

The unequal relationship

The unequal relationship is something very popular both in the world and within the church of God, it is something that causes many problems and difficulties, both emotionally and mentally in the family.

There are very professional people, such as in churches or governments, who are supporting this type of relationship within their churches as in their countries, where they do not give low-income people any opportunity to prepare or have a decent job and study a career professional.

Not only are parents responsible, great religious and political leaders are responsible as well. Unequal relationships are never made out of pleasure, always out of necessity.

Why does the family accept their children to have an unequal relationship?

Since parents cannot respond to their needs, due to misery or lack of preparation, they must accept all the bad decisions of their children. The solution is to be with an older man who can cover your personal expenses and those of your parents. That home has lost all rights, the parents will never be able to react against the children, because the incapacity allows them to sell their integrity to survive.

Needs cause all the wrong decisions to be made inadvertently.

What can happen with an unequal relationship?

That relationship destroys many families and leaves many children orphaned, without mom or dad. There are children from birth to adults, who never know their parents, because of the "unequal", children pay for their parents' mistakes.

If we want a world without misery or abuse, where love can reign over the whole earth, each individual must make a reflection for his life and his descendant, where they can control a little "the unequal relationship".

Where can we find the fragrance of love again in all uneven homes? There are two categories of "unequal relationships": ages and ranges. Many people who are saying that in love there is "neither age nor rank", although it may be a reality, but not totally true, because there are many risks in these types of relationships, especially when you are in love with emotion.

No love relationship can work well with two people who are not the same age: there are many people who are very old who are having a romantic relationship with a young guy. It is a fatal risk for both sexes, especially if the man is older than her, because he will not be able to satisfy her in sexual relations without the viagra. There will come a time when the pill will not work at all.

As a young lady, she has to find another alternative. There he will begin to pay for his irresponsibility. All things can forgive a person, but age will never forgive anyone.

What should you do to avoid this type of relationship in your family?

You must prevent it before marrying someone; Warn you that you must know how to choose a partner, you must have a professional career, a stable job before getting married, or a business or your own company. Where money will not be an obstacle in your home. Because absence of money means presence of misery. Nothing good.

There are many men who think that money is enough to maintain a happy relationship, it is one of the ingredients, but it is not the only one. The couple needs four things for the relationship to work well:

1.- God as the center

When God is the center of your house, that home will become a nest of love, where peace, joy and happiness reign.

2.- The economy

The economy is a tool that the family can take on the path of total happiness, because no family can live without the economy in this century, where all things count. The economy causes disunity, infidelity, bad temper, suffering, sadness, boredom, etc...

3.- Romance

All women in the world like pleasure in privacy, no woman likes to be with a rooster in bed, or a man who has premature ejaculation problems. In order to respond with this tool, you have to have two things: good nutrition and a reasonable age.

Now there are therapies that can revive all the dead cells of the body, all women feel good when their partners are able to extract two or three orgasms in privacy. When you can do that, she will feel good with you.

4.- Good conversations

Good conversation is one of the factors that can recover any relationship that is about to break. It is one of the qualities that can help interaction and sincerity. No one should neglect this aspect in their relationship.

Why are there so many homicides in the world?

Because of the unequal relationship problem, when the man cannot solve sexually, he feels humiliated. His shame makes him aggressive; Possibly she will look for someone to make her sexually happy. There the problems will come. 80% of homicides, crimes, lawsuits, jealousy, femicides, verbal and physical assaults, comes from an unequal relationship.

The unequal relationship does not mean that everything is doomed to failure, there is always an exception but you must think for the future. If you are 45 years old now your partner is 24, they can all work well. When you get to 70 and she's 49, be prepared: trouble will plague the family.

Social rank in relationships

Social rank can also cause a very serious problem between the two, more if the numbers are in favor of women. If you are professional and have more input than the husband, the relationship may work, but in your heart you are unhappy. No woman feels good when she is superior to her spouse, she can bear it perhaps for the Christian faith or for her children, but she is not happy.

Because she was born to be a little less than or equal to the husband, automatically she feels superior that relationship does not last, because she will never feel good socially with a man who does not represent her.

The gentlemen are making a very serious mistake by not preparing professionally, in all the universities 70% of the graduates are women. Where are the men?: in vices, robberies, making easy money, doing corner, playing in the banking of ball, etc... And the profession for when? Who will suffer their mistakes are the children. In this century the two must be equal. When the two are equal, each feels more comfortable with the other in the relationship.

The great mistake of most men who come out of poverty, overcome themselves and marry, financially help their wives to finish their degree. A great gesture without a doubt, but they do not think about their future. Bad idea.

No woman likes to work to support a man, she was not created for that, she is the man who was created to maintain the home. That is why man is the priest of the home, and blasphemer in running a home without capacity. Sure, in the distorted state of values the world is mired in, examples of bum-keeping women abound just because they get their hands on the bed.

If you want to live a better future tomorrow, all gentlemen must prepare well, to face the cost of living; so you can have an exemplary family.

Chapter 11

The uneven yoke

There is a great problem that is shaking the religious world, those who claim to be followers of Jesus, who are not. Even within the true church of God the parishioner is following and complying to the letter, the decision of the enemy, through the "unequal yoke."

What is a yoke?

Instrument to join two oxen or mules in a yoke, made up of an elongated piece of wood with two arches that fit the head or neck of animals, and which is attached to the lance of a cart or the rudder of a plow, allowing them to pull on them.

The yoke is a wooden artifact to which the mules or oxen are attached, forming a yoke, and on which the spear or pole of the cart, the rudder of the plow, etc… are attached. Two oxen working together, joined by a yoke, are called a yunta. The expression derives from this last word and also applies, by extension, to other animals that work together, or to a couple of people who do the same. It means "union" in Latin.

It is a sentimental relationship between two people who do not share the same Christian faith and belief, each one has his own belief.

What do psychologists say about inequalities?

There is an association of psychologists in Madrid called AMS, women for health, where they have commented very seriously on the unequal yoke that is shaking the world, precisely in the Christian family.

Inequalities and inequities in couple relationships

This highly professional and studious group sees the situation almost the same as the Bible suggests, and they argue: "Through the following articles and the testimonies of various experiences on couple relationships.

We reveal the most common cheating mechanisms that any heterosexual couple encounters, from the moment they decide to marry or live as a couple and explain why both he and she do not perceive them as inequalities, think that they are both the same and believe that the fact that they are pairing will not affect them in their daily life".

We will talk about inequalities and inequities that usually remain hidden within traditional couple relationships, and which, however, are sufficiently contrasted in studies that confirm that marriage is a risk factor for women's health, while it is a protective factor for men. Thus, it is proven that married men have better health than married women, unlike single women, who enjoy better health than single men.

Both he and she do not perceive it as inequalities, they think that they are both the same and they believe that the fact of pairing will not affect them in their daily life.

Another important risk factor for women's health is having two or more children, which does not affect men in the same way. This is due to the difference assumed in parenting workloads and the different meaning of traditional motherhood and fatherhood. In this traditional model, the burdens of raising children fall on the women, who must make a physical and emotional effort in the multiple tasks of care.

However, men represent a nominal and social fatherhood, free from the tasks of care and the blame that this entails. By the same construction of gender, the meaning of the children is different in the ideal of masculinity and femininity. For women, sons and daughters are part of their integrity, the core of their being, which does not happen in the same way and intensity in the case of men.

These gender psychosocial aspects differentially influence the health of fathers and mothers, causing the worst health in women.

In order to understand the complex framework of traditional couple relationships, we start from the critical analysis of the ideas imposed in our society by the gender training for the gender training on the" Romantic Love "model. We depend, much more than most of us would like, that others love us, living focused on the lives and needs of our partner and our sons and daughters.

Aspects very well developed by the psychologists of the Espacio de Salud Entre Nosotras, in the articles "I renounce myself in the name of love" and "Affective dependencies in couple relationships".

In our therapeutic experience, for large numbers of women, these relationships become" addictive "and mutually exclusive, so that at some points in their lives they feel trapped and at a dead end. They experience what in AMS we have called a Gender Psychosocial Disorder (TPSG), which manifests itself in the form of Gender Depression or a Gender Syndrome (nº XXVIII and XXIX of La Boletina).

In the article" The invisible bond ", causes and consequences of incorporating and living unequal models of couple relationships are shown, as well as the traps, myths, love beliefs and" hooks "that they emerge in the ruptures of these sick and unequal relationships.

The exit to this crossroads is not easy, it takes a lot of personal work, a lot of pain and a lot of courage, to become aware of the insane consequences of patriarchal couple relationships, and find ways to establish new models of couple relationships, as reflected in the article "Personal space and shared space".

Finally, in the article" Obligatory shared custody, another form of Gender Violence ", we expose the false speeches and the tricks used by the neomachista movement that claims" egalitarian paternities", because, according to these men, they want to dedicate themselves," in equality "with the mothers, to take care of their daughters and sons.

Claims that in theory are very good, but that the reality of the data denies».

The common characteristic is that they are parents who, during the coexistence, argued that they could not be responsible for this care due to lack of time and not possess the necessary skills. Many of them have even exerted gender violence on their women and daughters and sons. However, it is only after divorce that they claim their right to exercise parenthood and care for them "equally."

Apparently, now they do have the time and the skills of caregivers... We also make visible the traumatic consequences that occur in the lives of mothers, sons and daughters, when in the wrong separations and divorces, the wrong call is legally imposed on them joint custody, or when the mothers are accused of alienating and guilty of the false syndrome of parental alienation (SAP).

A paradigmatic example of this new machismo" for the equality of the parents ", is the one that assiduously show judges and judges in their conferences and articles and, what is more serious, in their judicial decisions.

Public figures with great power in the judiciary and with great media influence, opponents of the Comprehensive Law against Gender Violence, ardent defenders of the majority existence of "False Reports" of women for ill-treatment, and vindicators of the false Alienation Syndrome Parental.

(The Bulletin nº XXVI and nº XXVIII). As we can see, ma.chismo, misogyny and arrogance are also shared by our highest representatives of justice.

I totally agree with that group of professional women, who take their time to analyze and see the opposite of others, although that situation affects the Christian family more than the worldly family, because they are the ones who suffer the most from this plague.

What does the Bible say about that contagious disease that is shaking almost all religious families, God is in favor of the unequal yoke between his children and those of the worldly?

The messenger of God spoke about that great and terrible virus that was shaking the parishioners of the church in Corinth said: «Be ye not unequally yoked together with unbelievers: for what fellowship hath righteousness with unrighteousness? and what communion hath light with darkness?»: [2 Corinthians 6:14].

In this new generation, this deadly virus has been changed by an incurable disease, because no Christian wants God to enter their relationship, where he is saying "we choose the people who love us and with whom we feel good."

Although the Apostle Paul has ended his Bible quote with two personal questions to all of God's parishioners, the spirit of pleasure and the flesh does not allow him to understand and practice God's standards. For centuries Christians have had no fear and respect for God, they have reacted according to their tastes and feelings.

Why does God not want his children to unite with unbelievers?

Because God does not want any of his children to suffer. God wants everyone to live harmony, a lot of peace and happiness, no sheep can be fine when he joins a wolf, at first the wolf will go through a sheep much healthier than all the others, with good treatment, but it is a way of weaving his trap.

The wolves inside the church

There are not only carnivores outside the church, they are inside the church as well. They are everywhere, the wolves that are inside the church are fiercer than those that are outside; they are very difficult to discover because they have sheep's clothing but their hearts are that of wolves.

They are carnivores, although they are in sheep's clothing they never eat herbs because they are wolves. We can only discover them through prayer and their behavior.

Wolves in sheep's clothing will never stop being wolves. Sooner or later they will manifest what they really are because no darkness can stand in front of the light.

What happens when a Christian unites with an unbeliever?

You will have an unhappy life, suffering, bitterness, demands at all times, because no unbeliever wants to have a single partner, his pleasure is to have many women/men and vices. The path of all unbelievers is perdition and the path of Christians is eternal life in Christ Jesus, they are two groups of people with two very different paths.

What will their offspring be like?

Possibly they will be more dangerous than their parents because they have two different bloods, your descendants will not be able to be lambs or wolves because they are two different kingdoms, all married people must choose who their descendants will be if they want a better future for their children.

Being married to an unbeliever can be one of the most difficult challenges in the Christian life. Marriage is a sacred covenant that unites two people together in one flesh. (Matthew 19: 5). It can be very difficult for a believer and an unbeliever to live in peaceful harmony: (2 Corinthians 6: 14-15).

If a spouse becomes a Christian after marriage, the inherent struggles that come as a result of living under two different authorities become very apparent.

What is injustice?

Action contrary to justice, total illegality. Injustice is the lack or absence of justice, either in reference to an event, act or factual situation. It can be referred to a subject or a social group. Injustice —and by extension justice— can be considered differently according to the legal systems in force in the different countries. The term injustice generally refers to unlawfulness, negligence, misconduct, or abuse that has not been corrected.

Violators are those who say there is no law, do not respect the law of God or earthly. Someone who always has a problem with justice, someone who does not know God, someone who has no judgment, they say they are free from all laws. If someone does not follow the law, then he is above it.

Most people who practice injustice are womanizers, they never want to have a single woman, they are vicious too, if they are vicious their homes are experiencing bad needs. It is a danger to the other person, because it can affect them with different deadly viruses.

Why do unbelievers practice injustice?

Because they have no fear for the owner of justice, as their characters are of injustices; they rejoice greatly in injustice. King Solomon has clearly explained about the person who is practicing injustice, he said: "An heart that deviseth wicked imaginations, feet that be swift in running to mischief.

A false witness that speaketh lies, and he that soweth discord among brethren": [Proverbs 6: 18-19].

Solomon goes on to say: "Lying lips are abomination to the Lord: but they that deal truly are his delight": [Proverbs 12:22].

The author said: that all injustices are liars and abominable before the eyes of God, it is one of the factors that allows God to destroy all the people who have practiced injustices. They rejoice when they discredit others with their lips, but God will never be left without doing anything against them.

The prophet Micah gave another example of why God has to execute people who practice injustice, he said: " Woe to them that devise iniquity, and work evil upon their beds! when the morning is light, they practise it, because it is in the power of their hand. And they covet fields, and take them by violence; and houses, and take them away: so they oppress a man and his house, even a man and his heritage.

Therefore thus saith the Lord; Behold, against this family do I devise an evil, from which ye shall not remove your necks; neither shall ye go haughtily: for this time is evil": [Micah 2: 1-3].

The apostle Paul said: «That no man go beyond and defraud his brother in any matter: because that the Lord is the avenger of all such, as we also have forewarned you and testified»: [1 Thessalonians 4: 6].

If you heard Jehovah's voice, none of this would happen. It is we ourselves who seek deception, because we make wrong decisions. Because of all this, God does not want us to get together with unbelievers and people who practice injustice, because God will never stand idly by without punishing them.

Chapter 12

The compromise covenant

When two lovers have finished understanding each other perfectly well, they should change the dating relationship for one that is more important in the life of all of them, which is the commitment to marry.

The covenant of commitment must be in the consultation of the two bride and groom, before meeting the two different relatives in a general and public consultation, where the two must be free in this relationship, to carry out this consummation, both must be of sufficient age and preparing at all levels to be successful at all steps, where happiness can reign for life.

Being engaged to someone is an important step between the two sweethearts the step of engagement does not mean that they have finished getting to know each other, each one has to continue with their discoveries, to see if they can change the engagement from dating to marriage for life.

Even if you are committed, you still do not have all the right to do anything, all your rights will be valid after the marriage covenant. Now if both of you have full unlimited rights to each other's bodies, now you are not the owner of your own body: it is your partner.

They can break thousands of pre-marriage relationships, but not a marriage, because the two have been married for life, only death can separate them. No person should accept this great commitment to anyone if he is not very sure of any mistake that he is his ideal partner; There must be true love between the two without deception or falsehood.

What is a covenant of commitment? How should a compromise be made? Before whom should this pact be made?

It is an agreement, an alliance, a deal or commitment whose stakeholders agree to respect what they stipulate. The pact establishes a commitment and sets fidelity towards the agreed terms or towards a declaration; therefore, it requires compliance with certain guidelines.

The covenant of commitment is it is a covenant that will lead them to the marriage that is the final consummation of the relationship.

There is a person who makes this stipulation with rings that represent the sign that he is committed to another guy, the ring represents a seal in the presence of the true witnesses who are the closest parents or families or friends. Where they have all the liberties to go out and talk without fear.

There are other groups of people, who do not use any ring, make the pact with words in the presence of very close families and friends, according to their cultures or religious norms. The pre-marriage covenant is the preparation of the true covenant that is marriage.

That relationship should last from six months to one year. The covenant of commitment comes after the courtship and before the marriage vow.

What requirements must we have to make a commitment pact?

We need to have five important elements to fulfill that mandate:

1.- A good family, professional and religious formation.

2.- A good amount of money in the bank.

3.- A stable job or business.

4.- A vehicle.

5.- Have a good common vision of your future.

When the individual meets these requirements, he is prepared to face those two relationships: pre-marriage and the marriage vow. Having a commitment to someone does not mean they are already married, because there are many people who confuse pre-marriage with marriage, they are two different things.

If you want to enjoy all the privileges, you must make the marriage vow before God, the government, the parishioner, the witnesses and the guests.

We are living in a society where anything goes, but even if we face the demands of society, no bad habit can change our custom, the biblical norms. People who want to build a successful family must make a difference.

If there is understanding and preparation between the two, true love is seasoning their hearts, they are fulfilling all the requirements they have asked to marry. What can prevent them from choosing a close date to join through the marriage vow!

When an individual seeks to have a loving relationship, he is telling society that he is financially ready to provide for his own family, he no longer wants to depend on his parents as he wants to be equal to them. Because no one should spend 34 years in their parents' house. You have to create your own home, it is the law of life.

We were born in homes, where from newborns to adults, we are taking the training on how we should support our own families in the future. We learn theories in our homes to put them into practice in independent living.

What do you learn at your parents' house?

Each individual learns something different than another in their schools, because all teachers do not teach in the same way, nor do they have the same techniques. No one teaches what they did not learn, if teachers are good, good things can be taught, and students can learn good things too.

When they are grown up they will teach all the good things learned from their teachers. If the teachers are bad, they will teach bad theories, the students will learn all the bad theories that their teachers teach, and they will transmit it in their practices.

If one has a bad theory and the other a good one, they will never have a good practice, because that is very important to know well before joining the marriage vow. You must fully discover who is the guy who will live with you for life.

The man who wants to have something safe with his partner, must think about marriage from the first day of dating, must start planning what his home will be like with that lady, what he would do so that the home can be very successful, etc. You must begin to analyze the rules that you will have within the marriage.

Likewise, no one should think what he would do with wealth at the moment of opportunity, he should think before that moment arrives; no one should think what he would do when he is in the bosom of the marriage, he should think it before, for when the time comes and to have an agenda prepared.

All things in life need a very deep study before facing it, because a good agenda, more budget, more vision, more goal, is equal to total success, because you will never know your partner. The human mind changes every five seconds, but you can have an idea at least.

The time of knowing and discovery has ended since the day of the wedding vow if you have married him/her it is because you have known him/her enough for the final agreement.

When the engaged are ready to marry, in consultation between the two and the parents, they will set a date so that they can join in the marriage vow. They are the two most important dates for future married couples. The day of the marriage vow and the firstborn.

In those two days, they cannot explain the emotions, the feelings, the joys that they feel, because each one of them was waiting with enthusiasm. They are two dates that mark the history of their lives forever. Now, if those two dates have been met by wrong people when they remember them, they will feel pain, bitterness and much hatred.

That is why it is very important to marry the authentic partner, with whom you can enjoy those beautiful moments in life.

True love is natural, without condition. The true feeling is something without malice, without deception, without interest. That love manifests itself as the two young doves who make their decisions to be with each other for their entire lives.

Chapter 13

The marriage vow Part 1

What is the marriage union?

It is the union of two people through certain rituals or legal formalities and is recognized by law as a family.

Marriage is a social institution present in every great culture, which establishes a conjugal bond between natural persons, recognized and consolidated through community practices and legal, customary, religious or moral norms. It is the union of a man and a woman.

What do scientists say about marriage?

Cecilia Zinicola (Sep. 15, 2017) said: «According to science, marriage can improve physical and mental health for a long and happy life. After studying men for nearly 80 years as part of the Harvard Study of Adult Development, one of the world's longest studies of adult life, scientists have gathered a considerable amount of data on physical and mental health.

In it, the health benefits of a stable marriage are highlighted, so, although it may be a path full of difficulties, according to scientific evidence it is worth taking that path if you want a long and happy life».

Cecilia confirms that marriage can extend your life. According to science, marriage can improve physical and mental health for a long and happy life.

Can marriage lengthen your life?

As one of the study's conclusions, people who have strong social relationships are less likely to die prematurely than those who are isolated. Isolation leads people to be less happy, have weaker health, and a shorter life.

According to the collected evidence, the solitaries were dying before, reason why the scientists affirm that "the solitude kills" and its effect is as powerful as the cigarette or the alcohol.

However, it is not "being with someone" that makes a true contribution, but the quality of that relationship and the level of commitment present. The study highlights warm and close relationships such as those that, by containing a value of belonging, allowed physical health and less mental deterioration over the years.

The researchers found that women who felt strongly attached to their partners were less depressed and happier in their relationships two and a half years later, and also had better memories than those with unhealthy marital relationships. The more commitment, the more health.

This data reaffirms what another study, published in the British medical journal British Medical Journal a couple of years ago, observed about the variability of these protective health effects according to the type of relationship, for example between cohabiting and being married.

The greater the commitment to the couple, the greater the health benefit. This could explain why married couples live longer: because marriage involves a deeper commitment than cohabitation. Marriage can keep your mind sharp.

Study director Robert Waldinger, a psychiatrist at Massachusetts General Hospital and professor of psychiatry at Harvard Medical School, in his TED talk, said: "Good relationships not only protect our bodies, but also our brains".

And according to the evidence, those good relationships don't have to be smooth all the time. Some of the couples could quarrel every day as long as they felt they could really count on each other when things got tough, allowing those arguments not to hurt their memories.

The researchers found that marital satisfaction has a protective effect on people's mental health. Part of the study found that people who had happy marriages in their 80s reported that their moods didn't suffer even on the days when they had the most physical pain, while those who had unhappy marriages felt both emotional and physical pain.

Studies show that stressful relationships, both short and long term, have a negative impact on mental health. On the contrary, those who maintained warm relationships lived longer and happier. From my point of view, all scientists are right about the virtues of marriage, all those who have married have a new life.

It is true, they are happier than before, and eat well at the exact time. One is always taking care of the other. What scientists don't say is that happiness comes directly from God.

Marriage multiplies the lives of individuals. Scientists claim that married orgasm is vitaminic. In my case, I am convinced that marriage is an institution that God has established from the Garden of Eden so that man can enjoy all the joy and sweetness of that relationship, because all the things that God has done for man, they are good in a big way.

Man has invented different types of forms of marriage, but the original one comes from God himself even though science does not know the existence of God.

God has created sex so that man can enjoy it only in marriage in the name of the Lord, and although God created that institution, not all marriages come from God.

Nor does God know all kinds of marriages; nor has he blessed everyone. God is never where his name is not respected or mentioned. He has his rules where individuals can fulfill, if they wish, his mandates. Even within his own church.

What does the bible say about marriage?

God gave a good example of how the human race should celebrate or choose a person as its fit for life. "And the Lord God said, It is not good that the man should be alone; I will make him an help meet for him": [Genesis 2:18].

If God made that decision for Adam, it is because he knew that no man can be alone in life, that is why he decided to create a companion to the taste of Adam.

How does the man react after the wedding?

He spoke such sensual and pleasant words in her ear: "And Adam said, This is now bone of my bones, and flesh of my flesh: she shall be called Woman, because she was taken out of Man. Therefore shall a man leave his father and his mother, and shall cleave unto his wife: and they shall be one flesh": [Genesis 2: 23-24].

All married guy must express the same expression of Adam, not only in theory, but in daily practice.

Not only in sexuality in coexistence as well, all married people must change into poets to fall in love with their partner just like adam and salon, with good treatment they can put into practice all the teachings of Palblo, who said: "The wife hath not power of her own body, but the husband: and likewise also the husband hath not power of his own body, but the wife.

Defraud ye not one the other, except it be with consent for a time, that ye may give yourselves to fasting and prayer; and come together again, that Satan tempt you not for your incontinency. But I speak this by permission, and not of commandment": [1Corinthians 7: 4-6].

What is the mandate for them after marriage?

Moses said: "And God blessed them, and God said unto them, Be fruitful, and multiply, and replenish the earth, and subdue it: and have dominion over the fish of the sea, and over the fowl of the air, and over every living thing that moveth upon the earth": [Genesis 1:28].

No one gets married to not have production. Everyone who has accepted that rectum must bear fruit and multiply the earth with their offspring. That mandate will end when we are transformed to go to heaven with Jesus. But if we are still on earth, our duty is to populate it with our descendants.

Chapter 14

The marriage vow Part 2

Wedding vows are the promises with which the engagement is sealed at the wedding ceremony. They represent the will of the couple to be united, not only through the wedding rings, but in respect and love, even in the most adverse circumstances.

What do professionals say about the marriage vow?

Marisol Rendón, February 6, 2019, commented on the page [marriage.com.do], that: «During the last month of planning, in which they must perform the last test of the groom suit and wedding dress, establish the distribution of your guests at the tables or define the song or soundtrack for your first day of marriage, verify that the decoration for the event room is correct with the provider, comes another important point to which you must spend time: the votes married.

We dedicate this article so that they know what they mean, what is said and what other options exist». And he continues: «The wedding vows are the promises with which the engagement is sealed in the wedding ceremony. They represent the will of the bride and groom to be united, not only through the wedding rings, but in respect and love, even in the most adverse circumstances.

If you have chosen a religious ceremony, you can choose one of the following formulas of vows; If you have opted for a civil celebration or something symbolic, there is more flexibility and you will be able to write them yourself.

My opinion about that beautiful ceremony is that it is a culmination of a process in a quasi-blood ritual. Well after a long wait, finally the day comes that everyone was waiting for, especially the bride and groom. A day that marks history in the lives of both, where they will sign a great commitment before God and humanity. A day that they will never forget; where they will enter the last stage for life.

On the exact day and time, all the families, the church and the guests will be waiting to witness this infinite relationship they will sign before God for life.

First step in the wedding ceremony

The father of the bride has to accompany her in his arms until he arrives in front of the groom, in the presence of everyone, where he will deliver his own daughter to the groom. That sign has great significance, where the pastor and guests witness the delivery.

In the same minute of receiving the bride, the groom says that I am now responsible for your daughter; I will treat her as well as you have given me.

It is a very solemn moment, where the pastor of the ceremony invites the Creator to bless that relationship by singing a prayer. Never forget, there is no marriage without knee prayer, if married people want God bless that union, both have to comply with the rules of the bible, because what God unites, cannot be disjoined by any man, so the covenant that is going to be signed.

After the marriage vow ends, they lend themselves to living and practicing the good teachings they received in their homes.

When a guy signs the marriage vow, he is saying: I am taking responsibility before God and the witnesses, to support and love her, be with her in good times as well as bad times, etc. After that vow, God will write that covenant in the book of heaven, no one can erase it only because of unfaithfulness.

Are you saying I accept you my young dove to make you happy from today until death do us part. In this relationship, there cannot be two different checks or salaries, nor two bank accounts, nor can cell phones have passwords, so as not to create doubts between the two.

The marriage vow means that from today I am blind to other guy, I agree to carry that relationship until death separates us. You are saying from that moment, nobody can discover my nakedness, only you.

What will the life of the two be like in practice within the home?

That home should be a love nest, a refuge, a spring, a source of fresh water where all the birds and animals can come to rest and feed. That new home should become a flower garden where all kinds of birds and insects can come to take refuge under its sanctified fragrance.

That new home should change to a palace where all kinds of aromas and fragrances can exist around all kinds of flowers. It can change like a little heaven on earth where children can make and grow in all harmonies.

In coexistence life, there should be no mistrust, the fruits of zeal, illusion, doubt, insecurity, malice, suspicion or fear.

If you have discovered one of those elements before marriage, you should end this relationship automatically because you will never have happiness in this nest. No one has built a home for destruction, everyone wants to build their home until death do them part.

The life of married people before having children

Elizabeth González Torres, a lawyer from Mexico City, commented on [families.com], the following: «Just married? Three important things to do before having children. If you recently got married and do not know if it is the right time to have children, this will certainly interest you.

One of the most frequently asked questions of all newly married couples is" and when do you plan to have children? ". Faced with this questioning, most couples tend to hesitate in the answer and ask themselves "when will be the right time to take the step of being parents?".

Certainly, there is no single answer to this question that hundreds of couples ask after getting married. And each answer varies according to the circumstances and people's opinions. However, be clear that before making such an important decision, some spiritual, temporal and emotional aspects must be developed as a marriage project, which will be very helpful».

So, if you just got married and don't know if it is the right time to have children, I share with you three important aspects that you and your partner should do and cover before making that significant decision:

1.- Economic stability

We live in a time when it is increasingly difficult to have a good job, a home of your own, a car, a business and even savings. It is a reality that now, more than in other times, due to this panorama, making the determination to start a family becomes difficult. Therefore, it is important that you and your partner work hard - during their first years of marriage - to achieve financial stability.

Of course, being financially stable doesn't mean having a luxurious home or a late-model car. On the contrary, it implies having three basic things to lead a healthy and dignified life: a job, a place to live and savings to cope with any emergency.

Whether they rent or own the place where they live, whether there are many or few savings they accumulate, it is of utmost importance that before having children, as a couple they have the essentials to support their own home.

Likewise, it will be essential that both have a medical service that in due course can be of great help to them when facing a health problem of their own or of their future children.

2.- Emotional and spiritual fullness as a couple

As you may have noticed, you and your partner have different ways of behaving emotionally and spiritually. Being individuals with different customs and ways of thinking, it is normal that in these early years some quarrels arise.

However, they must take advantage of that period of their marriage to stabilize themselves as a couple. Now is when they can learn to be two individual beings as members of the same team.

At this stage of your marriage focus your efforts on laying the spiritual and emotional foundation that will direct your family. Decide from now on how you will solve and face your challenges, define what faith you will follow as a couple and determine the direction to follow as the team you already are. This will allow them to be better parents and husbands.

3.- Get to know and enjoy yourself

Having children is a great reason for couples to unite more. However, this union is much greater when - prior to the arrival of the children - the couple has taken the time to get to know each other and enjoy each other's company. Talk as much as you can. Get yourself and pamper yourself. Enjoy this time alone wisely.

Love each other intensely right now so that in the future, when you decide to have your children, you can love and direct them as an excellent marriage.

Finally, remember that children will be a blessing to your marriage that only you two will decide when to have them. They may arrive soon or they may be late; However, keep in mind that being prepared for that great moment will make you enjoy, more fully, the beautiful experience of being parents.

Elizabeth focuses her study on the majority of young people who are married without professional and economic preparation, when they have those two great elements before getting married, if the blessing of being a father comes, they have something to correspond with.

How long should couples take before having their first child?

Each couple should take one to two years before the first pregnancy, so that they can have enough time to enjoy each other. Because in the time of dating there were many privileges they could not enjoy outside of marriage, now they are legal to enjoy all the pleasures, which they desire without any fear, because they are allowed by divine and earthly law.

If they have children before the time, they will not have enough space to enjoy each other, their time will only be for the care of the creatures, sometimes when they are in the act of intimacy, there they are asking for attention, they have to leave it to go attend them, because each stage has its time.

Also in the time of married life they must use more intimate expressions between the two. On behalf of the wife: "my king, my prince, my daddy, my heaven, my treasure, my chocolate, my sweetie", etc.

As for the husband: "my queen, my princess, mommy, my candy", etc. That is to say, each one must look for romantic qualifications to address the other.

When they are at work, the office, they have to take time to call each other, they have to try to keep it fixed, they have to ask how are you spending the day there, my little chocolate, my sweet love? Did you eat my little angel? I am thinking a lot about you my dear beloved. Everything naturally and spontaneously.

When one goes to eat, the other has to warn, so they can go out to eat at the same time. You have to agree on the menu you will choose, since the two are one meat, try to have a good conversation between the two.

You have to notify when you leave work, when you are in the vehicle, how far you are from the house, etc. Whoever arrives first has to start doing the chores, never forget we are two in one, if they both work, the two also have to cooperate with the services inside the house.

There are many men who reduce their love delivery to 20% in the day to day of married life. That emotion should not go down, they have to keep it at a higher level than the time of dating. The man has to be a gentleman in all deals.

A good husband never comes home without bringing even a mint for his wife. The man must be very detailed, not pessimistic. All women feel good about a gentlemanly man, who is attentive to everything. Remember, it is not the quantity that is worth, it is the quality, it is the gesture.

Women always value whatever their husband brings. The two have new ideas to improve their relationship, they always have to invent something different to surprise the other.

When a dog realizes his master is coming, he receives it with emotion and joy. Same for spouses. They must use the same strategy of the animal to receive their partner with kisses, hugs, to welcome them home. The first expression you should use after kissing is "how was your day today daddy/mommy?". Because half of your body was not with you during the day, each one can feel is special for another.

The honest answer must be that he/she considered it during the hard day of work; Both can enter hand in hand or embrace towards the house with much love.

If she arrives first, she can change her husband's clothes for one from the house, the man equal to his wife because they are two in one; after a few minutes, the two have to go to bathe together, each has to bathe the other, there is no better time when the couple is making love under the shower and the water falls on them, they feel they are sucking a honeycomb.

If the food was not ready, prepare it collaboratively. If the wife is not in the house, the husband has an ethical commitment to do so. A good gentleman must know how to cook, clean, wash, iron, etc. All women are proud to eat the food prepared by her husband, although the food lacks seasoning, for her it is the best food in the world.

If it is the lady's turn and the food has some mistakes... Well, she is a human being and since everyone can be wrong, you have to know how to say it to her so she doesn't feel bad. If her seasoning is good, you have to congratulate her. Every time the husband compliments the wife on something, she feels good.

Intimacy between the couple

There are many men who do not know how to get into sexual relations with their wives, although the two are one, there must be an agreement between the two to enjoy these beautiful moments together. All those men who know their wives without their wills committed a violation against her.

Also, many men who do not know how to ask that sweetness of their pretty ladies — for as there is no school where people teach — they must learn alone; They must have good sensuality to get to that moment.

If the husband is looking for her and she does not want to, he should not force her, he wants to know what the reason was, sometimes she can feel pain, discomfort or a bad state; sometimes there are things she is not going to say if the husband does not seek to know it.

How the couple should indulge in intimacy?

Two steps are inevitable:

1.- The husband must excite his wife very well before penetration.

Without excitement the husband will never be able to please her. It is the worst time for a woman when her partner cannot reach his weak point in intimacy. Before penetration, the wife must touch him on all sensual points. Each must please the other very well in privacy, before...

2.- Both must know exactly the weak points of the other.

Each one must experience several orgasms, in the case of the woman even before penetration. But they must avoid sinning against the Holy Spirit and nature when they are in this act, although both have rights over the body of another, there are parts in the body that are totally sexually forbidden, because God has created all the parts that are in man to fulfill a well-defined mandate. If we use an opposite part in intimacy, such as anal penetration, we sin against God.

Women are very different from men. Sometimes she is making love to her husband just to please him, not because she wants to. The good man must know his wife very well, if she is not encouraged, his duty is to put her on a very high level where she can reactivate again. You must know how to activate the erogenous zones of it even if you have no desire.

There are many men who like to tell their wives to spread their legs. It is not like that to make love, it is she who will open them when she cannot take it anymore, because you have already reached all her weak points, and she changes her voice as desperate: she is ready for the fight. There are also many women who are used to lying with their legs open, and do nothing else, like saying to the husband: "Kill yourself and kill me."

She is definitely not a romantic or cooperative lady. The man must feel he is going up to heaven by the same ladder that Jacob dreamed of; both must be at zero level before penetration. The sweetest moment in that intimacy is when the mutual orgasm occurs with mathematical precision.

Paul asks all those Christians who want to make love like worldly a good question, he said: "What? know ye not that your body is the temple of the Holy Ghost which is in you, which ye have of God, and ye are not your own? For ye are bought with a price: therefore glorify God in your body, and in your spirit, which are God's": [1 Corinthians 6: 19-20].

If you are servants of God, you cannot make love like them, nor marry them, because we are two peoples with two different cultures. Each has its owner, if you mistakenly joined them, you should know that there is a place that is totally forbidden in sexuality "anal sex".

In penetration, the two have to do it with a lot of passion, never forget that there is no feeling very fast. If you want to enjoy good sex you must make it soft.

In order for a person to eat a good, well-seasoned food, he must eat it gently and slowly, it is the excitement between the two together that will ask for speed. Each one has to try to please his partner in moments of emotion, never forget all men have been born especially to love their wives and make them happy at all times.

The journey within marriage

The newlyweds should have the small luxury of traveling together to other countries, to meet other cultures, climate, other people, even if it is in their own country.

They have to get to know other cities together, go to enjoy the landscapes, nature, historical places, etc. They have to take some romantic massages together during the honeymoon, which makes them feel like they are truly on the moon.

All activities to be done during this trip must be chosen by the wife, because the lady knows how to buy more than the gentleman, the man must say to his beloved, "Mommy, what are we going to do today?" When the husband gives her the priority of deciding or choosing, not because she is the dominant one, it is so that she feels confident.

Going on vacation to different countries together is essential for newlyweds. The man must let her make the choice the country of her dream, when she has the freedom of choice, she can feel his dream comes true.

Vacation is very important, not only for the newlyweds, for all the people who have spent a whole year working from sunrise to sunset. There are also men who have a long time without pleasing their partner due to lack of time, due to work. The only time they have to please each other is vacation.

That little window is a moment where the person is disconnected with all their work, both mental and physical. Many people save a monthly amount especially for vacation. It is a necessity for all human beings, whether rich or poor.

So, all newlyweds should take time before the child's arrival to enjoy their romance as it should be, if possible they can go on a trip every six months depending on the entry.

Chapter 15

The husband's papers at home

The Great Architect of the Universe, gave a great responsibility to man as the priest of the home, not the head of her. A good priest is a leader, an honest, responsible person; who is always looking for the ideal way to guide your home with total success.

What is the difference between the boss husband and a leader?

They are two totally different things in every way. The difference between leader and boss is that a boss is an imposed authority, who uses his power to command others. Instead a leader is one who leads and motivates a team of people without imposing their own ideas.

Leadership is a capacity that not everyone has, so not everyone can be a leader. Who are you especially inside your home? How have your wife and children seen you inside the home? Are you a dominant male or a corporate male? All macho men think they are the head of their homes, that only they rule.

Everyone has to do what he tells them to do. Gross mistake. Men and women are equal with different leadership roles.

Who causes male children to be sexist: men or women?

Are the mothers, because they prioritize the females: tasks the males cannot do, only the females. Sometimes even in food, they have more priorities over them. When that happens, males think they are superior to females.

Good teachers should treat everyone the same, they should teach both to do the housework. If they are well prepared wherever they arrive they will be able to live together in a useful way, because they will not be inside the house forever.

There was a similar problem of ours, which was happening with the people of Ephesians. God commanded his servant Paul how husbands should treat wives. He said: " Husbands, love your wives, even as Christ also loved the church, and gave himself for it": [Ephesians 5:25].

Christ never verbally and physically mistreated the church, on the contrary, he loved her so much, he died for her.

No woman should receive sexual, verbal or physical aggression from any man, she was not created to receive any type of aggression, on the contrary she was created to be loved, protected, the man must give protection to a wife like Christ to the church; she is like a fragile glass; she is like an egg that needs a lot of care and protection.

All those who are mistreating their partners in all ways must be punished by heavenly and earthly law. The thing will never be solved with aggression. On the contrary, aggression will make it worse.

Adam, as the first model God created on earth, never mistreated his beloved wife, on the contrary, his love for her made him sacrifice the very immortality of the Garden of Eden, just to be with his beloved. If he has to die, the man must die to save or defend his family.

The man who loves his wife suffers with her in any pain, because if one member of the body is suffering, all the members feel the same pain. It is the same for the couple. The man must be patient in everything, he must speak less, if he wants to save his home.

Many men talk and argue more than a parrot. The man must speak little and think more, the man does not aggravate the situation, he seeks a correct solution; man has been created especially to solve, not to create complications.

What happened between the first Adam and the second Adam?

The first for love, lost all the privileges he had, all the promises, for his error comes perdition and eternal death. With the second, also out of love, he came to rescue the human race. His death bequeathed us eternal salvation.

The apostle John said: "For God so loved the world, that he gave his only begotten Son, that whosoever believeth in him should not perish, but have everlasting life": [John 3:16].

What a deep love God has for humanity, it is a love that has no comparison. If we want to wear that beautiful fragrance called "love," we must love our wives with all our hearts, souls, and bodies. We not only have to say it, we have to demonstrate it in every way.

We must live 70% in theory and 100% in practice. In many homes, children and wives feel good when husbands are gone, when lions enter, there are many sadnesses, anguishes, fears and discontents... No family can live that horrible and caustic life. All men must sow love if they want to reap more love, where much peace and happiness can reign in their homes.

Man cannot be a monster to his own family. When a father or husband crosses the threshold of the door of the home, it must be lit with the happiness of wife and children.

The apostle Paul gave another explanation about filial love, because there was another serious problem that the Colossian people were going through, he said: "Husbands, love your wives, and do not be harsh with them": [Colossians 3:19].

Paul was saying husbands love their wives, and don't be male chauvinist with them. As much maleness as there is in this world, God is against maleness, where that pathology exists, love cannot be, nor should the "I" exist between the couple. All those who want to be successful in their relationships must eliminate or kill ma.chismo and the "I".

Even within the true church of God, what is kept by the commandments of God and the testimony of Jesus, there are harsh Christians who rejoice in the "I", who think their wives are inferior to them. This barbarism produces verbal and physical aggression; that problem causes many separations between married Christians as pagans.

There are many men who are holy within the church but in their houses they are rude. They are double-faced, they are Christians in the church and wolves in the house. They forget if Christianity begins within the home.

The treatment inside the home

Since God is against ma.chismo, he wants love to reign in every home. Peter said: Likewise, ye husbands, dwell with them according to knowledge, giving honour unto the wife, as unto the weaker vessel, and as being heirs together of the grace of life; that your prayers be not hindered: [1 Peter 3: 7].

God wants all men to respect their wives, to care for them like a more fragile glass, to live wisely with them, never to offend them with ugly expressions, nor should they adore them, adoration only for God, because God does not hear the prayer of a abuser, you have to convert and confess your sin first before...

What are the husband's responsibilities at home?

Each of them must fulfill their responsibilities at home, the apostle Paul suggested to married people, he said: "Let the husband render unto the wife due benevolence: and likewise also the wife unto the husband.

The wife hath not power of her own body, but the husband: and likewise also the husband hath not power of his own body, but the wife. Defraud ye not one the other, except it be with consent for a time, that ye may give yourselves to fasting and prayer; and come together again, that Satan tempt you not for your incontinency": [1 Corinthians 7: 3-5].

Neither of the two should deny, but because of discomfort or pain, each must respond to the need of his partner, it is very comfortable if the two must sleep half naked to enjoy each other when necessary; there must be good communication between the two, if there is any discomfort or misunderstanding, you should never reject the desire of your partner even if they have not yet found a solution.

There are some women who never want to give anything to their husbands for any misunderstanding or foolishness, they might be a little unhappy indeed, never reject their husbands' requests.

No woman should neglect when her partner wants something from her, any rejection is sending her partner to the street. Worst moment for man when his upper part demands something, and it is not reciprocated. Because of this great need, man can make a thousand negative thoughts.

The wife must deny the husband for three reasons only: for her menstruation, illness and ill states. The husband also has reason to deny the wife, but he must always do so with tact and delicacy, so that she understands.

What should you do so that each one has their eyes on another?

The wife must be very wise to discover all the tastes of her husband, if he likes the woman with a miniskirt, she must please him but only inside the house, even if it is not her style. If he likes sexy women, she should go to the gym to get sexy too.

If you want to save your marriage you must be competitive, if he has found all his fantasies in his wife, he will never look at other women.

Many women who, being Christian, do not like going to the salon. It is a great mistake on their part, they must get pretty and well groomed for their husbands. Faith is not against beauty and highlighting feminine attributes. No man wants to be with a nasty or poorly dressed woman.

There are many things that can attract a married man to temptation with other women: physical fitness, clothing, the fragrance of his perfume... But if he has found all three in his wife, he will not look for them in another. So it is very important to see and know the tastes of their husbands. Several times it is the wife herself who allows her husband to be unfaithful by mistake or carelessness.

All women must live wisely with their husbands to infect them, they must be antidotes, antivirus to eliminate or block all the viruses that want to harm their relationships, if they want to be successful.

The two must sleep holding each other, her head must be on the husband's chest or arm, neither of them can sleep with the opposite head; if there is a problem between the two, never let the sun lie down on this problem without resolution, nobody should sleep angry or in a bad mood.

How should the husband speak to the queen of the home?

You should use contagious expressions to always make your partner fall in love. Expressions of love must never end.

Solomon explained to us how we should deal with and talk to our wives, he said: "Let thy fountain be blessed: and rejoice with the wife of thy youth. Let her be as the loving hind and pleasant roe; let her breasts satisfy thee at all times; and be thou ravished always with her love": [Proverbs 5: 18,19].

Solomon was one of the best knights that has ever existed in human history, that man had so many beautiful expressions of love. All men must copy from him to make their wives fall in love every day until death separates them bodily, since it will not disunite their souls.

The source of a woman is the pleasure and the rapid and violent emission of a liquid, especially semen, that she gave when she is intimate with her partner.

All good husbands must continue to conquer their wives with sweet words: your spring is sweeter than honey; I feel happier than ever when I am dipping in your spring that refreshes so much, they are expressions that can take it to such a high level that a minute can never pass without its presence.

In each intimate moment, the husband must become a poet to describe the moment the two have spent together, he must say something so she feels pleased and happy. After intimacy, the husband must change to a Solomon, to praise her entire body.

Expressions of love for the wife

The love poet said to his wife: «Until the day break, and the shadows flee away, I will get me to the mountain of myrrh, and to the hill of frankincense.Thou art all fair, my love; there is no spot in thee. Come with me from Lebanon, my spouse, with me from Lebanon: look from the top of Amana, from the top of Shenir and Hermon, from the lions' dens, from the mountains of the leopards.

Thou hast ravished my heart, my sister, my spouse; thou hast ravished my heart with one of thine eyes, with one chain of thy neck. How fair is thy love, my sister, my spouse! how much better is thy love than wine! and the smell of thine ointments than all spices! Thy lips, o my spouse, drop as the honeycomb: honey and milk are under thy tongue; and the smell of thy garments is like the smell of Lebanon.

A garden inclosed is my sister, my spouse; a spring shut up, a fountain sealed. Thy plants are an orchard of pomegranates, with pleasant fruits; camphire, with spikenard, Spikenard and saffron; calamus and cinnamon, with all trees of frankincense; myrrh and aloes, with all the chief spices: A fountain of gardens, a well of living waters, and streams from Lebanon».

Awake, o north wind; and come, thou south; blow upon my garden, that the spices thereof may flow out. Let my beloved come into his garden, and eat his pleasant fruits»:[Song of songs 4: 9 -16].

Solomon continues to tell his beautiful wife: «I am come into my garden, my sister, my spouse: I have gathered my myrrh with my spice; I have eaten my honeycomb with my honey; I have drunk my wine with my milk: eat, o friends; drink, yea, drink abundantly, o beloved»: [Song of songs 5:1].

The poet continues to praise his beloved wife he said: «How beautiful are thy feet with shoes, o prince's daughter! the joints of thy thighs are like jewels, the work of the hands of a cunning workman. Thy navel is like a round goblet, which wanteth not liquor: thy belly is like an heap of wheat set about with lilies. Thy two breasts are like two young roes that are twins.

Thy neck is as a tower of ivory; thine eyes like the fishpools in Heshbon, by the gate of Bathrabbim: thy nose is as the tower of Lebanon which looketh toward Damascus. Thine head upon thee is like Carmel, and the hair of thine head like purple; the king is held in the galleries.

How fair and how pleasant art thou, o love, for delights! This thy stature is like to a palm tree, and thy breasts to clusters of grapes. I said, I will go up to the palm tree, I will take hold of the boughs thereof: now also thy breasts shall be as clusters of the vine, and the smell of thy nose like apples»: [Song of songs 7:1-8].

No woman can bear or resist with that kind of compliments from her husband, she will feel that she is rising in the clouds with those expressions so sweet and soft, the man must use a very contagious sweet voice, so that he can make her fall in love every second more. Man must say it in theory and apply it in practice. All women have fallen in love with what they have heard, home should be the source of love verbs.

Solomon teaches all men who do not know how to fall in love, who do not know how to value a lady, from his songs, he tells us how we should treat a lady, what kinds of expressions we should say to them. No woman in the world can resist those poems on her husband's lip.

Any man who values such a woman can never live without her presence. We must reject the werewolf that we are, the ma.chismo that creeps inside us like a snake that makes us fall again and again.

We must sacrifice our wives with all kinds of love, with beautiful songs, love poems and all kinds of flowers; we must make them fall in love more and more, we must create or invent new ideas and strategies to surprise her more, and more, as good hairs of Jehovah we are.

All Christian men must follow the example of Solomon, they must become artists to draw the body of their wives with all the expressions of love that exist in the world. We cannot have two faces, we must live by example.

It is not possible for a Christian man to behave worse than the worlds with his partner, he must be an exemplary husband, because he has the Holy Bible as a mirror or guide of his marriage towards success, if he does everything that is written in it with his wife will be a total success.

Expressions of love for the husband

Shes said: «What is thy beloved more than another beloved, O thou fairest among women? what is thy beloved more than another beloved, that thou dost so charge us? My beloved is white and ruddy, the chiefest among ten thousand. His head is as the most fine gold, his locks are bushy, and black as a raven. His eyes are as the eyes of doves by the rivers of waters, washed with milk, and fitly set.

His cheeks are as a bed of spices, as sweet flowers: his lips like lilies, dropping sweet smelling myrrh. His hands are as gold rings set with the beryl: his belly is as bright ivory overlaid with sapphires.

His legs are as pillars of marble, set upon sockets of fine gold: his countenance is as Lebanon, excellent as the cedars. His mouth is most sweet: yea, he is altogether lovely. This is my beloved, and this is my friend, O daughters of Jerusalem»: [Song of songs 5:9-16].

Are expressions that can elevate man to the clouds; and can allow him to stay in the house, without having his eyes towards other women. No man can stand bombarded with such flattery. For a man to fall madly in love with a woman, she must know all the strategies, because she is the same woman that allows her partner to be unfaithful, or to be on the street.

The wise woman controls her husband with good treatment, sweet verbs and love.

Hopefully all the married people who have read this book can transform their home into a little heaven where all the little ones can receive all the good formations.

Chapter 16

The wife's papers at home

There are many women who are father and mother in the home, due to the wrong choice. No woman was created for that heavy responsibility, it is not God's plan, it is her decision. God created her especially as a suitable husband, but it is not she who has all the responsibility for the home.

The woman is very cooperative, she never wants to be at home without doing anything, she has learned some professions to bring food around the house, the husband should appreciate her effort for her pleasant cooperation so there is more income in the house.

There are many men who have the mentality of lions, they do not like to hunt at all, they spend all their time asleep, they leave all the burden and responsibilities on the females, the work they like to do is: fight with other males for the territory, when they realize their interests or territories are threatened.

Each has their own role or responsibility to fulfill both inside and outside the home. After the fall of Adam and Eve in the Garden of Eden, God gave each member their role within precious garden that is home.

God said to the woman: «Unto the woman he said, I will greatly multiply thy sorrow and thy conception; in sorrow thou shalt bring forth children; and thy desire shall be to thy husband, and he shall rule over thee you»: [Genesis 3:16].

After the fall she had three great responsibilities within the home: she gives birth to children, work inside the house, and the children's teachings. For this reason, no woman finishes her work inside the house, she always sees something that is not in her place. A house without a woman lacks everything.

The role and responsibility of man after the fall. God said to him: «And unto Adam he said, because thou hast hearkened unto the voice of thy wife, and hast eaten of the tree, of which I commanded thee, saying, thou shalt not eat of it: cursed is the ground for thy sake; in sorrow shalt thou eat of it all the days of thy life; Thorns also and thistles shall it bring forth to thee; and thou shalt eat the herb of the field.

In the sweat of thy face shalt thou eat bread, till thou return unto the ground; for out of it wast thou taken: for dust thou art, and unto dust shalt thou return»: [Genesis 3: 17-19].

After the fall, God has done three things with them. First: the investigative judgment. Second: the final sentence on each case. Third: the daily work they must do or perform to survive. Because of the curse of sin, man must sweat with great pain to get the daily bread for his family, but it is not God's plan that man be in that situation.

But for disobedience, man has to pay for his own mistake he changed his happiness for sadness and bitterness. Due to the shortage of bread at home, the lady makes her own decision to work like a man and sweat with great pain so that food is not lacking in her home. Although that hurts a lot in the heart of God, the law of God must be fulfilled, because God is not the human to change his decision.

When two people of different sexes are working, due to the nature of their bodies, everyone can see the great difference that exists between the two, both at work inside the home and outside. All men should honor their wives for their daily chores to bring bread home. Because if there are two entries each month, there will never be a shortage of bread in this home, if they know how to manage it.

The couples agreement at home

In the houses of the first Christians in Colossians, a very critical situation was taking place: they did not respect any marriage norm within their homes, as followers of Christ their homes were the same as the pagans. Where there was no couple love.

God informs his servant Paul how followers of Christ can make a great difference between Christian and pagan homes. Because God wanted them to set a good example for their children as continuators in the next generation.

Paul said: "Wives, submit yourselves unto your own husbands, as unto the Lord. For the husband is the head of the wife, even as Christ is the head of the church: and he is the saviour of the body. Therefore as the church is subject unto Christ, so let the wives be to their own husbands in every thing.": [Ephesians 5: 22-24].

The married woman must submit, obey her own husband, as the Lord, because the man is the head of the woman as Christ is the head of the church. They are two very different things, which have nothing to do with the "maleness" of the "boss" of the home.

What is the role of Christ within the church?

Christ has always connected with his church, He has never disconnected for a second with it; he cares a lot about her; He cares for her at all times; he died to save her. The man must do the same with his wife. The home priest must be a leader to guide your relationship to success along with all family members. Everyone must have one word like Christ with the church.

All married women must assume their husbands as priests of the home. All women are born to obey their husbands. If the husband has lost his leadership due to lack of spiritual or intellectual knowledge, she will take over and become a priestess of the home. Possibly she can search for a leader, because by nature, she was not born for this position.

The church was created to obey Christ, but not Christ to the church, it is the same for the husband with the wife, so if the home does not have a man as leader, that house has no respect at all. It does not mean only the man rules inside the house; they both rule because they are two people in one body.

The priest guides his house to comply with all the rules to the letter, according to the will of the great Master, he is like a shepherd of sheep that leads them where there is a lot of green grass with plenty of water.

The priest must have a plan of spiritual, intellectual and economic growth, he must guard his herds against all cannibals. If there is an attack, he has to fight hard in every way to protect his flock. Being a priest is a great responsibility, cowards, the weak cannot take priestly office, because they will find many attacks along the way.

What is the priest's behavior at home?

You have to scrutinize the word of God, you have to eat it every day of its existence, because all the knowledge is within it, through the Holy Spirit, you will be able to discover and find everything you need for that great "priestly" office. No one can do it well without the presence of God.

Head of household

The Bible clearly explains man is the head of the home, not woman. No woman should seek that position, nor can she covet it. There are many women who are seeking their rights to be equal to men in everything. True, the two are the same, but not in all respects. There are positions that never correspond to any woman, only the man.

Today women think they are smarter than the Creator, where they want to supplant the leadership God Himself gave to man. His slogan is that if the man can, the woman can too. They have allowed themselves to be washed away by absurd and chaotic ideologies, enemies of the order has allowed humanity to advance for millennia.

That has created great competition between men and women for two positions, God never gave to any woman: "the priest of the home and head of the church." When a person is looking to have a position does not belong or corresponds, he will never live happy, for that reason everyone should live with what he has.

A lady can have all the positions that exist in the world, but the priestly position and shepherds a religious congregation, never belongs to any woman, only to the man. All men must fulfill their positions as good priests of their own houses.

Likewise, the problem is caused by the loss of leadership of many men, whether due to moral, intellectual, spiritual, professional and economic incapacity. Qualities without which it is impossible to fulfill that position.

Who between the two can give the fulfillment of the law of the home, the man or the woman?

Paul said: "For the woman which hath an husband is bound by the law to her husband so long as he liveth; but if the husband be dead, she is loosed from the law of her husband": [Roman 7: 2].

The wife has no power to create law within the house, only the husband. It is a command from God. The wife and children must abide by that law, the husband must exercise it.

The priest must take care of all the laws of his home and be obeyed, nobody should be above the law. All women should be subject to the laws of their husbands, but not to their whims.

What category of law should the husband enforce at home?

You can compare home fulfillment as a business. There are three things that can enable the company to function well:

1.- The rules all collaborators must comply to the letter if they want to be part of that company.

2.- A good goal the company must meet every month or annually.

3.- The budget.

Without all three it is impossible that such a company can function and last for long. All households must have those three elements if they want to be successful.

Husbands are not only there to make and be to keep the house law, they must also submit to it. There are many men who like to be followed the law, but never want to fulfill it. They themselves have to set the example of how to obey it.

What preparation should the husband have to create the law of the home?

Man must have two main preparations to fulfill that mandate as a good priest: spirituality and intellectuality.

No illiterate man can make and be comply with any law within his house, if the wife is more educated than he is, it is a great danger for both sexes. If the husband is inferior to her, the wife will never follow any instructions come from him. All men must be superior to or equal to their wives so that all standards can be met within homes.

Of the 100% of marriages, there are 80% who have divorced due to this problem, due to lack of leadership. Many men confuse the leader with the boss within the home, if there is leadership in the home the final goal will be reached; but if there is a "boss", they will end in divorces: all the mediocre, harsh are the head of the household, but all the wise are leaders who carry out their priestly works.

Fools carry out their mandates of chiefs, and with their foolish decisions lead their homes to ultimate destruction, wise leaders maintain total happiness and success. No one wants to be with a mediocre or a boss, because everyone wants to be with a leader.

Can a servant of God marry any woman?

The answer is no. She must be a virtuous, wise and intelligent woman, attentive to the needs of her home. Solomon gave the character of the fearful woman, he said: «The virtuous woman is the crown of her husband; But the bad, like woodworm in his bones»: [Proverbs12].

A virtuous woman has seven characterized:

1.- She is God-fearing: a God-fearing person always keeps his commandments. He never does anything against the will of God.

2.- Take care of his family: he is a responsible person who likes to fulfill his position.

3.- Pious: it is the virtue that, for the love of God, a person inclines to carry out acts of compassion and love towards his family and neighbor.

4.- She is cautious: she is a woman who acts with caution or a person who thinks and arranges things in advance. She is a prudent woman.

5.- It is economic: she is a woman who knows how to economize, who thinks about the future.

6.- She is busy: she is a woman who does things with passion. A lady who does her errands eagerly to achieve her goals.

7.- She does not speak ill of her husband: she always keeps all the secrets of her husband. Above all, she is a responsible woman, who likes to fulfill everything in favor of her husband.

What must the man of God do to get a woman of this stature?

You must pray a lot. Total surrender to God, because the virtuous lady is difficult to obtain, the virtuous is not seen by the face, nor by good expressions, nor by good human educations. No man can get such a woman on his own, or for anyone, only by God's blessing.

The virtuous woman has other qualities that draw attention to all men: she is an honest, discreet woman; a woman who can do well all that corresponds to her, who has the moral to do the right thing; an intelligent woman, pure, upright, good, kind, forgiving, benevolent, charitable, merciful, etc.

3.- She is generous: she is a good human being who has a habit of giving or sharing with others without receiving anything in return. A person who has a good attitude, who has good behavior.

The tastes of the couple at home

The couple must know they are two different people, with different tastes, characters and cultures, each one must live with great wisdom; they must respect each other's rights, there must be a lot of patience between the two.

No one can fulfill that rule without love, that's why love comes first after God. The root of all the destruction of the home is fed by bad treatment, so communication is essential to bring your relationship to ultimate success.

The vast majority of men like to watch action movies, news and sports. And most of the ladies like novels. They are two totally different tastes, although there are two televisions in the house, the good couple must accompany the other in their tastes.

How should everyone's taste be met?

There must be an agreement between the two, each must please the other: one week the two will watch soap operas together, the other week it is the husband's turn. The two must be very comfortable, without any displeasure, but many kisses and hugs.

Both must win, both must feel happy, because if one is looking for superiority, the expression "I", the "ego", which victimizes us out of self-love, will automatically enter.

No one makes a decision on the same day. Little by little to form and nurture the thought, until one day it explodes, spreading a disintegration virus the couple must counteract.

The beach, rivers and the countryside in married life

Every weekend, married couples must go to three important places where they can enjoy nature together: the beach, the river and the countryside. Perhaps one likes the beach and the other likes the river. They must agree between the two so they can enjoy each other's taste together as married. Without disagreement.

They can divide the time like this: one weekend for the beach, one for the river, two to enjoy in the fields. There is no better experience than enjoying a sunrise in a field, listening to the melodies of all kinds of birds praising their creator.

Each couple must have houses in two different places: one in the city, to respond to the needs of the family; another in the countryside, to enjoy the good life there.

Why the family should have a house in the countryside; What difference between country life and the city?

There are several reasons for the family to enjoy a country life:

1.- They are two different airs, the lungs breathe the pure air without toxins, where all the parts of the body can function well, the peasants get sick less than those who live in the big cities, the food is healthier.

2.- The peasant mentality is more innocent than the city, they have a life with less stress, because they are in direct contact with nature. Spending a night in the countryside is an unforgettable moment, it is something has no comparison.

Enjoying a rich bath in the river of a field that is in the middle of the trees, is an incomparable experience. But especially if you live as a couple. The three hours of the day suitable for such an experience are: 6 a.m. when the sun is up, in the middle of the day and 7 p.m. when the sun is setting.

Sex with the couple in the river is a sublime moment. It is like a baptism in the waters of the Jordan, or a song of praise of the bodies to the creation of God.

Life in the big city is not the same as that of the country, all the basic necessities should ideally be bought in the countryside where the air is not polluted by the smoke from cars and factories. There are many people who work, negotiate and study in big cities but who live in the rural area. They know about the dangers of cities.

It is an unforgettable and incomparable moment to contemplate the growth of plants, flowers and wildlife every morning in order to understand a little better the power of God through nature. We must enjoy all those rich family moments to know and see the greatness of the Creator.

Why do birds never suffer from need?

It is because they respect all the rules that the Creator has given them, they always comply with all the mandates, at dawn both the great and the chicks wake up and praise the Creator before going out to look for their food. They always find something to survive, God never leaves them without eating anything for the day.

The human being has been created in the image of God, man has more privilege than birds, the great problem is: he does not want to obey the Creator. If man takes the birds as his example, he can have a life far superior to them. Country life is not only good for health or to have a beautiful experience as a couple, it is also good so that we can learn from birds how we should worship and respect God as Creator.

The other example the couple should learn from birds and animals is time. They do not have clocks to control time, yet they are faithful and responsible. During the day they work, but before twelve o'clock everyone returns to the trees to praise the Creator.

Before twelve noon, all the animals are resting under the trees, to contemplate the owner of the Universe who is Christ Jesus. Always happy, because the Creator took care of them at all times. All those who want to build a successful family must learn from them.

Chapter 17

The profession and the finance of the couple

In creation before sin, man had the privilege of enjoying all the trees God had created, he had a life full of blessing, much peace and happiness, because the glory of God was upon him. He did not need the moon or the sun, neither sowing nor harvesting, because God always took care of him.

Before the fall, God spoke face to face with man at all times because he was perfect, without any fear he could see and contemplate the face of God without fear because the glory of God dwelt in him, he could enjoy all Benefits and God's Blessing Now, hearing the voice of the enemy, who is the father of deceit and lies, God had to separate and hide his face in order for man to live.

The man who was immortal changes into mortal, from perfection to imperfection, from incorruptible to corruptible, from saint to sinner. Now he will have to bend his back to eat, "disobedience problem".

And to the man God said: "Because you obeyed your wife's voice and ate from the tree that I commanded you saying: You shall not eat from it, cursed will the earth be because of you; with pain you will eat of it all the days of your life, thorns and thistles will produce you and you will eat plants of the field. With the sweat of your face you will eat the bread until you return to the ground, because from it you were taken; for dust you are and to dust you will return": [Genesis 3: 17-19].

As the land was cursed for man's disobedience, day by day the land is giving less production than before, the trees do not give the amounts of fruits they used to give, the man has to learn a profession so as not to till the land any more. You have to support your family, you have to get a job with what you learned in college.

Nowadays you can make money with two things: a profession or a business, but you must obtain the daily bread with dignity without any deception and fraud. All those who have practiced injustice and deceit to have wealth will never go unpunished, because God is always against injustice.

All those who have made easy money leave in the same way. All professionals must carry out their duties with honesty and clarity. If they have used their knowledge to unfairly deceive their neighbor, all that person's curses will fall on their shoulders.

Conversely, those who have earned their wealth with sincerity and justice will last for generation after generation, each moment will double, because God likes justice and fidelity. He wants to prosper in everything, to be faithful all the time.

What is a professional career?

Habitual activity of a person, generally for which it has been prepared that, by exercising it, they have the right to receive remuneration or wages. The term profession designates the trade, employment or occupation that is exercised in exchange for remuneration.

Likewise, it defines the set of professionals who practice it. Professions generally require specialized and formal knowledge, which is usually acquired after tertiary or university training. The trades, on the other hand, usually consist of informal activities or whose learning is based on practice.

Why should you study a professional career?

Studying a university degree is important for several reasons. It gives you a bigger picture of the world around you. In addition, studying at a university will teach you a sense of discipline and responsibility and will allow you to meet people from many fields.

A career can help you land a stable, profitable job so you can meet the high cost of living. Therefore, all people must acquire a professional career before taking that great and prestigious responsibility of being a husband.

What do scholars say about having a professional career?

On February 08, 2019, Paulina Santibáñez commented on UNITEC: "There are six reasons to study a university degree":

1.- You will have more possibilities of finding a better job

Did you know that a person with a degree earns twice as much as someone who only has a high school? [Source: National Survey of Occupation and Employment 2015]. Today more than ever, employers are seeking to hire people with a college degree. And this is even more important when deciding who will grow within a company.

If you aspire to a good job, having a career is not only an "extra point" in your favor. To develop yourself in many professions, it is simply something indispensable.

2.- You will feel more sure of yourself

Having completed a career, acquired a theoretical knowledge base, practiced to reinforce what you have learned in the classroom, and formed a wide network of contacts - classmates, teachers and more - will allow you to gain self-confidence. Of course, you will project this security. Being a prepared person — and sure of yourself — will open many doors for you.

3.- You will develop a broad and critical vision

College is meant to prepare you to successfully meet the challenges of "out there." You will know the beautiful part and also the most difficult aspects of the profession you choose; You will face dilemmas very similar to those of the real world and you will have to make difficult decisions.

In addition, you will meet countless people with ideas similar and different to yours, and you will acquire knowledge that will allow you to have a more critical view of the world around you. In short: the university will broaden your horizon so that you cannot even imagine.

4.- You will become an independent person

Studying a college degree is nothing like studying high school. In high school, teachers and your parents "run around" to attend classes and do homework. At university, you are solely responsible for your education. The teachers will be your counselors, but they will not be chasing you to get good grades.

This is more positive than it sounds: it forces you to become an independent, responsible person, capable of making your own decisions. Not to mention that studying a career gives you more possibilities of finding a job, and therefore, having your own income.

5.- It prepares you to work as a team

Believe me, few attributes are as essential to succeed in the workplace as learning to work as a team. In some professions it is more important than in others, but in all you will have to work with other people to achieve your goals. The university teaches you to be an independent person, but at the same time, collaborative. Team projects will be a very important part of your academic development.

6.- Graduate will make you feel invincible

Few sensations are as satisfying as graduating from a university career, taking the podium and receiving your diploma.

Obtaining a degree is undoubtedly one of the highest reasons for pride you could give your family, and it will always be one of the great achievements of your life. Just imagine the moment you receive your diploma and throw your mortarboard towards the sky... You will feel capable of overcoming any other obstacle that stands in your way!

Why is there so much poverty in the world; Has God created one group to enjoy wealth and another to suffer from poverty?

Evangelist Matthew said: «For the kingdom of heaven is as a man travelling into a far country, who called his own servants, and delivered unto them his goods. And unto one he gave five talents, to another two, and to another one; to every man according to his several ability; and straightway took his journey.

Then he that had received the five talents went and traded with the same, and made them other five talents. And likewise he that had received two, he also gained other two. But he that had received one went and digged in the earth, and hid his lord's money. After a long time the lord of those servants cometh, and reckoneth with them.

And so he that had received five talents came and brought other five talents, saying, Lord, thou deliveredst unto me five talents: behold, I have gained beside them five talents more. His lord said unto him, Well done, thou good and faithful servant: thou hast been faithful over a few things, I will make thee ruler over many things: enter thou into the joy of thy lord.

He also that had received two talents came and said, Lord, thou deliveredst unto me two talents: behold, I have gained two other talents beside them. His lord said unto him, Well done, good and faithful servant; thou hast been faithful over a few things, I will make thee ruler over many things: enter thou into the joy of thy lord.

Then he which had received the one talent came and said, Lord, I knew thee that thou art an hard man, reaping where thou hast not sown, and gathering where thou hast not strawed: And I was afraid, and went and hid thy talent in the earth: lo, there thou hast that is thine»: [Mattew 25:14-25].

God is a God of justice, he hates injustice, He has not created anyone to be poor. He wants everyone to have a lot of wealth, he is the man who has made his choice or his decision to be what he wants to be, and God is sad when he sees his children are suffering from misery.

God has distributed talents to the whole world, now it is you who must know what you want for your life, how your future will be tomorrow, it is you who have to decide if you want a successful future or not; if you want to overcome or not; if you want to study a professional career or not; If you want to sweat to get your daily bread or if you want to be lazy, it all depends on you.

Lazy people, should they eat according to the bible?

The apostle Paul said: «For even when we were with you, this we commanded you, that if any would not work, neither should he eat. For we hear that there are some which walk among you disorderly, working not at all, but are busybodies.

Now them that are such we command and exhort by our Lord Jesus Christ, that with quietness they work, and eat their own bread»: [2 Thessalonians 3: 10-12].

The Importance of Home Finances

Some professionals express themselves about the most important ingredient in all families. We know very clearly that no one can live without that resource called "the economy."

Janeth Pérez Alegría (June 26, 2013), commented on [gestiopolis.com] said: «Life is full of unforeseen events, so prevention is better than regret. Some people work just to pay debts, others invest it in fun, gambling, or unnecessary products and activities, for example.

However, there are also those who prefer to "spend" a certain amount of money on a business that may bring them benefits in the future. In other words, there are multiple ways in which we can "spend" our money, the difficult part is knowing how to distribute it».

Each individual must know what tools they have, to plan their finances when acquiring a vehicle, a home, starting their own business or buying shares in an existing one, paying school fees and extra curricular activities for their children, vacation trips and countless activities, both personal and work.

All those who have poorly guarded their talents, afraid of sweating to survive. God called them useless, lazy servants.

God gave each one talents according to their ability. Where have you invested the wealth God gave you? What have you done with his talents? Have you spent it on useless things or have you invested it in things that have value for the future? You must take advantage of all the good times and moments to prepare, because you will never recover the time requested.

Finance and growth at home

Undoubtedly, today the good management of personal finances has a significant and direct impact on the family economy, individuals need to know how to properly organize and manage their monetary resources to ensure future well-being, not only their own, but that of their family.

Also, whether it is for the education of your children, to get real estate, cars and even to have a good retirement fund and thus live without worries before any unexpected eventuality that you might suffer at any time.

Our life is governed by finances and money, regardless of the profession we have and the ups and downs that arise in the different stages of life. In this sense, it is important that we have a good management of our personal finances, because this way we will be able to reach the middle age financially and retire comfortably.

Without forgetting the importance of finances, there is also another situation that commonly happens when people start saving in a bank account to buy something in the future, say home or car: they realize that over time inflation is higher to the interests that you have obtained and that the prices of the good or goods that you wanted to acquire rise faster than expected.

After the time, they will have to acquire something of lesser quality than the one desired or go into debt to complete it. Here are the pitfalls of saving, since most people think that because they have limited savings or investment capacity, they have to resort to traditional alternatives. That is, to banks: which offer very low returns.

In many cases, especially in people who live on the proceeds of a settlement, retirement or the savings they managed to collect during the course of their productive lives, they commonly say that they live on their interests.

But they realize over time that it is not possible to live adequately with the product of the low returns they receive, and they begin to withdraw part of the capital. And having no income or reinvestment of capital, they sadly realize that after a short time their savings have disappeared.

These situations arise basically due to a lack of financial culture and not knowing how to manage personal finances. The basic principles and rules of personal finance seem very complex to those who do not know them, but they are really very easy to understand.

I very much agree with the idea Janeth Pérez, all families should put it into practice, although I see things from a different perspective for each individual.

Finance is something that is very important in human life, no one can live without it, every human being needs finance to survive on earth, even the church of God stops working without that element. There are two elements that each family needs to be happy: "God and finance."

What must man do to have growth at home?

The first thing the guy must do is to look for a decent job that guarantees a good future. There are many companies that pay biweekly, others monthly.

Each individual must have three agendas: one biweekly, monthly, and yearly. To reach your goal you must reduce expenses, you cannot buy anything unnecessarily, you must have control over food, you cannot live for others or for appearance, you should never buy in grocery stores, you must buy biweekly, you must have a list of all the things you need during the fortnight.

All people who do not belong to a magnate family, must go through suffering first if they want to be successful people in the future, they must never try a life of appearance, never demonstrate what they are not, avoid all debts. Each person must be their own butler.

If you want to have a better tomorrow, you must start from today.

Chapter 18

The couple's economy in married life

Dr. José Antonio García Higuera, member of the team at Psicoterapeutas.com, whose consultation is at the Center for Clinical Psychology and Psychotherapy García Higuera, expressed the following opinion: «The economy affects all aspects of life and, therefore, also to the love relationship. It mainly influences several aspects:»In decision making.

In our society, whoever has the money is the one who decides, although under normal circumstances the roles can be distributed and each member of the couple specializes in different areas, for example, one is in charge of household expenses, the other of the car, holidays are mainly assigned to one of them, etc.

But, finally, whoever has the source of the money has the ultimate power of decision.

How should they share their finances together?

The couple is a social unit and as such must have its own well-established economy. That there is a common money and that decisions are made about it together and by consensus, is a fundamental element in the functioning of the couple. How this common money is contributed depends on the characteristics of each couple.

It should not be forgotten that, even in the separation of property regime, each member of the marriage has the obligation to contribute to the couple's economy in proportion to their income.

An important difference between the separation of assets and the profit regime is that the earnings of each of the exclusive assets are yours and you do not have to ask the other for permission to do with them what you want, that is, the separation of assets it gives an independence to the parties in the management of their assets, which does not exist in the community property regime.

You have to be careful with the differences between the assets of one and the other when they are important. If the difference is very large, in the separation of goods, the "poor" member of the couple may feel "grateful" to the other for their generosity.

Thus, the economic relationship is clear and explicit. In the case of community property, the one who enters the most "gives" the difference to the other and does so implicitly. The "poor" are entitled to half the income.

When the differences are not very great, the regime only influences the way of sharing life. The important thing is to make the economic relations between the members of the couple very clear, explicit and legally supported, because, if things go well in the couple, there are no problems; but if they go wrong, many annoyances are avoided.

Economic relationships can be sources of problems that arise when one member feels that the other is abusing. For example, a common theme that works in the separation of assets model. One has bought an apartment before being in a couple and living together the finances in common are inevitable, thus, one pays for food so that the other pays for the apartment.

When the non-owner of the apartment realizes that he or she is actually helping to pay the apartment to the other, discussions may arise.

It is a good illustration. Dr. José Antonio has explained about the home economy, you should not have two checks or two bank accounts, because the two are one flesh.

Can a Christian be a tycoon?

Of course. There are many people who think a servant of God cannot be a tycoon or wealthy, nor can he have a good house, or a luxury vehicle. For them only the poor can serve God. It's a big mistake on their part, It is contrary. They are the followers of Christ who had to be rich because they are princes.

What does the bible say about that?

The first faithful character of God is Abraham. [Genesis 13: 2]. And Abram was very rich in cattle, in silver, and in gold.

That servant of God had a lot of wealth, but he never put his wealth above God. God was always in the first place of Abraham's heart, that's why the Spirit of God was always over him at all times. As a rich man, he never departed from his Creator at any time.

The second character was Solomon, the author said: "So king Solomon exceeded all the kings of the earth for riches and for wisdom. And all the earth sought to Solomon, to hear his wisdom, which God had put in his heart": [1 Kings 10: 23-24].

Not only did Solomon have much wealth and much wisdom, there has been no king over all the earth who had the wealth and wisdom of Solomon. So God never gave his children enough, always in abundance. With God you never lose or tie, you always win. The children of God always have the vision of an eagle, they always fly high in both wealth and wisdom.

The third character who was very rich was Hezekiah. "And Hezekiah hearkened unto them, and shewed them all the house of his precious things, the silver, and the gold, and the spices, and the precious ointment, and all the house of his armour, and all that was found in his treasures: there was nothing in his house, nor in all his dominion, that Hezekiah shewed them not": [2 Kings 20:13].

When a servant of God has a lot of wealth and power, he must listen and do only what God says, and if he does the opposite he will pay the consequence, Hezekiah made a great mistake: he should not teach his wealth to enemies. Because no enemy wants to see a good gift from their enemy.

The fourth character was Job. "His substance also was seven thousand sheep, and three thousand camels, and five hundred yoke of oxen, and five hundred she asses, and a very great household; so that this man was the greatest of all the men of the east": [Job 1: 3].

That servant had a lot of wealth over all the eastern ones, because he trusted God. God gave him a lot of abundance. Fifth character who was very rich in the New Testament was Joseph of Arimathea.

Evangelist Matthew said: «When the even was come, there came a rich man of Arimathaea, named Joseph, who also himself was Jesus' disciple: He went to Pilate, and begged the body of Jesus. Then Pilate commanded the body to be delivered.

And when Joseph had taken the body, he wrapped it in a clean linen cloth, and laid it in his own new tomb, which he had hewn out in the rock: and he rolled a great stone to the door of the sepulchre, and departed»: [Matthew 27: 57-60].

As a rich man in the area, even the kings had respect for him, which no disciple could do, he did it with his power, he went to ask Pilate and he listened. He buried the Master in a millionaire grave, because he was one of Jesus' believers.

Jesus said unto him, "Thou shalt love the Lord thy God with all thy heart, and with all thy soul, and with all thy mind": [Matthew 22:37].

No one can serve two masters together. All the things a person wants above God, his presence cannot be, because God does not like second place, always first place.

No family can be afraid of having wealth, their wealth can function to advance the work of God, also many Christians can survive with their company, also many people can know their God through their wealth. They can do their work with money.

The children of the poor

The great improvement of the workers are the children of the poor or the middle class, the tycoons's children never work with anyone, as they are relieved by their parents, since they were little they are taught to run the companies, they are always in the savings banks, or in all the departments where the parents are.

They also teach them how to run their own businesses and fortune. They were born in money, educated in money. They have an entrepreneurial mind for inheritance and education. They give work but they don't take work.

Can the children of the poor be magnates?

This world is a world of opportunities, anyone can be a billionaire if he puts the rule into practice, each individual can never miss any opportunity, he must take advantage of all the good opportunities arise in his favor, because the lost opportunity never returns.

Each person must be very vigilant to catch good opportunities. How many opportunities do we not miss without taking advantage of anything? There are people who are thinking to get rich they must find a sack of money on the street or in the world, it is a crazy vision, because that will never happen.

To grow you must start from scratch, you must fight hard to fulfill your vision. All things starting from scratch are difficult, you will find many stumbling blocks, many mountains, many opposing winds want to destroy your vision, never give up, you must fight even with giants. You never lose hope, because the darkest moment precedes the dawn.

You can fall millions of times, but never stay on the ground. You have to get up again if you have to die, you must die fighting. Everyone has their struggles, their battles, all the struggles do not come in the same way. Adapt, fight hard to fulfill your dreams.

The moment you are fighting, never think that you are a hen, you always think you are an eagle, one day without waiting for it, you will shake its feathers, its wings and you will take flight. When you are flying, never look at the land where you were: look up, try to fly much higher, until you reach the summits of the eagles.

Even if you are eating with the hens, you must be aware you that do not belong to that species: your lineage is that of the eagle.

The famous credit card

What is the credit card?

The credit card is issued by a bank that allows certain operations to be carried out from an ATM and the purchase of goods and services on credit; it is generally made of plastic and has a magnetic stripe on one side.

It is money the bank makes available to you, with an interest rate for each transaction you have made. It is very tempting, it is money that is not yours, that card can get you in trouble, in a debt where you can lose all your belongings. It is sweet to spend what is not yours without knowing how you will pay, without thinking about the consequences.

Why should you use the credit card?

Some professionals comment on the use of the plague called the credit card. The card has a good and bad part, it depends on how it is used. María Alejandra Moncada, (7/19/2016) commented on the account of [Finanzaspersonal.com], about the credit card:

"The simple fact of having a credit card implies that you must receive a fixed monthly salary or some income that serves as a support to the bank in which it is demonstrated that you have how to pay what you are going to buy."

According to María Teresa Macías, expert in pocket economics at the Universidad de la Sabana: «The main disadvantage of having a credit card is the psychological effect that it produces in which the person who thinks they have more money available as if they were own. This immediate availability makes you believe that it is yours and, therefore, leads you to spend more money than you should.

On the other hand, it is healthy to have it, but as a backup for an emergency eventuality »When the person uses it, a usury rate of 32% is a very big problem if they do not know how to handle it, although in most banks they have a lower rate if deferred to few installments

Rodrigo Nadal, manager of Solve your Debt in Colombia, is emphatic that credits should not be demonized because: «The most important thing is to understand that credit card and loans are not extensions of salary or additional money, they are a method of payment that provides benefits and like any financial instrument, has a cost and a responsibility. The secret to success is to have a clear capacity to borrow and to keep control of income and expenses».

Additionally, it must be borne in mind that having this "plastic" means that you started a credit life that will open up a field for you, not only in your working life, but also in your financial life.

So what should you consider before agreeing to have a credit card?

I agree with Moncada for the very clear explanation he gave about the use of the card. However I have some ideas that I can add about the credit card.

Positive or good part

You can have a credit card, if you have a good salary, because you have the means to pay the fees without affecting the family. You can use your credit card to pay bills if you don't want to walk with cash. Many people use it for security, for so many criminals on the street.

If you are traveling, it is important to use a credit card because you will be outside your country, because you will not be able to buy with national currency, you must purchase a credit card. But it is easier to have a national or international debit card, because what you have on the card is yours, you do not have to pay any fee if you want to be debt free.

Negative or bad part

It is when you do not have a good fixed salary, you are using it because your friends have, you want to demonstrate equality, you live for the appearance, and that will generate a big problem that will be very difficult to get rid of, because the money that is on the card, is not yours. You will have to pay what was spent and the fee as well.

What will happen if you cannot pay the loan?

It will automatically change the face of the guy who invited you to enter that risk. You will receive many calls daily, including legal procedural threats. Possibly you lose your house or car; your account will be in all the banks, you will never be able to get any document without paying that money; they'll sign you as a defaulting customer

If it is a mortgage loan on your home or other property, the entity will request a foreclosure from a judge. You will have another term of more or less one year to pay off the debt — which will be considerably longer than at the beginning—, but if you don't do it, your house will be auctioned and you will have to abandon it, losing any right as owner.

If the house cannot be auctioned for the full amount due to the bank, plus expenses, because even after losing your home, you will still have a debt with the bank and the latter may demand payment from your guarantors or seize your other assets.

If it is a personal loan, do not think you are getting rid of it. By contracting a personal loan (consumer loan) you guarantee all of your present and future assets. In the event of a prolonged default situation, the entity could get a judge to seize these assets, which include your home, your car, your bank accounts, part of your payroll or pension, etc. In short, everything you need to pay off the debt.

To be happy you must avoid all temptations, think about it fifty times before taking out a loan.

Chapter 19

The expenses of the two at home

Your expenses depend on the monthly or biweekly profit, nobody can spend more than they earn monthly, if they do, it is lost because nothing can be thrown for the future, and they have to shed even one dolar. Although your friends and neighbors earn the same, less or more than you, you cannot have competition in expenses.

You have to be in competition even from misery and poverty. The growth budget should not be personal, the two have to make all the decisions together. All those who want to be great in life have to start from today, because tomorrow will be too late.

Negative people

What is it to be a negative person?

Negative concept. A negative thinking person is one who is able to see the bad or irremediable of facts or things, "the glass half empty" instead of observing what is good or positive. For example: "I have two healthy and hard-working children, but I am distressed to think that they are not rich enough."

Negative people are dangers against economic growth, against his own family and against himself. The negatives do nothing but inoculate the poison of your opinion. And even if you are a positive person, that person's negativity can affect you even on an energetic level.

There are ten negative things that can defeat any religious family or not, professional or not; they are poisons that can venerate even the successful family, each family must eliminate them from their center, they are not only dangerous for the family, but for anyone who wants to live a noble life.

1.- The gossip

Gossipers delight in the misfortune of others. At first it can be fun to snoop on the personal or professional stumbles of others, but over time he gets tired, makes you feel bad, and hurts others. There are a lot of positive people out there and you can learn a lot from interesting people to waste time talking about other people's misfortune.

What is a gossipy person?

The researchers say: Gossiping is a human activity that involves talking about someone or something, both in good and in bad, although generally in an unfavorable way, without the person in question being present. Some synonyms of gossip are gossip, gossip, rumor, gossip or gossip, the latter being in the colloquial field.

The gossiper likes to give false comments and news about others, he can never remain silent for any reason, he is like a reporter who is looking for the information to comment on it.

There are gossips who comment even their own privacy, because of their language it can cause many problems in the center of their home, even inside the church there are many members who are more gossip than worldly ones.

What should be done to stop gossipers?

The psychologist Irma Socorro Rodríguez, gave a good recommendation on gossips, she said: «When you get information as a gossip, you should go through certain gangs, which are nothing more than questions to assess how important the information is. The first questions to ask ourselves are: Is what they tell us useful for anything? Does it benefit me in something? Does it do the person you are talking about good? If none of those responses is positive, then gossip should get there.

If that information or rumor falls directly on the person who listens to it, how good is it to approach the person who issues it?

The first step is to enter to see what is being said about me, deep down ask ourselves if it is true or not, how true it is. It is also important that the person who is involved confronts him, without forgetting that many times our brain sees what it wants to see and not reality. Many times the fact of inquiring and asking makes a topic go long, as opposed to leaving it like that so that it dies right there.

Many people also make the mistake of taking everything personally and things may not be for them, so it is best to land all the information in the first place.

We must enter to evaluate how much we are counting our personal life so that this is a common conversation throughout the company. We cannot expose our intimacy, if we expose our life to the public light it simply becomes public.

So the first question to answer is how much information do I give about my life? Surely a person who does not count beyond what he must count will be exposed to gossip. The type of personality also influences a lot.

When a gossip person is detected that affects the work environment, how to approach the subject? We must confront it, do it with all the people involved in the gossip. We should not neglect the person's gifts or qualities but it is good to be firm and tell him the implications that his attitude could bring, if he continues to publish things that do not concern him.

Failure to do so in time, the rumor will grow and not only that, because the gossipy person will be the most affected since they will end up receiving social rejection. It is helping her to see that the information she brings and carries is not benefiting others, much less her.

The formula that psychology Irma uses to describe the gossip is very effective, there are also gossips who like to listen only to what they need and it is necessary to know about others to put all kinds of negative ingredients in order to make the conversation more enjoyable.

What does the Bible say about gossipers?

The wise Solomon said: «An ungodly man diggeth up evil: and in his lips there is as a burning fire. A froward man soweth strife: and a whisperer separateth chief friends.

A violent man enticeth his neighbour, and leadeth him into the way that is not good. He shutteth his eyes to devise froward things: moving his lips he bringeth evil to pass. The hoary head is a crown of glory, if it be found in the way of righteousness.

He that is slow to anger is better than the mighty; and he that ruleth his spirit than he that taketh a city. The lot is cast into the lap; but the whole disposing thereof is of the LORD»: [Proverbs 16: 27-33].

The psalmist said: «He that walketh uprightly, and worketh righteousness, and speaketh the truth in his heart. He that backbiteth not with his tongue, nor doeth evil to his neighbour, nor taketh up a reproach against his neighbour»: [Psalms 15: 2-3].

All those who do not slander their tongues against their neighbors, are whole people who do justice all the time, never accept the gossip of others, gossip is the enemy of justice, we must be fair in all circumstances, if we want to be happy.

The wise Solomon continues saying: "The integrity of the upright shall guide them: but the perverseness of transgressors shall destroy them": [Proverbs 11: 3].

A gossiper is only interested in sharing juicy information, no matter how it affects the people he/she is talking about. Often when things are said in trust, he promises not to tell others, so by revealing such secrets, the gossiper betrays the trust placed in him and is dishonest.

But a faithful friend keeps secrets and cares for the interests of his friends. He/she only reveals a secret when one wants to help the friend (in cases such as abuse, drugs or suicide threat).

What does the Bible say about the expressions of Christians?

The apostle Paul said: "Let no corrupt communication proceed out of your mouth, but that which is good to the use of edifying, that it may minister grace unto the hearers": [Ephesians 4:29].

No corrupted word should come out of his mouth, his expressions should be edify everyone around him. All those Christians who are more gossipy than worldly people, if they want the Holy Spirit to dwell within their homes, they must stop being gossipy.

Many men are more gossips than women, they cannot keep any secrets, because their tongues are so hot, their repentance is to say it with the others, if they want to bring good fruit they must control their tongues before expressing themselves. The wise Solomon said in his book: «He that hideth hatred with lying lips, and he that uttereth a slander, is a fool»: [Proverbs 10:18].

Gossip is a violation of human rights, if you want to be at peace against youself, you must respect everyone's right. Gossipers always have two temperaments; one to search for information, the other to disseminate it. Satan refines his ear and tongue, turning them into honey for idle curiosity.

What is envy?

Envy is a feeling or mental state in which there is pain or misery for not possessing oneself what the other has, be it in goods, superior qualities or other kinds of tangible and intangible things. The SAR has defined it as sadness or regret for the good of others, or as a desire for something that is not owned.

How much damage can envy cause in a home?

Envy can come in different forms, because a good partner who has a profession, a good job that is envious is danger to their own family. His mind is to covet what does not belong to him, he is going to live a life of bitterness, sadness, hate, he can never be happy at any time.

All people should avoid all the envious fruits if they want to live without stress and bitterness. The envious are never satisfied with what they have.

Pickers are people who immediately tell you what's right and what's not. They have a way of judging what you are passionate about and they make you feel terribly bad. Instead of valuing and learning from the people they are different from, the picky eyed look down on them.

Critics steal your desire to be passionate and expressive, so the best thing you can do is take them out of your life and be yourself.

Arrogant people are a waste of time because they consider everything you do to be a personal challenge. Arrogance is lack of confidence and always hides great insecurity. A study from the University of Akron found that arrogance is linked to a number of problems in the workplace.

Arrogant people generally don't perform well, are more unpleasant, and have more learning problems than the average person.

Bradberry is absolutely right in ensuring that the negative person does not progress at all, nor does he want another person to grow, he is a threat to himself and to society, if a couple is negative they will never grow professionally or financially.

There are many types of individuals, and each with their strengths and weaknesses. Without a doubt, one of the biggest defects that human beings can have is a negative attitude towards life, because we all know that day to day is not always a paradise, and the way we interpret and face the events that happen to us influences in our happiness and in our ability to solve problems.

While there are optimistic people, whom everyone wants to have by their side, there are also negative people, who see everything as black. In this article we will talk about the latter.

Gossip is the true or false comment that is made about a person, regardless of the consequences. A gossiper makes the rumors spread even if he is not sure of them.

Some experts in psychology think that envy is the origin of gossip, because as a result of these opinions many couples live in mistrust, families disunite and friends stop being so because they allow themselves to be influenced by intrigues.

What psychological problems can envy cause in the person?

First definition: Sadness, or regret for the good of others. Understood in this way, it is possible to conclude that envy is the mother of resentment, a feeling that does not seek that one does better but that the other does worse.

Second definition: Emulation, desire for something that is not possessed. Oscar Castillero Mimenza on the page [psicologiaymente.com], said: there are five keys to understand an envious person.

1.- Different types of envy

However, it is worth asking if envy occurs in the same way in all people, a question that seems to have a negative answer. This is due to what is known as healthy envy. This term refers to a type of envy focused on the envied element, without wishing any harm to the person who owns it.

On the contrary, pure envy supposes the belief that we are more deserving of the object of desire than the one whom we envy, and joy can be produced in the face of its failure.

2.- Disadvantages to consider

Envy has traditionally been conceptualized as a negative element, due to the deep discomfort that it causes together with the hostile relationship that it supposes towards other people, which is related to lack of self-esteem and the fact that it comes from the feeling of inferiority and inequity.

Also, according to numerous studies, envy may be behind the existence and creation of prejudice.

Envy towards other people can make defensive reactions appear in the form of irony, mockery, heteroaggressiveness (that is, aggressiveness directed at other people, be it physical or psychological) and narcissism.

It is common for envy to become resentment, and if it is a prolonged situation in time it can induce depressive disorders. Similarly, it can induce feelings of guilt in people who are aware of their envy (which correlates with the desire that the envied do poorly), as well as anxiety and stress.

3.- Evolutionary sense of envy

However, despite all these considerations being scientifically based, envy can also be used in a positive way. Envy seems to have an evolutionary sense: this feeling has fueled competition for the search for resources and the generation of new strategies and tools, elements that have been essential for survival since the beginning of humanity.

In this sense, envy makes a situation that we consider unfair, a reason to try to reach a situation of equity in areas such as employment (for example, it can lead to fighting to reduce salary differences, avoid favoritism, or establish promotion criteria clear).

4.- Neurobiology of envy

Reflecting on envy can lead to wondering, and what happens in our brains when we envy someone?

This reflection has prompted various experiments. Thus, in this sense, a series of experiments carried out by researchers from the National Institute of Radiological Sciences of Japan have indicated that various areas involved in the perception of physical pain are activated at the cerebral level.

Likewise, when volunteers were asked to imagine that the envied subject suffered a failure, the release of dopamine in brain areas of the ventral striatum was triggered, activating the brain reward mechanism. Furthermore, the results show that the intensity of the perceived envy was correlated with the pleasure obtained by the failure of the envied.

5.- Jealousy and envy: fundamental differences

It is relatively frequent, especially when the object of desire is a relationship with someone, that envy and jealousy are used interchangeably to refer to the feeling of frustration caused by not enjoying that personal relationship.

The reason that envy and jealousy are often confused is that they usually occur together. That is, jealousy is given to people who consider themselves to be more attractive or have qualities than oneself, thereby envying the supposed rival.

However, these are two concepts that, although related, do not refer to the same thing. The main differentiation is that while envy occurs with respect to an attribute or element that is not possessed, jealousy occurs when there is fear of the loss of an element that was available (usually personal relationships).

Another difference can be found in the fact that envy occurs between two people (envied and subject who envies) with respect to an element, in the case of jealousy a triadic relationship is established (person with jealousy, person with respect to whom they are jealous and a third person who could snatch the second).

The third difference would be found in the fact that jealousy comes together with a feeling of betrayal, whereas in the case of envy this does not usually happen.

The psychologist Mimenza gives many meanings, all the things that can happen to an envious person, and all the things that this great phenomenon produces. He expressed himself as a human professional, but the psychologist of psychologists expressed himself from a superhuman plane, more transcendental and eternal, his laws are not subject to time.

What does the Bible say about envy?

The wise Solomon said, "Let not thine heart envy sinners: but be thou in the fear of the Lord all the day long. For surely there is an end; and thine expectation shall not be cut off": [Proverbs 23: 17].

God said through King Solomon, no human being should have an envious heart, because all evil thoughts are stored in the mind's archive. That is why we must have our mind free of all false thoughts, which can cause us harm.

Apostle Paul said: "For we ourselves also were sometimes foolish, disobedient, deceived, serving divers lusts and pleasures, living in malice and envy, hateful, and hating one another": [Titus 3: 3].

The apostle Paul was saying to all those who have envious hearts they are foolish, because a wise person will never envy the things of others. All those who want to have prosperity in all must sow their own fruits.

Paul continues saying: «Charity suffereth long, and is kind; charity envieth not; charity vaunteth not itself, is not puffed up, doth not behave itself unseemly, seeketh not her own, is not easily provoked, thinketh no evil; rejoiceth not in iniquity, but rejoiceth in the truth; beareth all things, believeth all things, hopeth all things, endureth all things.

Charity never faileth: but whether there be prophecies, they shall fail; whether there be tongues, they shall cease; whether there be knowledge, it shall vanish away»: [1 Corinthians 13: 4-8].

Love never goes with envy, they are two different things. If you love your neighbor you cannot be envious of his, if someone is looking for his in others, love is never in him, no one can hate his neighbor for his belongings, nor can he enjoy injustice towards his fellow man. We should only enjoy the justice that is the production of legality.

Doctor Lucas said: «But the Jews which believed not, moved with envy, took unto them certain lewd fellows of the baser sort, and gathered a company, and set all the city on an uproar, and assaulted the house of Jason, and sought to bring them out to the people.

And when they found them not, they drew Jason and certain brethren unto the rulers of the city, crying, These that have turned the world upside down are come hither also; whom Jason hath received: and these all do contrary to the decrees of Caesar, saying that there is another king, one Jesus»: [Acts 17: 5-7].

Other difference between jealousy and envy

Both envy and jealousy are "negative" or non-constructive emotions. Both refer to the belonging or non-belonging of something; be they material goods or abstract goods, like someone's affection. These emotions are among the most natural and inherent in the human being.

However, they are also among the most damaging and destructive a person can experience. In many cases, envy and jealousy result from the insecurities of each person.

That is why it is desirable to learn to control these emotional responses. Only in this way will a person be able to build healthy interpersonal relationships.

As for the differences, the main one is that while envy is the feeling of coveting what another person has, jealousy is the emotion related to the fear of losing something or someone. Envy produces rancor, hatred, coveting what does not belong, and jealousy produces anger and fear of something, but both do the same damage.

There are two types of jealousy, one positive and the other negative. Each one has its own fruits.

The apostle Peter said: "Wherefore laying aside all malice, and all guile, and hypocrisies, and envies, and all evil speakings, as newborn babes, desire the sincere milk of the word, that ye may grow thereby: If so be ye have tasted that the Lord is gracious": [1 Peter 2: 1-3].

God has a good recipe for the envious, if they want to have prosperity, happiness. Without this remedy it is impossible to have total change. When the individual lets the Holy Spirit work in his heart, all kinds of malice, deceit, hypocrisy, envy disappear. In a second he will change like a newborn, he will drink the spiritual milk every day of his life for eternity.

Moses said, "But unto Cain and to his offering he had not respect. And Cain was very wroth, and his countenance fell": [Genesis 4: 5].

Envy caused Cain to kill his own brother Abel, because he coveted the blessing that he had received from God, envy does not come from God, all people who feel envy against their neighbor, are servants of the enemy.

The wise Solomon said: "Wrath is cruel, and anger is outrageous; but who is able to stand before envy?": [Proverbs 27: 4].

Envy can cause cruelty and anger against the other person. When a guy is dominated by envy, he can never resist against its fruits. There we have Cain and Abel as the example.

The apostle Paul said: «Being filled with all unrighteousness, fornication, wickedness, covetousness, maliciousness; full of envy, murder, debate, deceit, malignity; whisperers, backbiters, haters of God, despiteful, proud, boasters, inventors of evil things, disobedient to parents, without understanding, covenantbreakers, without natural affection, implacable, unmerciful.

Who knowing the judgment of God, that they which commit such things are worthy of death, not only do the same, but have pleasure in them that do them»: [Romans 1: 29-32].

The fruits of envy can inspire the other person to commit verbal and physical aggression against his family or neighbor.

The apostle Paul continues saying: «Now the works of the flesh are manifest, which are these; Adultery, fornication, uncleanness, lasciviousness, Idolatry, witchcraft, hatred, variance, emulations, wrath, strife, seditions, heresies, envyings, murders, drunkenness, revellings, and such like.

Of the which I tell you before, as I have also told you in time past, that they which do such things shall not inherit the kingdom of God»: [Galatians 5: 19-21].

Definitely, the great psychologist of the universe explains the thing more clearly. Much is the damage that great mistake can do, when one does not allow God to guide his heart.

Chapter 20

Growths within the home

There are many authors who have written and commented on family growth, their opinions coincide: no couple can live without economic growth. The lack of entry causes many separations both in the religious world and outside.

According to the Women's Institute for Financial Education, Wife.org, a nonprofit organization dedicated to providing financial education to women in their quest for economic independence: "The way we earn, spend, and save Money is a practical expression of our beliefs and lifestyle.

For Kathleen Gurney and Ginita Wall, authors of the book "Love and Money: 150 financial tips for couples", it is important to analyze the couple in the financial field during the courtship to be clear how will behave during marriage.

According to NOHRA MALDONADO on the page of [fucsia.com], There are five financial rules for newlyweds.

1.- Clean history

In many cases, the bride and groom agree to be honest about their romantic past and even agree to reveal to their partners how many relationships they had before they met, but they never mention debts, legal problems or complications with inheritances.

In this topic it is important to also include the issue of financial responsibilities acquired with seniority and from which debts are generated. It is essential to make clear if after marriage these will become shared or if each will be responsible for their financial commitments.

2.- When you have everything

It is more and more frequent that the bride and groom marry at a more mature age, when they are established, they have work, solid bank accounts and properties such as cars or houses.

In a good percentage of the cases, gathering all the assets from the beginning can generate high levels of stress, seeing that the other spends what he has achieved with years of work. Therefore, the first step is to analyze and discuss what portion of your finances will be shared.

Just because they are now married does not mean they are no longer financially independent. It is correct to manage personal accounts, for personal expenses, but you should never lie about it, let alone hide them. A healthy recommendation is to create a shared account that is used for the usual household expenses such as rent, utilities, food and other extras.

3.- Prepare a budget

An Excel chart will be of great help to organize and make clear the assets and liabilities they have. It is also important to indicate one by one the expenses that they must assume month by month and the income of the couple with whom they will bear them (It must be established how much each one earns to make an equitable distribution).

The most recommended is that one of the two is in charge of keeping track of expenses and managing the money in the shared account, paying receipts or obligations.

4.- Shared decisions

Usually, one partner is more financially facilitated than the other, so it's okay for him to be in charge of managing finances, but that doesn't mean he has to make individual decisions like what or where to invest. All issues related to money must be agreed to avoid misunderstandings and future problems.

5.- Think ahead

The only way to grow financially is to maintain high levels of savings and make the right investments. If so far they begin their life as a couple, they may have plans to buy a more comfortable property or invest in real estate, if they plan to have children, they must consider the great expense that this implies, so it is important to have a good level of savings from Start.

It is very true that when it comes to money there are many people who do not have as much capacity to handle it, compulsive shopping without necessity and vices do not allow it. All married people must manage their income with monastic discipline if they want to have a prosperous future.

Also economic growth should be between two people who have the same temperament, two positive people, if one is contrary, it can cause chaos in the financial lives of both. They must both have the same vision, the same goal to reach ultimate success.

Why should the couple have the same positive thinking in development?

Because the force of negativity is much more contagious than that of positivity, there is only one way not to fall into your networks: do not approach or accept any negative person at your side.

The negative person is a danger even to himself, no growth will ever be experienced if there is negativity in the partner. If one of the two is negative it can affect all the good positive thoughts that the other had.

In electricity a negative with a positive can work, but in the family economy it is totally different, there must be two positives.

No positive guy should share his thoughts or listen to any negative person if he wants to reach the heights of growth. Negative people are afraid to risk anything; the positive never thinks of defeat or failure, growth dwells within her mind.

The negatives always remain at the level of conformity; "They do not sow because of the birds" as an old Hindu saying goes. The positive rises to the level of triumph.

The family equation is God + money + love + communication equals the end success.

Chapter 21

You and I

Science is talking about the existence of humanity, who can talk about the existence of creation, God or science? Who is right between the two? What is science?

It is the branch of human knowledge made up of the set of verifiable and objective knowledge on a given subject that is obtained through observation and experimentation.

The explanation of its principles and causes, and the formation and verification of hypotheses characterizes it, in addition to the use of an appropriate methodology for the object of study and the systematization of knowledge. It covers the different branches of human knowledge, especially those that have the natural or physical world or technology as subjects of study.

Who created humanity according to science?

Johann Beckmann [1739 to 1811] was a German naturalist, mycologist, economist and agronomist and scientific writer, who coined the term technology, in the sense of the science of the trades.

He was the first person to teach technology, and wrote about it as an academic subject. Where were human scientists in the first evolution? Who told them, for the first time, that we humans come from the monkey?

What is the monkey?

It is a domestic or wild animal does not have the reason, the moral, the thought or the emotion, it is an animal that reacts totally by its instinct. It is an animal like all animals, which exist without a curiosity or need beyond reproducing or eating.

Who has created the monkey according to scientists?

Evolution or an explosion. Who created that explosion? For nothing comes from nothing, you must have a spirit created it. A monkey is an animal that reacts on instinct. Instinct is unconscious behavior and reflects that it is generally transmitted between living beings of the same species and that makes them respond in the same way to certain stimuli.

Man cannot come from that animal in any way. Charles Robert Darwin said that humanity comes from the monkey: did Darwin really say that? No scientist can speak of the existence of humanity without inserting God into the equation.

Who Was Charles Robert Darwin?

Scientists know him as the father of evolution. He was an English naturalist born in Shrewsbury, England, on February 12, 1809.

In April 1882 he was recognized for being the most influential scientist at that time along with Alfred Russel Wallace, for developing the idea of biological evolution through selection natural, justifying it in his 1859 work "The Origin of Species", with numerous examples taken from observing nature.

He postulated that all species of living things have evolved over time from a common ancestor through a process called natural selection. Evolution was accepted as fact by the scientific community and by much of Darwin's living public, but was not considered the primary explanation of the evolutionary process until the 1930s.

What was Charles Robert Darwin's religion?

Today it forms the basis of modern evolutionary synthesis. With its modifications, Darwin's scientific discoveries still remain the founding record of biology as a science, since they constitute a logical explanation that unifies observations about the diversity of life.

Charles Darwin's religion was Anglicanism and Agnosticism. If his religion was Anglican, he could not say that humanity was created by evolution, because he had a belief.

Anglicanism could be defined as the faith, practice and spirit of the member churches of the Anglican communion, that is, churches in full communion with the Archbishop of Canterbury.

The archbishop is a bishop who has jurisdiction over other bishops who form an ecclesiastical province, while also exercising episcopal functions in his own diocese, such as the Vatican. It means Charles Darwin was a very active member in Catholic doctrine or Catholic religion.

What is an evolution?

It is a gradual change or transformation of something, such as a state, a circumstance, a situation. That was the idea of Charles Darwin. The idea, in turn, is a thought that can be real or false. The theory on its part is an organized set of ideas that explain a phenomenon, deduced from observation, experience, or logical reasoning.

That is why Charles Darwin joined Alfredo Russel Wallace, to develop evolution with the theory according to his thoughts and the observations of a second.

Charles Darwin is known for his work as a naturalist and for developing a theory of evolution to explain biological change. In 1831 Charles Darwin embarked on a five-year journey around the world on HMS Beagle. His studies of specimens led him to formulate his theory of evolution and his views on the process of natural selection.

In 1859 he published "The Origin of Species." Died on April 19, 1882, Charles Robert Darwin belonged to a family with a long list of scientists. Her father, Dr. R. W. Darwin, was a physician, and her grandfather, Dr. Erasmus Darwin, was a recognized botanist. Darwin's mother Suzanna died when he was only eight years old.

If it is Charles Darwin who comes with the theory of evolution, that means that his grandfather Dr. Erasmus Darwin did not know that theory. Before Charles Darwin the theory of evolution did not exist.

In October 1825, at age 16, Darwin enrolled at the University of Edinburgh, along with his brother Erasmus. Two years later, Charles Darwin became a student at Christs College Cambridge. Her father expected her to follow in his footsteps and study medicine. But Darwin had a passion for the natural sciences and natural history.

On December 27, 1831, the brig HMS Beagle set out on his voyage around the world with Darwin on board. Over the course of the journey, Darwin collected and observed a wide variety of natural specimens, including birds, plants, and fossils. Through practice in research and experimentation, he had the unique opportunity to closely observe the principles of botany and biology.

The Pacific islands and the Galapagos archipelago were of particular interest, as was South America. Upon his return to England in 1836, Darwin began writing his discoveries in a research journal. The trip had a monumental effect on Darwin's vision of natural history. He began to develop a revolutionary theory about the origin of living beings that was contrary to the popular opinion of other naturalists of the time.

Theory of evolution

Charles Darwin's experience on the trip raised important questions for him. Other naturalists believed that all species were either made at the beginning of the world's origin, or had been created throughout natural history. In either case, the species was believed to remain almost the same over time.

However, Darwin, noting the similarities between species around the world, along with variations based on specific locations, led him to believe that they had gradually evolved from common ancestors.

He came to believe that species survived thanks to a process called "natural selection," where species that successfully adapted to meet the changing needs of their natural habitat thrived, while those that failed to develop and reproduce became extinct.

In 1858, after years of deep scientific research, Darwin publicly presented his groundbreaking theory at the Linnean Society. On November 24, 1859, he published his best-known work, "The Origin of Species through Natural Selection."

According to John Lozano, in all of Charles's theory, nothing can be explained about the foundation of the world and where man comes from. There is no human scientist who can explain the creation of the world, no human theory can explain that beautiful wonder that is creation.

Big Bang Theory

In 1931, the idea was proposed that the universe originated in the explosion of a "primeval atom or cosmic egg or hulem." British astronomer Fred Hoyle, a philosophical supporter of a model of the eternal universe, coined the pejorative expression Big Bang to ridicule the ideas developed by Lemaître.

Astronomer is the one who studies the physics of the universe, investigates stars, planets, galaxies, and other celestial bodies, analyzes data, and uses theoretical models to study objects. Hans Lippeshey invented the discipline of astronomy; Hans Lippershey also designed the first telescope.

What does John say about science about the existence of the world?

Juan de Ciencia explained it in another way. He said that the beginnings of our universe, which started 13.8 billion years ago, hold great mysteries without answer. However, we know that galaxies are huge collections of stars, gas, and dark matter. Their number depends on their size, which can range from a few million stars to several hundreds of billions.

When and how did the first stars form?

In this lesson we are going to discover the answer so that you know better the confines of our universe. 550 million years after the Big Bang.

Knowing when the first stars of the universe formed is a complicated question, they did not do it about 450 million years after the Big Bang, as previously believed, but 100 million years later, according to observations of the Planek satellite on the polarization of microwave background radiation.

According to the study on human scientists, everyone is in contradiction with themselves, where Fred Hoyle said that the universe was created from an explosion of a primeval atom. Who created that egg and the explosion? Because nothing can create itself. Only divine indecency could have detonated, with a creative purpose, such an explosion.

Georges Henry Lemaître, a Belgian astronomer who owes a first formulation of the Big Bang cosmological theory of the origin of the universe, was greatly mistaken in his studies of creation.

He allowed himself to be guided and dominated by the great prince of darkness, who sows doubts in the hearts of all the great intellectuals, with false arguments against the existence of God.

What is the theory?

An organized set of ideas that explain a phenomenon, deduced from observation, experience, or logical reasoning. A theory is a logical-deductive system consisting of a set of tested hypotheses, a field of application and some rules that allow consequences to be drawn from the hypotheses.

So there is no clarity or truth in the theory of evolution, because no rule can be created by itself, to have that logical-deductive system, you must have someone who created it.

Who is the main author of that false idea?

The apostle John said: «And prevailed not; neither was their place found any more in heaven. And the great dragon was cast out, that old serpent, called the Devil, and Satan, which deceiveth the whole world: he was cast out into the earth, and his angels were cast out with him.

Therefore rejoice, ye heavens, and ye that dwell in them. Woe to the inhabiters of the earth and of the sea! for the devil is come down unto you, having great wrath, because he knoweth that he hath but a short time»: [Revelation 12: 8.9, 12].

He knows very well how it was created. As he is the great deceiver, he is deceived by men of letters and great scholars, so that they can put doubts about the creation of man, because he knows that only with lies can he have followers.

How has John of science answered his followers?

He said: the beginnings of our universe, created 13.8 billion years ago, hold great mysteries. Why has the scientist used that explosion? What did he mean? First, we must define what is a mystery to understand John's concern for science.

Mystery is defined as something very difficult to understand, something strange and inexplicable to understand or discover because of how hidden it is, or because it belongs to some arcane, that is, a fact or thing whose nature, cause, origin or reason for being does not have explanation or cannot be understood. It is a secret or reserved matter.

Why did he say that creation is a mystery?

Because all the things that a person cannot understand or explain, are superior to his knowledge that is very limited. All visible things are for man, but invisible things are for God. No scientist can explain the existence of creation without using the Bible as a laboratory.

What does the Bible say about the creation and existence of man and the universe?

The architect Moses said: «In the beginning God created the heaven and the earth. And the earth was without form, and void; and darkness was upon the face of the deep. And the Spirit of God moved upon the face of the waters. And God said, let there be light: and there was light.

And God saw the light, that it was good: and God divided the light from the darkness. And God called the light Day, and the darkness he called Night. And the evening and the morning were the first day»: [Genesis 1: 1-5].

The author of creation was Jehovah God. He created it before the existence of man, no one was present or witnessed his creation. No human can explain this great work but Himself.

God created man after the existence of the universe, the Creator had different works to perform with different structures. Each day he did a different thing, before moving on to the next stage. He first checked the work of his hands to see if everything was perfect From the first to the fifth day He created the universe.

Who created all the animals?

Moses goes on to say, "And God made the beast of the earth after his kind, and cattle after their kind, and every thing that creepeth upon the earth after his kind: and God saw that it was good": [Genesis 1:25].

Then animals were created before man, they witnessed how God dirtied his hands in the mud to give existence to man.

Moses said: «And God said, Let us make man in our image, after our likeness: and let them have dominion over the fish of the sea, and over the fowl of the air, and over the cattle, and over all the earth, and over every creeping thing that creepeth upon the earth.

So God created man in his own image, in the image of God created he him; male and female created he them»: [Genesis 1: 26-27].

Man was created in the image of God. As steward and administrator of all the things that God had created. He was created for two things, as Jehovah's administrator and worshiper.

What elements does God take in the creation of man?

The architect said, "And the Lord God formed man of the dust of the ground, and breathed into his nostrils the breath of life; and man became a living soul": [Genesis 2: 7].

Man is equal to dust plus water, plus the breath of God is equal to the living being, man is a descendant of the living God.

What difference is there between man and animals?

Animals are a mass of primary instincts; man has reason, morality and thought. Man was created to dominate all animals, they are two totally different living beings that have nothing like it. No man is an animal descendant, even if he behaves like one. Clear thing, which happens very often.

What really is the breath of life that is within man or humanity?

The breath of life that God blew into man's nose is his own life, his own spirit, for that reason, man has so much knowledge to create because his knowledge comes from the Almighty, man is limited, God is unlimited.

Never forget that Lucifer was a created being too; their knowledge is limited. Only that the human being was created inferior to him and the angels.

What is the breath of life?

The breath of life that is within man is a philosophical, psychological, artistic, spiritual component, his knowledge, mind, intellect, emotion, passion, fear, creativity, awareness, understanding, memory, his image and his personality.

Without that breath, the human being changes into a corpse, into a lifeless body. That is why Jesus sentenced: "I am the way, the truth, and the life: no man cometh unto the Father, but by me": [John 14: 6].

It is an immense opportunity and privilege for humanity to be graced by the attention of Jehovah, who is the source of life, no one has life without Christ Jesus because he is the author of life. For that reason only he who has the power to know and understand all the bad and good thoughts within your heart, no created being has that privilege, only Christ Jesus.

He is the way and the life, no one can live without him, and no one can go to the Father without going through him.

As the Father has given his son, he does not accept any created being without the intervention of the son. Whether you like it or not, all humans are connected to the source of life that is Jesus. He never stops calling you, because he knows that it is impossible to have life without him.

Chapter 22

The first temptation in the Garden of Eden

The disobedience of man:

The architect Moisés said in his book: «Now the serpent was more subtil than any beast of the field which the Lord God had made. And he said unto the woman, Yea, hath God said, Ye shall not eat of every tree of the garden? And the woman said unto the serpent.

We may eat of the fruit of the trees of the garden: But of the fruit of the tree which is in the midst of the garden, God hath said, Ye shall not eat of it, neither shall ye touch it, lest ye die. And the serpent said unto the woman, Ye shall not surely die: For God doth know that in the day ye eat thereof, then your eyes shall be opened, and ye shall be as gods, knowing good and evil.

And when the woman saw that the tree was good for food, and that it was pleasant to the eyes, and a tree to be desired to make one wise, she took of the fruit thereof, and did eat, and gave also unto her husband with her; and he did eat.

And the eyes of them both were opened, and they knew that they were naked; and they sewed fig leaves together, and made themselves aprons»: [Genesis 3:1-7]

What is a cunning person?

Person who shows ability to understand things and obtain profit or benefit by cheating or avoiding it. We must be very careful with the human wisdom that we acquire in the universities, so as not to be fooled by the false theory of evolution. There are many who were deceived, but it is not too late for them to wake up.

Eve was deceived, but she recognized her mistake, although she paid the consequence God forgave her. God is willing to forgive even Satan's representatives. Everyone has a chance to repent.

When Satan called Eve in the middle of the forbidden tree, it was the first time that she heard such a soft and delicious voice like that. She made a serious mistake of going to talk to that dangerous and wise adversary without knowing who she was dealing with.

Her mistake is the mistake of all women in the world, they are always hungry to see and know, that is why they always fall into the networks of the enemy. Because of that great mistake, sin entered the world.

Did God warn Eve "you shall not touch the forbidden tree"?

In no way. She wanted to defend Jehovah before the enemy, without knowing who she was talking to. As a great accuser and a liar, he sought a subtle way to make them fail with his misrepresentation of the creative verb, the gift of the word, for his purposes.

He knew well that he had only one chance. He did not want to fail in any way, so he used all his wisdom and intelligence to succeed: and he did it! Eve, for her part, made three big mistakes.

1.- she wanted to defend God with lies, and since the enemy is the father of lies, no one can win him.

2.- out of curiosity, she agreed to converse with that voice so sweet, soft, sensual, pleasant. There can never be deception without interaction.

3.- Eve had never seen a snake talking in her life.

What did God really say to the couple?

Moses said, "And the Lord God commanded the man, saying, Of every tree of the garden thou mayest freely eat: But of the tree of the knowledge of good and evil, thou shalt not eat of it: for in the day that thou eatest thereof thou shalt surely die": [Genesis 2: 16-17].

There are two different expressions between what God has said with the misinterpretation of Eve. When a person misinterprets the word of God, He will never be by their side to defend themselves, because God hates lies. Because of her misinterpretation, she was alone in front of the enemy.

What should Eve have done in that situation?

Run away from that temptation. Prophet Zacharias said: "And the Lord said unto Satan, The Lord rebuke thee, O Satan; even the Lord that hath chosen Jerusalem rebuke thee: is not this a brand plucked out of the fire?": [Zechariah 3: 2].

If he wanted to tempt whoever created him, what will happen between you and me? The big problem is the enemy will never come as the cartoon devil in front of you, but as an angel of light, as the savior; their mission is to make you fall and suffer.

When a person is in front of someone who is promising and offering so many beautiful things, you must take time to enter into yourself; you must ask yourself what hidden secret is behind all those promises? What about change between those offers?

What should you do when you are facing that problem?

You must seek the presence of the most high with a secret prayer, then you must rebuke him in the name of the Lord, because Jesus will never come to your aid without his invitation. There are many women who are making the same mistake as

Eve, they are in front of some modern tempters, without knowing who they are talking to.

First they will come with many misleading promises, cute well-calculated expressions to beat their hearts, when they return to normal it will be too late.

When they come to open their eyes in the middle of the networks, their homes are already destroyed, the divorces signed, their homeless children... They will want to die but death will avoid them like a plague.

What modern network does the enemy prepare for Christians?

Envy of accomplishing something without sweating, unequal relationship and unequal yoke, are three main elements the enemy uses to attract all followers of Christ to his network. With all three, the enemy is in the center of their home, where the presence of Jesus will not be for any reason.

80% of those who claim to be followers of Jesus are trapped by one of them, that is why there are so many sufferings, chaos, afflictions and tribulations within the family of God.

Who is behind all the temptations?

The apostle Paul said: "For we have no struggle against blood and flesh, but against principalities, against powers, against the rulers of darkness of this century, against spiritual hosts of wickedness in the heavenly regions": [Ephesians 6:12].

Satan as an evil spirit, has used all his spiritual forces against the followers of Christ. They can come in two forms:

1.- taking human appearance and their expressions to deceive you.

2.- Using the human thoughts against and in favor of deceiving yourself, you must be very diligent at all times if you want to defeat the evil one with his acolytes.

What must we do to overcome them?

The apostle Paul continues saying: "Take therefore all the armor of God, so that you can resist in the bad day, and having finished everything, be firm. Stand firm, therefore, girded in your loins with truth, and clothed in the breastplate of righteousness, and shod your feet with the readiness of the gospel of peace.

Above all, take the shield of faith, with which you can extinguish all the fiery darts of the evil one. And take the helmet of salvation, and the sword of the Spirit, which is the word of God; praying at all times with all prayer and supplication in the Spirit, and watching with all perseverance and supplication for all the saints".

They are the powerful weapons of all Christians who want to overcome all temptations in the name of Jesus, because we cannot overcome them with our forces, they are more powerful than all humans. Every time we realize that we are faced with a temptation, we must seek the help of the great overcomer through prayer.

All Christians must connect with Christ at all times as he has connected with their Father, if they want to be overcomers, when he was on earth.

What are the other three networks the enemy has for Christians?

The three main networks the enemy has prepared against all the followers of Christ, are fame, money and pleasure. It is not bad to have all three, it depends on the place they occupy within your heart. God never accepts second or last place, always first. In his holy word, God explained how Christians should have wealth, not as the enemy wants.

Chat in marriage

Chat is very important in this century, everyone is being updated by all kinds of pages that exist in cyberspace. The internet is so important that you can read any book; you can buy and sell everything on their platforms; any transaction can be made from bank to bank. It can also be used to find a partner, lover or pleasures. You can use it to find a job too.

All companies use it to interact or pass any message to their employees. The internet offers all the things that human beings need. There are two categories of people that are connected on all pages: the good and the bad. In the case of social networks they can help you build your home, they can also destroy it to pieces. They give and take too.

All religions, politicians, followers of Jesus as well as those of Satan, are all connected to social media. Children, adolescents, young people, adults, the elderly... they are all up to date out there. Christians use them to evangelize, looking for people for Christ, a Christian evangelist must be everywhere where there are people to bring them to the feet of Jesus.

Chatting is an easier way to communicate with loved ones, if a person is looking for their family, which they haven't seen in a long time, they can find it through social media. Networks are useful for all things. You can be talking to more than twenty people at the same time from different countries.

Equally, it is something that can destroy your family in pieces, you must control all kinds of emotions that can harm your life and that of your family. No one can be against your family. You must spend little time on the networks and a lot of time on the family without wanting to save them.

A faithful family should not have a password on their private cell phone, the password casts doubt on their partner, even if they are not committing infidelity, with that measure they say that there is something that is not correct. Children may not know something, but your partner should know it.

It is also not recommended that couples check another person's cell phone with malicious intent, because what is sought is always found. Neither partner should raise doubts in the other's mind if they want to be happy in this relationship.

Chapter 23

Children in marriage

What do some professionals say about their lives with their children?

Mauricio Cohen Salamá, Executive Coach and consultant in Organizational Development 21 Oct. 2016, responded as follows:

"For most of human history, having children was not a kind of lifelong burden but a medium-term investment. It was about securing the supply of young labor to assist with routine tasks and then replace parents as they grew older. In our society this is no longer the case".

Today, children give only work: they require time, attention, effort to obtain the necessary economic resources for their well-being, responsibility to make decisions favorable to their development, unconditional support when they are already undergoing a crisis, etc., etc.

By the way, they complicate your life and yet, most people want to have them and do not regret, in addition, having had them.

There are people who have children only because of social pressure and then suffer from it. Leaving aside these cases, which deserve separate treatment, it seems to me that parents who do want their children seek through them to be part of this great human history that we all share and that has neither started with us nor will end day that we are no longer.

One of the fundamental conditions for having a good life is that it has a meaning, that it embodies a meaning.

When our existence makes sense, efforts, eventual sacrifices, setbacks and anguish can be coped with integrity because we are aware that we are committed to something that transcends us. Well, we have children to give more meaning to our lives and to be transcended.

I totally agree with Salamá, all married people should have their children, because it is they who are going to replace them in old age. From 18 to 40 years old, man has all the physical forces to develop anything, because he is very strong both sexually and physically.

At the age of 45 to 65 years, he loses 40% muscle strength, he is going to start feeling tired, he is never going to be able to do what he had done in youth, even if the man is exercising every day, you will never be able to have the strength you had before.

How many years must man last on earth after sin?

The psalmist said: "The days of our years are threescore years and ten; and if by reason of strength they be fourscore years, yet is their strength labour and sorrow; for it is soon cut off, and we fly away": [Psalms 90:10].

After 40 years, man is slowly dying from the consequence of sin, when God told Adam if he ate the forbidden tree he would die, Adam did not return to dust immediately, but his body began to die every day until he reaches the grave which is your destiny.

What do some people think about those who do not want to have children?

Sira Sánchez, in [webpsicologos.com], gave ten reasons why a person should not have children:

«When you start obsessing about a specific topic, it seems that the Universe is conspiring to make EVERYTHING relate to your obsession: suddenly, the TV commercials fill up with babies, pregnant women, gadgets to find out if you are in a state (or if you can make love... DING, DING, DING!), milk prepared to complement your child's diet, super absorbent diapers (and super expensive!)...

In movies and series, characters who do not have children or cannot have them seem the most unfortunate beings in this world and those who have them thank Heaven for the joy they feel (Amen!).

Things get worse when it is your younger sister who has become pregnant, because then all the eyes of the family rest on you and you start to hear phrases like: "and what are you waiting for?", "Why don't you dare? Or, "Don't you want to give your nephew a little cousin?"..., "Well, hey, maybe not."

After thinking long and hard about this matter, I have decided that if I have children I will be very happy, but if I do not have them, I will cling to these reasons that I will explain below to survive with dignity.

1.- Fun

I will make the most of my youthful years. Long live the party!

2.- Money

Home economics controlled!

3.- Tranquility

I will spare myself the constant suffering that mothers report for the well-being and safety of their children.

4.- Aesthetics and health

My body will NOT suffer from pregnancies, deliveries, caesarean sections, and breastfeeding. Long live size 38 and firm breasts!

5.- Free time

I will have all the weekends and vacations to do what pleases my partner and me (even if it is lying on the sofa with no other obligation than to change diapers, I say... channel).

6.- Family

I will not bear daughters-in-law, sons-in-law, in-laws... With my family and that of my husband, I have plenty of it!

7.- Children

I will enjoy the best of my nephews and the children of my friends until they become unbearable... So, what do your parents put up with!

8.- Roles

I will be the funny aunt but never the heavy mother.

9.- Work and hobbies

I will be able to dedicate myself fully to my professional career, training and hobbies. Long live philately!

10.- Friends

I will have time and energy to keep my social networks updated: Facebook, twitter, google +... and why not? Real life ones too.

Everyone has the freedom to say and express their opinion in their own way, but it is not an obligation to accept it, because each person has their own thoughts.

What does the Bible say about this terrible thought?

God gave origin to all married people, he said: "And God blessed them, and God said unto them, Be fruitful, and multiply, and replenish the earth, and subdue it: and have dominion over the fish of the sea, and over the fowl of the air, and over every living thing that moveth upon the earth": [Genesis 1:28].

All married people sign a covenant before God in the wedding vows to fulfill that commandment they say multiply and fill the earth with their descendants. There is nothing so precious and wonderful when a couple is waiting for their first-born, there is such an emotional state that there is no psychologist who can define that moment, because it is something inexplicable in human eyes.

It is such a beautiful thing when the couple enjoys and rejoices with their children of blood. But it is a great tragedy for those parents who do not have any economic preparation to correspond to the needs of the little ones. Children are the inheritance of parents, they are their futures, that is why every human being must beget children.

The child out of wedlock

The honest and responsible man, faithful and compliant, never thinks of having any child outside of his marriage, because he knows that committing a crime puts at risk the beautiful relationship that the two had, condemning her to destruction. Because she will never have more confidence in him and the problems will appear.

If they are not separated due to infidelity, the child will receive all mistreatment from the stepmother, or the stepfather. A lot, but in this case, if she is a female, she runs the risk of being sexually abused.

The boy is not responsible for his birth, he is innocent of that act, he cannot pay for his father's bad decision, although the man complies with the rule, he was tempted by the enemy. That is why the couple must fulfill all the duties and seduce their partner so that this relationship can reach final success.

Life inside a wrong home

The vast majority of the stepchildren have not received the same treatment as the biological ones, because there is always discontent between the stepparents and stepmothers with them, they have to pay all the guilt and the consequences of the fathers and mothers. No child has been born to be abused. They are not responsible for any discontent of others.

The stepchildren are the cows without tails, the birds live in the middle of the desert, the ugly ducklings or the black sheep... but always the Creator takes care of them and protects them.

What do professionals think about the treatment of children outside of marriage?

There is a group of professionals called "Growing up healthy" who, on October 30, 2017, commented on the page [educo.org.], On the abuse of stepchildren at home:

"Psychological abuse is also known as psychological or emotional abuse. This type of abuse includes behaviors such as ridiculing, intimidating, insulting, rejecting or humiliating a child, and although it is difficult for you to believe it, it is even more frequent than physical violence.

In fact, according to a study at McGill University in Montreal, Canada, "one in three children in the world suffers from some experience of emotional abuse."

Emotional abuse is a kind of silent abuse whose actor is usually the parents. Why do we talk about silent abuse? Simply because brands cannot be seen with the naked eye, but the injuries caused by insults, contempt, rejection and humiliation are profound and can generate problems of self-esteem or insecurity, creating possible abuse or child victims of bullying.

If we register our memory, we may remember some case of emotional abuse. Perhaps we ourselves have been victims in the past. Not surprisingly, the ANAR Foundation has detected an increase in family abuse with a total of 2,952 cases in 2015: "1,229 cases of physical abuse, 882 cases of psychological abuse, 435 cases of sexual abuse and 406 cases of abandonment."

Let's see together what are the symptoms of this kind of abuse in children.

Psychologists have explained very well about the treatment of others, because all the bad things they do on earth, you have to pay for them before you die.

No one knows the thoughts of any child, because sometimes their own blood children abandon you; only the stepchildren who had been mistreated, abused, assaulted at every moment, are they in old age who can help. So no one does wrong against anyone because no one knows the future.

José gave a good example of how stepfathers and stepmothers should care for and educate their stepchildren, because everything has a reason.

What should you do to avoid this atrocious phenomenon?

You must marry a guy who you have discovered who loves you, who values you, who accepts you as you are, you must also try to have children in marriage, because God does not want anyone to have a life of unhappiness. If there is true love between the two, even in old age one will continue to love the other.

They can see the growth of their grandchildren together, so they can enjoy the grandchildren together, even in old age their home can be a nest and spring of love, where everyone can be nurtured.

The education of children

The education of children is something very complicated and very difficult at the same time, because of work they do not have enough time to educate them, it is the grandparents, servants, friends who are giving education for them.

God never said it is the strange people who must educate them, but the biological parents who have all the capacities to educate them according to the instructions they have received in their parents' house.

How can children be given a good education?

All individuals need to have three great things to give a good education to children, without them it is impossible to achieve the goal like a good father.

1.- Fear of Jehovah, respect the holy house of God.

2.- A good family education or teaching.

3.- A good professional education.

How does God want parents to educate children?

The wise Solomon said: "Train up a child in the way he should go: and when he is old, he will not depart from it": [Proverb 22: 6].

The most correct way for parents should instruct the little ones, is fear of Jehovah, even if they are outside the church, the Holy Spirit will always upload all the good teachings they have learned in the old school that is their parents' home.

What should be done with the instructions that parents have received from God and how should they be used?

The great "I AM" instructed all parents who want to have a successful family. He said: «And thou shalt teach them diligently unto thy children, and shalt talk of them when thou sittest in thine house, and when thou walkest by the way, and when thou liest down, and when thou risest up.

And thou shalt bind them for a sign upon thine hand, and they shall be as frontlets between thine eyes. And thou shalt write them upon the posts of thy house, and on thy gates»: [Deuteronomy 6: 7-9].

The mission of parents is to teach the little ones the good news of Jehovah before bedtime and when they get up, so that they can grow strong and with all the wisdom of God.

Doctor Lucas said: «And brought them out, and said, Sirs, what must I do to be saved? And they said, Believe on the Lord Jesus Christ, and thou shalt be saved, and thy house. And they spake unto him the word of the Lord, and to all that were in his house»: [Acts 16: 30-32].

All those who want to save their houses must put into practice the principles of God, no home can be happy without fear of Jehovah. If a parent wants to be successful in economic growth and health, he must obey the word of God.

What must be done to have wealth?

The wise Solomon said: "By humility and the fear of the Lord are riches, and honour, and life": [Proverbs 22: 4].

Although Satan gives wealth by deception, it never lasts long. God gives it for life. Not only did God greatly give wealth, he gave the wisdom to manage it.

The psalmist said, "Behold, the eye of the Lord is upon them that fear him, upon them that hope in his mercy": [Psalms 33:18].

The psalmist said: "Blessed is every one that feareth the Lord; that walketh in his ways. For thou shalt eat the labour of thine hands: happy shalt thou be, and it shall be well with thee": [Psalms 128: 1-2].

The wise Solomon goes on to say: "The fear of the Lord is the instruction of wisdom; and before honour is humility": [Proverbs 15:33].

The fear of Jehovah is not terror, it is wisdom, honor and humility, they are the three qualities a person must possess to be afraid of Jehovah, and prosperity is the good education that all parents should give their children, if they want a better tomorrow for their children.

There are two educations in the world: one is fear of Jehovah, the other is phobia or debauchery, each parent must choose which is the best for their children, whether it is the first or the second.

That is why there are so many criminals in the world, because of the way parents are educating them, the children never do what they did not learn at home, because the parents are shadows or mirrors and the path they must follow. There are never bad students if there are no bad teachers.

Instruct the child. It is the act of instructing, teaching, indoctrinating, communicating, which embodies true parenthood. All children are born with their memory blank, it is the parents who have to fill it with good or bad teaching.

Your memory is like a blank CD, which stores everything inserted into it; it is like the memory of a computer that archives everything we want inside a folder.

How does the fetus form in a woman's womb?

To have a child is not something as easy as people think, it is something that comes directly from God, when the husband is meeting his wife, God is doing a great job between the two at the same moment of intimacy; It is a miracle from God, He said clearly in his holy scripture through the prophet Jeremiah:

"Before I formed thee in the belly I knew thee; and before thou camest forth out of the womb I sanctified thee, and I ordained thee a prophet unto the nations": [Jeremiah 1: 5].

For that reason, no scientist can give an exact date when a woman will become pregnant. It is something supernatural that surpasses human knowledge.

What is the role of God in the intimacy of the couple?

God has a very special role when the couple is getting to know each other. Although He has the date of the pregnancy well determined, it is he who has to move her ovaries, among millions of spermatozoa that are in movement, it is the Creator who has to say which one is going to enter; none can enter without the conviction of God.

So it is not by chance that you are here on this earth: you are very special to God.

From the first day, God put you into his mother's ovum and is taking care of you until today. For that reason, all babies need attention, because every time an individual reaches sexual intercourse with a woman, he is saying he is ready to be a father.

All parents should know that their children are not theirs; they cannot do what they want with them, they are creatures of Jehovah, their missions as adoptive parents are to educate them in the correct way for the owner, no man has the power to create a son only God.

God gave a number of babies to raise, educate, care for even adults. Each father and mother will be accountable to God for how they have raised and cared for their responsibilities that they have asked of God.

All parents will be judged before God for the bad educations and teachings they gave their children. No parent can take earthly law as an excuse for not educating their children the right way. No government, nor grandparents, brothers, cousins, friends, can take the positions of parents in the teachings of children, it is their own responsibility as father and mother.

At what age should parents start educating children?

From the moment ejaculation enters your ovary, God is caring for that creature to this day. Therefore, do not make mistakes or neglect with that creature that is inside your belly. The child has different stages, each stage has a different education and discipline, from before three months, the baby begins to listen inside the mother's uterus.

What do professionals say about children's education?

LOLA ROVATI, June 8, 2011, commented on [bebesymas.com], about the five steps to raise a child from one year to eight.

1.- Calm down

The first step is the most important: knowing how to recognize the symptoms of anger and calm down when we feel that the volcano is about to erupt. Many times we feel overwhelmed, angry, full of anger, but we are adults for a reason and we have to learn to put the brakes on when we are about to lose control.

2.- Listen

Knowing how to listen is the basis of communication with children. Punishment is used as a measure of "shock" before listening to the reasons that have led the child to have this or that behavior. It is easier to raise your hand or scream, but although it appears to be an effective measure, punishment is an uneducating method.

You have to listen to the child, what version, then you can continue with the following steps.

3.- Talk

It is essential to teach children that conflicts are resolved by talking, listening to the arguments of others and exposing our point of view, always with respect. We must not forget that we educate by example.

If we explode when something we do not like, we are projecting that behavior also in our children, thus they learn that conflicts are solved with violence, and not with dialogue.

4.- Explain

Having put forward the views, we need to focus on explaining to the children why what they have done is wrong; why it hurts another person; why what they have done may have undesirable consequences; why it can be dangerous, etc...

If the child or we are angry, it is better to wait a bit to calm down to explain things calmly, so that they can assimilate and understand them better.

5.- Reach agreements

Just because we are parents does not mean we have the absolute truth. Children often give us great lessons. The last step is to reach agreements between both parties. As if it were a negotiation, there will be points where sometimes it will be necessary to give in, both from one side and the other.

The importance of establishing agreements lies in the fact that the child —and the parents, as the case may be—, undertakes to improve or correct attitudes towards the future. The next time, you will take into account what has been discussed and what we have explained, and you will try to do better or not.

And if not, we'll have to re-launch the five steps again until I can figure it out.

Yes, indeed, applying these five basic steps to raise positively and without punishment requires a great deal of patience, common sense and affection, three fundamental pillars for respectful upbringing. In my opinion, the only effective one.

It is a good illustration that Lola gives us about the education of children, but she speaks as a mother who wants to formalize her children to have a better future, but also as a human and professional one.

All children show the same behavior as the animals, and if they share this way, it is because they still do not have the ability to grasp the thing as adults. Parents have to take care of them as a person who is learning to drive a vehicle. Every time he goes to the mountain, the teacher will take the guide to guide him in the correct way.

If the teacher wants to achieve this, he must do it with great patience and total dedication. It is the same for parents with children.

From nine to seventeen years old, the child must receive another form of education. Parents should instruct him with good advice. The child should be their own friend, if they have found any inconveniences or some bad decisions due to the error, they must testify to the child, if they have had any success they must also say so. They should speak to him/her as good friends.

Parents must teach their children to respect their elders

We are living in a world where no one respects anyone, parents have taught their children how they should disrespect even their own family. They have no respect for older people, if we want a better world, we have to change the way we are raising or educating our children.

From small we must teach our children a great love and respect for older people, whether they are their grandparents, neighbors, brothers in the church, older acquaintances or unknown people who are on the Street.

When they grow up, they will never forget the good training they have received in the first school that is home.

Why is the generation of this century so perverse?

Lack of respect is a source of conflict and violence in our society. We must set a good example to counter the general trend. No teacher or church leader can look into the eyes of children outside this time, because their parents are not taking responsibility. Children feel supported, and that is a sure formula to create antisocials.

What difference between the children of before and now?

There is a big difference because all the children had immense respect for the elders, they called all the elders who were not their family uncles and aunts; they had a love for them, now there is no respect or compassion for anyone.

Now they say any bad word to the elderly, no one can attract their attention, the teachers fear the students and their parents, because they denounce any and send them to jail.

There are many young people who go to school with weapons to fight; they openly compliment their teachers. Now any boy has a tablet or a laptop with internet where they can watch pornography, because his parents have taught him to make love at an early age. The internet and television are their teachers.

In this new generation parents have the earthly law against them, they cannot discipline their children when they deserve punishment, for anything the Kindred call the police. For disciplining their own children, they can receive a sentence of two to three months in prison.

Governments are responsible for the downfall of an entire generation, as they are the ones who pass all those satanic laws and enforce them.

Children are raping their grandmothers, equal grandparents, even their own parents are having sex with their own children, the world has fallen lower than Sodom and Gomorrah. But there is still time. God can change your sinful character and reshape his image. It is never too late to make a change.

If you want to save your family, you must go back to the old days.

How does God want the young to treat the older in all ages?

The apostle Peter said: «Likewise, ye younger, submit yourselves unto the elder. Yea, all of you be subject one to another, and be clothed with humility: for God resisteth the proud, and giveth grace to the humble»: [1 Peter 5: 5].

The wise Solomon said: "The glory of young men is their strength: and the beauty of old men is the grey head": [Proverbs 20:29].

Moses said: «Thou shalt rise up before the hoary head, and honour the face of the old man, and fear thy God: I am the Lord»: [Leviticus 19:32].

Joshua said, "Then Manoah intreated the Lord, and said, O my Lord, let the man of God which thou didst send come again unto us, and teach us what we shall do unto the child that shall be born": [Judges 13: 8].

Who should parents listen to to educate children on the internet, tv, the kings of the earth or the holy bible?

God wants all children and young people to respect the elderly. For that to happen, they must find someone to teach them, because they cannot learn it alone, if there is no one to teach them.

We are living in an age where animals seem to be smarter than human beings, because animals communicate, they greet each other in their ways, children do the same, although this should not be the case, because we must love our neighbor. And we must teach our children to do the same.

There are many children who say, we don't greet people we don't know. Everyone, both young and old, has forgotten the first rule of good living, which is greeting, with a smile on their faces.

We have a generation corrupted in all kinds of vices, addictions, it takes the presence of God to change their immoralities and wash them spiritually, from bratty to well-bred, from disrespectful to respectful people. For that to happen, they must go back to the Bible.

What does the bible say about unbelievers?

The apostle Paul said to the Corinthians: «For the unbelieving husband is sanctified by the wife, and the unbelieving wife is sanctified by the husband: else were your children unclean; but now are they holy": [1 Corinthians 7:14].

God never errs in his words. Unbelievers teach their children all the garbage, the filth of the world, when their temperaments are great and their personalities are totally unclean and corrupt, wicked, because they were born and grew in wickedness; It is totally impossible to have another mindset according to the moral law.

Their hearts are hard as stone, evil is a glory to them, nor the police can with them, they are social spots from head to toe. They fear no one. Their minds and hearts produce and cultivate all kinds of the fruits of evil. The only solution is Jesus Christ.

How should parents educate their children according to the Bible?

The servant of God gave a good explanation of what the hearts of the wise will be like when their children have received and guided by the path of the Bible, he said: "I have no greater joy than to hear that my children walk in truth": [3 John 1: 4].

That phrase not all parents can repeat it. The cowards, the unbelievers, the irresponsible, the vicious can never utter that expression, only the fighting parents, who never give up, the parents who never see their own needs first, all those who do their utmost to ensure their children can be men and women of professional value and doers of the work of God or his nation.

They are parents who have very great visions, who will not want their children to be the same or worse than them; who aspire to say with joy and happiness "we have accomplished our missions because our children are at the levels or heights we dream of."

What a great joy for a father to achieve with a lot of effort to make his children specialists in medicine, great businessmen, deputies, senators "congressmen", even presidents of his country. No one can say what his son will be tomorrow, no one knows his destiny and his future, only God, his job as a father is to provide good teaching and preparation to them, the rest depends on God.

Father, never stop sacrificing yourself in the education of your children, never stop fighting on their behalf, never stop fighting, because life is a fight only persevering can reach the final victory. Cowards never win any war or contests or races, only the brave, those who have never been afraid of criticism from others, who say they do not live to please others, who seek a better life for their family.

In this war you will always face giants much stronger than you, never look at their size, nor their strength, even if you are fainting in the fight, never give up, good warriors never give up in the fight, and if they have to die, they will die fighting. Even if you receive mortal blows, if you do not have enough strength, hold on to the feet of Jesus. He will help you, but never stop fighting.

Your children are not blind or unconscious, they will appreciate your fight and it will serve as an example of life. Possibly they will help you in the fight too, they will have more strength to fight when they grow up, and they can value their strength, they will appreciate all the drops of blood you spilled for them, they will never forget that.

If your parents didn't fight for your future when you were kids, your children cannot pay the consequence, you have to make a difference, because children are the wealth of good parents.

If you want to have a good life in old age, you must prepare it from today, because tomorrow will be another day.

Chapter 24

The discipline and correction of children

What is discipline?

Set of rules of behavior to maintain order and subordination between members of a body or a community in a profession or in a certain community. Discipline is a commitment to any effective method of developing skills or aptitudes, or to following a certain code of conduct or "order." The term "discipline" can have negative connotations.

It is something essential, inevitable that must be at the heart of all homes "discipline" is the fundamental basis for developing all creatures. All children are born with their minds and memories blank. They need to fill them in with the good instructions they have received from their parents.

Parents should not confuse discipline with verbal and physical aggression to the child, although they are similar, but they are not the same, no type of aggression is appropriate in children's corrections. We must avoid all kinds of mistreatment of children because they are defenseless.

For them, their parents are their defenses, even if they are punished. After punishment they will return crying into the arms of their attackers.

There are three types of good teaching: that of the biological parents, the school and the religious. The main base of the three is that of the parents. At home they have learned theory and practice day by day, they will always repeat what they hear at home and, once grown, they will repeat what they saw inside the home.

You can never have discipline without rules of behavior, because they are the ones that will guide you in your actions, on how you should do things to go well. It is like a mirror, if you want to see if your face is dirty, you should check the mirror.

No person can give a good correction if he does not respect the rules, because nobody can give what they do not have.

Discipline and punishment of the disobedient son

What do psychologists say about discipline, child punishment?

Borja Quicios, Educational Psychologist (November 15, 2017), put it this way:

Children must learn that certain actions that are carried out have consequences, and that sometimes these consequences are not pleasant. Punishment should always be the last resort that parents have to apply in the face of this type of disobedient or challenging behavior of the little ones.

Furthermore, we should not react the same if it is a baby who has committed a fault, than a primary school child.

Therefore we give you guidelines to discipline or punish them according to their age. How and when to punish children. If we adults want children to learn to respect the rules and limits, the first thing to do is try to be an example to follow and act by reinforcing the appropriate behaviors of the little ones whenever possible.

However, there are times when it will be necessary to teach children the negative consequences of their actions, and one way to do this will be to use punitive punishments and to do it rationally with the aim of educating children. To achieve this, we must take into account that:

- It should never be detrimental to your self-esteem. Punishment should not be understood as a way to make children feel bad, but as the consequence of a certain action.

- When applying punishment, children need to understand why, and understand what happens when certain actions are carried out.

- Punishment should be understood more as a deal. That is, what we have to do to achieve something, or things that should not be done to put aside the negative consequences.

Ideas to punish or discipline children according to their age

As we already know, communication and positive discipline are the fundamental tools that should be used in the education of children. However, there are times when it will be unavoidable for adults to resort to punishment in order for children to learn between what is right and what is wrong.

For punishments to be effective, it is important that the age of the children is taken into account.

From 2 years to 5 years

At this preschool stage it is important that punishments are applied immediately so that the child understands that the punishment is related to his bad behavior. At these ages, the following punishments may be carried out:

1.- Speak to them in an energetic and firm tone

Children at this age are very susceptible to the tone of voice in which they are spoken to. Therefore, talking seriously to children helps them know that they have not acted correctly. To work, you have to use this technique sparingly. That is, not to be screaming all day.

2.- Withdrawal of privileges

At this age, when he is no more than five years old, the withdrawal of a favorite toy will be a punishment in which the child will clearly see that his misbehavior has consequences.

3.- Over-correction

It will be from the age of three in which consequences based on reinforcement are used that are useful to end those "bad" behaviors that the child continues to show after trying other techniques that have not worked.

4.- Thinking chair?

We must ask ourselves if it is really an effective technique for such young children. It is a widely used method in nurseries, and at home. But we have to ask ourselves before carrying it out if the child at that age is capable, consciously, of thinking about what he has done and reaching positive conclusions.

5.- Time out

It is an effective technique in the face of aggressive and disobedient behavior. It is about removing the child from the situation where he has committed a bad action giving him the opportunity to calm down outside the place where everything has happened. (Different from the "thinking chair").

The duration of time out will vary depending on the age of the child, so we will try to apply it no more than one minute per year. The child should not be permanently away.

From 5 to 12 years old

At these ages children are more aware of everything. Among those that already occurred in the previous stage we can continue to use over-correction. Withdrawal of privileges will also continue to be effective but changing some nuances: not watching your favorite cartoons on TV.

Do not go out to the park to play. To do this if the child is, for example, three years old would be unfair. Not being able to use the tablet. Time out continues to be used as it is still useful up to ten years.

From 12 years old

When children are in their teens, the withdrawal of privileges must change again. This time it will be effective: don't go out on the weekend with friends. Do not use the mobile. Restrict social networks.

When applying all these punishments, it must be taken into account that for it to be educational, they must be coherent, exceptional and balanced.

The psychologist Quicios expressed very clearly, all children do not receive the same punishment, the punishment depends on their age, from months of age the baby needs to receive discipline, although he does not know anything yet, he must start at a very young age.

For a child, the worst moment that he could spend during the day is when his parents forbid him what they like to do, a child can go the whole day without eating when he is playing, for him his toys are his priorities, he has never negotiated it with anyone, so parents can use that tool to discipline them.

At each stage in the child's life his spirit develops further, from the first day of birth to two years, the child does not remember anything, although his mind is recording is not at a level of remembering. At that age, he cannot eat all kinds of food. Parents must have wisdom and intelligence to correct it according to their age.

Many parents who have made countless mistakes, even having sex in front of children. They think they do not feel or grasp anything of what is happening right now, although they are not old enough to fully understand that act as an adult, however little they have grasped, it is enough to arouse their curiosity and encourage them to imitate.

When a child does something or says something, many times it is not because he has seen or heard it at the same moment, but rather that it was in the memory file a long time ago. All the things a human being has heard several times, the mind captures by the weight of repetition, regardless of whether they are good or bad.

For this reason, all the big companies do their advertisements on a daily basis, so since children's minds are fresher than adults, all the things they have heard and seen are stored.

Not only do parents have to discipline their children, they must have and respect the house rules first. It is the same as a teacher who is teaching a subject, the first person who has learned and respected that subject is the teacher, because they must know very well what they are teaching, so the teacher prepares and studies more than the student.

There are many parents who do not have any discipline or correction for themselves, and want to make the most vulnerable fulfill their duties, it is a big mistake. The first thing that the rules have to comply with is the parents in order that the children can comply with them. They must discipline by example.

No parent can discipline or correct if he does not have discipline in himself, nobody can give what he does not have.

The bad disciplines of children

There are many children who have misbehaviors and behaviors within the home, which they reproduce in school and church, because parents let children do what they want for so much love for them. It is they who have taken the places of the parents in the home.

Parents have no power over them, it is the same when a leader loses his leadership, all employees do what they want. Only with many difficulties can they resume leadership again.

Bad behavior or misconduct usually designates behavior or conduct, especially social behavior, which is understood as bad, negative, deviant or excessive according to the different types. When parents lose control of children, they educate themselves. That virus affects almost 90% of homes, Christian or not.

Such misconduct generally refers to actions of an object or organism, usually in relation to its environment or world of stimuli. The behavior can be conscious or unconscious, public or hidden, voluntary or involuntary.

It is a very mortal danger for all those parents who allow their creatures to educate themselves, because they have failed of their leadership as parents; because of their weaknesses they have been spoiled.

That virus automatically changes his characters and is very difficult to remove. Only the presence of God can make that change because Jesus has the power to change the stone into dust.

What do professionals say about the bad education we are giving our children?

EMMA E. SÁNCHEZ, DESERET NEW (2015-11-11), commented on the page [elsalvador.com], about the five things that allow children to be spoiled:

1.- Parents are too permissive

These types of parents are raising children full of energy and need to discover the world. But they do not want to fight with children, or are so overwhelmed with love for their little ones that the simple idea of limiting them in any aspect seems almost offensive to them.

For any of the two reasons, the child or young person, everything is allowed, everything is tolerated, including disrespect and rebellion.

2.- Children have no responsibilities at home or with the family

Parents are generally the ones who do everything at home for their children and for their children. Children and adolescents do not have the remotest idea of what it means to help with some housework, clean or organize their bedroom, cooperate with their siblings.

None and in no way do anything else except study because their mom or dad has told them that this is "their only job and responsibility."

3.- Parents avoid disciplining their children or setting limits

Treating, mentioning or asking a child to help or collaborate is a tremendous displeasure on the part of the child: there are ugly faces, tantrums or similar things; then the parents, to avoid confrontation, end up doing everything themselves and the child wins one more battle in the power and government of the home.

Some parents acknowledge that they have a problem with their parenting style but do not know what or how to discipline their children, do not know how to end a tantrum or avoid it and fear the judgment of being "bad parents", the "what will they say" and until you lose the love of your children.

4.- There are no routines, norms or traditions in the home

All good things have a structure and an order. The little ones and all of us require structure, order and programming to conduct ourselves with property, prudence and live in society.

There are many good things that come from having routines, rules and traditions at home because it is precisely these things that provide us with structure, order and programming. Whenever I say that teenagers like order and discipline, the parents' eyes want to get out of their sockets.

It is true, the order and the discipline give security, something that the boys eagerly seek when their body and their world are transforming so rapidly.

It should be very clear to our children at what time they go to sleep, that their hands and teeth are washed, that neither alcohol nor cigarettes are allowed, that there is an age and a time to have a boyfriend/girlfriend, and all those issues that you and your family understand valuable in their training.

When children are the ones who decide what time they go to bed, when and how they will do their homework - if they do it - or what they will eat, it is a fact that parents will face a really nightmarish adolescence.

5.- The world of parents revolves around children

It is amazing the power that children come to have over the adults around them. Many parents do not see it and believe that this is the way to live or that this is the best way to educate a child. Some marriages are even separated because one of the parents pours all his attention on the son and neglects the couple.

Others simply become void in the marital relationship and raising the child. Is seriously. It is incredible to be at a children's party or social gathering where children, children of overly permissive parents, assault other children and parents do nothing.

They break things, they damage other people's property, they hurt plants and animals and, the parents?: well thank you... they continue in their talks and do nothing to correct their children and, poor man who dares to correct or limit their child! Maybe this overly permissive parenting style works for you, makes you comfortable, and prevents you from trying harder.

The truth is that the negative consequences come sooner or later to your life and the lives of your children. I invite you to reconsider some of the beliefs that you may have regarding the education of children.

Talk to teachers and listen to the words of other parents, attend the school for parents, attend conferences or education seminars and, above all, talk to your partner to establish a home and train men and women who will contribute to the society. That is the best of the fruits of being a mom or a dad.

I very much agree with Emma in her presentation about the bad education that parents are giving their children, because they allow everything. When children have too many freedoms they do not take any correction from their parents, nor listen to them when they speak.

There are many people who have confused discipline with love, because discipline is an act of love, Jesus said through the apostle John: «As many as I love, I rebuke and chasten: be zealous therefore, and repent»: [Revelation 3:19].

There are many parents who do not punish or discipline their children for so much love, they think they are doing good for them. It is the opposite, they are damaged morally, emotionally, physically and emotionally. There are also many parents who are very aggressive towards children, with aggressiveness they think they are disciplining them. Bad idea.

They are hurting them, they are going to get aggressive with everyone, they will be a threat to everyone around them.

What does the Bible say about the discipline and punishment of children?

The unknown writer of the book of Hebrew, he said: «And ye have forgotten the exhortation which speaketh unto you as unto children, my son, despise not thou the chastening of the Lord, nor faint when thou art rebuked of him: For whom the Lord loveth he chasteneth, and scourgeth every son whom he receiveth.

If ye endure chastening, God dealeth with you as with sons; for what son is he whom the father chasteneth not? But if ye be without chastisement, whereof all are partakers, then are ye bastards, and not sons.

Furthermore we have had fathers of our flesh which corrected us, and we gave them reverence: shall we not much rather be in subjection unto the Father of spirits, and live? For they verily for a few days chastened us after their own pleasure; but he for our profit, that we might be partakers of his holiness.

Now no chastening for the present seemeth to be joyous, but grievous: nevertheless afterward it yieldeth the peaceable fruit of righteousness unto them which are exercised thereby, the apostle Paul said: «Being filled with all unrighteousness, fornication, wickedness, covetousness, maliciousness; full of envy, murder, debate, deceit, malignity; whisperers, backbiters, haters of God, despiteful, proud, boasters, inventors of evil things, disobedient to parents, without understanding, covenantbreakers, without natural affection, implacable, unmerciful.

Who knowing the judgment of God, that they which commit such things are worthy of death, not only do the same, but have pleasure in them that do them»: [Romans 1: 29-32].

If the child makes a mistake, the parent must correct or admonish him, with words first, not bad expressions or incorrect and indecent words. You must react seriously, if he has not heard your correction you must take another measure, which is the rod.

The punishment with the stick should be the last measure. Discipline is used to correct and guide people on the right path. All those who do not discipline their children when they are little, tomorrow they will all be against them. Even his own parents.

Why does Jehovah have to punish his children?

The wise Solomon said the reason why God punishes his children, he expressed it thus: "For whom the Lord loveth he correcteth; even as a father the son in whom he delighteth": [Proverbs 3:12].

All those who do not punish their children when they make some mistakes are enemies of their futures. When God expressed through the wise Solomon about the discipline of children, he was not saying parents should assault them. If emotions cause the situation to be handled incorrectly, parents automatically turn bad. The law of God and earthly have to face them. They must react as a good parent, not as an aggressor.

King Solomon gave another example of how the child should be corrected or punished, he said:"Withhold not correction from the child: for if thou beatest him with the rod, he shall not die. Thou shalt beat him with the rod, and shalt deliver his soul from hell": [Proverbs 23: 13-14].

"Foolishness is bound in the heart of a child; but the rod of correction shall drive it far from him": [Proverbs 22:15].

"When the wicked are multiplied, transgression increaseth: but the righteous shall see their fall": [Proverbs 29:16].

What did the wise Solomon mean by that expression? He was saying that parents should punish little ones with the stick so they can hear their corrections. Because no warning kills a child, on the contrary, it will free him from bad ways for his whole life.

You are what you are for the correction and discipline and punishment of your parents; if you want to save your children you must do the same.

The father must use two ways to correct them, "discipline or punish", one day with the words the other day with the stick, because if only with words, they will always stay the same because they know their father will not punish them with anything more forceful.

And the words are of air and return to the air, like flesh to dust.

Should children hate their parents for correction?

In no way, because in the 5th Commandment God said to all the children: "Honour thy father and thy mother: that thy days may be long upon the land which the Lord thy God giveth thee": [Exodus 20:12].

Rather, you must love them, obey them in all circumstances. No child has the right in any way to hit their parents or speak indecent words to them under any conditions, they will not only be punished by God, but by earthly law as well.

What does the Bible say about rebellious children to their parents?

The prophet Jeremiah explained what the home of the rebellious children will be like to their parents, he said: "But if ye will not hear these words, I swear by myself, saith the Lord, that this house shall become a desolation": [Jeremiah 22: 5].

Chapter 25

Spiritual discipline at home

What is spiritual discipline? Why should we give spiritual discipline to our children?

Discipline is a standard practice that all parents must adhere to within their homes; it is the regular or full-time performance of actions and activities undertaken for the purpose of inducing spiritual experiences and cultivating spiritual development both within and outside the home.

It is allowing oneself to be totally guided by spiritual things, whether they be from God or from the enemy.

Spiritual discipline is to be imparted by the priest of the home, because it was to him God gave all responsibility to guide and instruct all those who dwell in that worthy home. The ecclesiastic is responsible for holding family services two to three times a day. Since he is working at noon, he must do it through the social network, because the family must nurture himself daily physically and spiritually.

There are two categories of priests in every home: the good and the bad. Each man must know or identify what type of priest you are, who you represent, whether it's God or the enemy.

There are also two categories of spiritual disciplines in every home: that of Christ and the enemy, which one of the two are you teaching your children? Who is listened to? Each parent teaches according to his belief and his moral capacity. No priest can be neutral in the home, he has to represent God or the enemy.

There are also many people who say they are followers of Christ, who have two faces, one in the church and the other in the house, they are sheep in the church and wolves in the house, they do not live what they preach.

There are many ways to discover them "with the behavior of your children within the church." Because they will show what they have learned in their homes within the church or the street.

God has a warning for all who are practicing two faces, two ways within the church. God said through his servant Moses: "Thou shalt not bow down thyself to them, nor serve them: for I the Lord thy God am a jealous God, visiting the iniquity of the fathers upon the children unto the third and fourth generation of them that hate me": [Exodus 20: 5].

The home dwellers

There are three main categories of people who dwell in almost every household, father, mother, and children. Each has their own role to play within the home, and each must join the smooth running of the home. Each one has his own responsibility.

The father's job as a priest is to guide the family at the feet of Jesus every day. The good shepherd grazes his herd day and night where he can get many green herbs and a lot of fresh water. He checks if the sheep are wounded by any wolf, if they are in good health, they are protected from any predator; they fight hard to defend their young.

But bad priests or shepherds neglect their herds in all circumstances. They are irresponsible, they only see their stomachs, they leave their own herds looking for their own food without taking care of any of them. When they are in charge of wild animals, they can never defend themselves, lacking strength and faith. They are always victims of the irresponsibility of their own shepherds.

Good shepherds have Jesus as their model, but false ones have the enemy.

What must the good shepherd do to take care of his sheep?

The herd must have two types of daily food so that the sheep can grow strong and healthy: daily and spiritual bread. Since the human body needs three meals a day to stay strong and healthy, it is the same for the spiritual.

What are the three spirit foods that the physical body needs to live strong and healthy?

These are the three family services must be celebrated daily in the home: the morning service, at twelve o'clock, and before going to sleep, no one can be spiritually solid without one of these three meals.

How should the priest celebrate the services without boredom of the children?

Each must have a role to play in the nest, must interact, the worship should not last more than 25 minutes. The priest must have an itinerary with night and day services, but the noon service should last only 10 minutes. When children make mistakes in their participation, never draw attention to them, better congratulate them.

A teacher makes a big mistake in repressing a student, because they close and lose the initiative to participate.

All children begin to develop in their home first. When they are in front of their parents they feel much safer than ever, that is why when they are inside the church, they sit in the middle of the father and the mother, that sign means absolute security. No parent should neglect even one of the ingredients if they want to achieve ultimate success.

What can happen at home if the priest neglects family services?

Total failure is like a soldier who goes to war without a rifle, without preparation. No Christian should go to sleep or leave the door of his house without praying or doing family worship. The evil spirit works more with the person when he is sleeping, nobody can spend a good night without recommending it in the hand of the Lord.

When a person goes to bed without praying, he does not sleep peacefully. All the people who do family worship and pray before bed never have a bad night.

A Christian who does family worship, prays and reads psalms before bed, heavenly angels always watch over his sleep throughout the night. When the enemy comes to harm him, he will meet the angels of God and the presence of Jesus.

The psalmist expressed it very clearly with all his security, he said: «He that dwelleth in the secret place of the most High shall abide under the shadow of the Almighty. I will say of the LORD, He is my refuge and my fortress: my God; in him will I trust. Surely he shall deliver thee from the snare of the fowler, and from the noisome pestilence.

He shall cover thee with his feathers, and under his wings shalt thou trust: his truth shall be thy shield and buckler. Thou shalt not be afraid for the terror by night; nor for the arrow that flieth by day; Nor for the pestilence that walketh in darkness; nor for the destruction that wasteth at noonday. A thousand shall fall at thy side, and ten thousand at thy right hand; but it shall not come nigh thee.

Only with thine eyes shalt thou behold and see the reward of the wicked. Because thou hast made the LORD, which is my refuge, even the most High, thy habitation; there shall no evil befall thee, neither shall any plague come nigh thy dwelling.

For he shall give his angels charge over thee, to keep thee in all thy ways. They shall bear thee up in their hands, lest thou dash thy foot against a stone. Thou shalt tread upon the lion and adder: the young lion and the dragon shalt thou trample under feet»: [Psalms 91:1-13].

Wicked spirits are attacking at any time, but they are fiercer at noon and midnight. The psalmist was saying that no matter what they are up to, he is not afraid, because his life is assured on the rock that is Jesus Christ.

A Christian who does the morning prayer service before leaving will always spend the day full of love and blessing, because Jesus will clean the path that his feet will tread. If you face some problems, you will not be alone, Jesus will always give a positive exit.

A guy who went out with morning worship and prayer is like a well-equipped soldier going to war; protected by the wings of the Holy Spirit. There will never be a day of boredom. Everyone will testify that he is a true child of God.

Before leaving the home, he must dismiss the flock with kisses and hugs in the name of God. If they are the sheep that will leave first, they must do the same. At lunchtime, the flock must have a specific moment where each sheep will receive a call or a blessing message before sharing the meal.

There should never be a lack of communication and fellowship within that home, the entire flock should be content and happy when the shepherd is within the flock. The shepherd must be a big pack for some of the little sheep, the whole flock must listen and love when his presence is inside the home; they must obey and trust his words.

When there is such good behavior, that home will change to a little heaven on earth. The pastor must not be a boss, he must be a good leader all the time.

The priest's job is to connect his herds to Christ Jesus every day through family services. The mission of the Holy Spirit is to convince and guide all the human spirits of the family to Christ.

Chapter 26

The true worship of the Creator

Many people are talking about worship, not knowing what worship is, why we should worship, who we should worship and how we should worship, how important it is to worship.

Worship is a contemplative spiritual state in which the human being is overcome with wonder, establishing an intimate communion with a Deity. Worship means "loving the extreme." When applied to a Deity, it means "loving a Deity to the extreme."

The prophet Hosea said: «My people were destroyed, because they lacked knowledge. Because you rejected knowledge, I will cast you out of the priesthood; and because you forgot the law of your God, I will also forget your children»: [Hosea 4: 6].

God's people are ruining for lack of knowledge, for that reason they cannot give or offer a sincere and worthy worship to God. All created beings are worshiping their creator as they should be, except humanity has been created in his image. Man was created especially to give sincere worship to the Creator, for lack of knowledge it does the opposite.

Worshipers must take all precautions when offering worship to the Creator, because God does not accept all kinds of worship, we must know how we should offer worthy worship to the Creator, the plan of the enemy is to put confusion among humanity so no one can worship as God asked.

There are two category of worship: one true and one false. Both are very common in the world, sometimes they are similar according to the culture of the individual. What is the enemy's plan? Since he knows that man was born especially to worship, he has falsified the way God wants or asks for worship.

In the mind of the individual he thinks he is giving a worthy worship to the Creator, in the end he is giving or offering worship to the enemy, nobody worships in vain. If the Creator does not accept his worship, he is pleased and the enemy laughs.

How should worshipers know if God accepts their worship?

Worship can be defined as the act of honoring and loving a Deity, it must be from the heart: you can never give good worship without loving the Deity with all your heart and you must have a redeemed heart, occupied by God at all times, if you love God with all your heart you can worship him with an act of grace.

For all this to happen, you must meet all the criteria he has requested. There are two things that are very important to God: "worship and praise."

What is praise?

In the religious context, praises to God are an integral part of the liturgy. For example, in Christianity to Jesus Christ, they hold God is a supreme being worthy of praise. The Biblical Book of Psalms is a collection of hymns and poems mostly praise God.

Although God has never negotiated with anyone, but worship and praise are unmatched, if a person wants heaven to open in his favor, he must give worship and praise worthy to Jehovah.

The only supreme who deserves all the glory, honor and praise is the great "I AM". One way that earth must have direct contact with heaven: through prayer, worship and praise.

Does God accept all kinds of worship and praise?

The architect Moses said in his book: "Thus the heavens and the earth were finished, and all the host of them. And on the seventh day God ended his work which he had made; and he rested on the seventh day from all his work which he had made.

And God blessed the seventh day, and sanctified it: because that in it he had rested from all his work which God created and made": [Genesis 2: 1–3].

God is a God of order, He does not accept all kinds of worship, He has his own criteria of how worshipers should praise Him. We must worship every day, but God has a well-determined day where he can receive all the adorations, the praises for ever and ever, no one should question because this day, when God says something, the worshipers must say amen, which means! So be it!

How should true worshipers worship him on his holy day?

God said through the prophet Isaiah: «If thou turn away thy foot from the sabbath, from doing thy pleasure on my holy day; and call the sabbath a delight, the holy of the Lord, honourable; and shalt honour him, not doing thine own ways, nor finding thine own pleasure, nor speaking thine own words.

Then shalt thou delight thyself in the Lord; and I will cause thee to ride upon the high places of the earth, and feed thee with the heritage of Jacob thy father: for the mouth of the Lord hath spoken it»: [Isaiah 58: 13, 14].

There are many people who are inside the church, who have a personal encounter with their friends, they are not worshipers, they come out of habit, not because they come to worship. God gave the condition as he can accept our adorations and praises, if we do the opposite, he is the enemy that takes that adoration, because if we do not accept the condition of God, we accept the other.

Worship is a demonstration of love and respect for the Creator. "The Lord is in his holy temple, the Lord's throne is in heaven: his eyes behold, his eyelids try, the children of men". [Psalms 11: 4].

Jehovah is in his holy temple; Jehovah has his throne in heaven; his eyes see, his eyelids examine the sons of men.

The author said, "And he said, Hear thou therefore the word of the Lord: I saw the Lord sitting on his throne, and all the host of heaven standing by him on his right hand and on his left": [1 Kings 22:19].

King Solomon's expression means, all who dwell in heaven are before him to praise and worship him in his holy day, if they were before the throne of God, it is because they were worshiping him with much reverence and fear. Earthly worshipers have no respect or reverence when they stand before God in his holy temple.

What is the new Jerusalem?

John said: "And I John saw the holy city, new Jerusalem, coming down from God out of heaven, prepared as a bride adorned for her husband. And I heard a great voice out of heaven saying, Behold, the tabernacle of God is with men, and he will dwell with them, and they shall be his people, and God himself shall be with them, and be their God": [Revelation 21: 2-3].

The servant of God had the great privilege of seeing that beautiful city Jesus is preparing for all the saved, which is the New Jerusalem. According to the prophet Isaiah, the day all the saved will gather together with the great liberator who is Christ Jesus to worship the Creator is the 7th day that is the rest for Jehovah of armies.

What is reverence?

A bow is an action in which a person bows his body or part of it as a sign of respectful greeting or veneration. On many occasions, a bow is nothing more than a quick bow of the head, but it can also consist of a deep bow from the waist or a genuflection. Reverence is love, respect for the presence of God.

Samuel said: "Only fear the Lord, and serve him in truth with all your heart: for consider how great things he hath done for you. But if ye shall still do wickedly, ye shall be consumed, both ye and your King": [1 Samuel 12:24].

Why should the parishioner bow in the temple of God?

The prophet Habakkuk gave the correct answer why everyone should have reverence in the holy temple of God, he said: "But the Lord is in his holy temple: let all the earth keep silence before him": [Habakkuk 2:20].

Because not a simple man who is inside the temple, nor a human king, is the King of kings and Lord of lords, the whole earth has to be silent before his presence.

How are living beings worshiping the Creator in heaven?

Daniel explained very clearly how living beings are worshiping the Creator in heaven, it is something incomparable inexplicable, he said: "I beheld till the thrones were cast down, and the Ancient of days did sit, whose garment was white as snow, and the hair of his head like the pure wool: his throne was like the fiery flame, and his wheels as burning fire.

A fiery stream issued and came forth from before him: thousand thousands ministered unto him, and ten thousand times ten thousand stood before him: the judgment was set, and the books were opened": [Daniel 7: 9-10].

You cannot have the trial without the penal, civil books, neither without the witnesses, nor the lawyers, the accusers and the accused. God sits on his throne in the most holy place as the great judge, thousands of thousands of angels are present at this trial as witnesses, the accused are us, our defender and advocate is Christ Jesus.

Daniel saw four books that were opened before the old man of days: the book of the ten commandments, the book of life, memory and death. Which of the three will your name be written?

There is still a chance, Jesus as the faithful lawyer can issue a positive sentence in your favor if you have recognized that you are guilty of your crimes, even the door of grace is open, but at any time the old man of days can close it, like no other know when that will happen, you must take advantage of today before it will be too late.

There are three categories of trials in heaven, the investigative judgment, the order to investigate, and the sentence. On the day of the three the accuser will never be present because the faithful lawyer, who is Christ Jesus, defeated him on the cross of Calvary.

If a person has the enemy as his lawyer he can never win any case, he does not have enough strength or argument to overcome the great lawyer who is Jesus Christ.

Jesus as the great defender is defending all his clients, against all attacks from the enemy, the good news for all those who have chosen Christ Jesus as their Advocate, himself who will give the final sentence. All those who do not want to offer a worthy worship service to Jehovah according to the treatment, will go before the great tribunal of Christ because they have obeyed the voice of the enemy than Jesus.

The apostle Paul said: "For we must all appear before the judgment seat of Christ; that every one may receive the things done in his body, according to that he hath done, whether it be good or bad": [2 Corinthians 5:10].

The rich, the poor, the whites, the yellows and the blacks, trained as disabled, all of us must appear before the judgment seat of God. God is not a human judge where money can buy Him. Whether you want it or not, you will have to appear before the great court of God.

Nor is the great lawyer human to sell or negotiate the cases of his clients. All those who have had Christ as their advocate will win.

Does God live in the house that manufactures with the human hand?

No way. God is not human who lives in the house that manufactures with the human hand. Since humans cannot go to heaven in person to adorn him, he came in spirit to receive all the adorations and praises of his children. God revealed to Apostle Paul, said: "Heaven is my throne, and the earth is my footstool."

Dr. Lucas said, "Heaven is my throne, and earth is my footstool: what house will ye build me? saith the Lord: or what is the place of my rest?": [Acts 7:49].

He is in contact with the earth when we are offering a worship in the way he asked us, not because he comes to dwell in the home where we manufacture, the temple is a meeting place between the parishioners with heaven.

Jesus said,"For where two or three are gathered together in my name, there am I in the midst of them": [Matthew 18:20].

God has made his own sanctuary with his hands and his intelligence; He did not ask anybody for advice because before Him there was no one because he is alpha and omega, the first and the last, He lives forever and ever.

It is the same for all those people who want to have families, they must build their own roofs before making that great decision or responsibility.

All the faithful must know that God does not dwell in the earthly temple; He came to receive worship services like us, then he goes to his heavenly sanctuary, he will always be with us every day in the Spirit until the end of the world according to his promise.

Why can't humans see the face or forehead of God?

Jehovah God said to Moses: "You will not be able to see my face; because man will not see me, and he will live": [Exodus 33:20].

After the fall of Adam and Eve, nobody can see the presence of God to be alive, because He is too holy, his face is pure fire, because of our sins he has to hide his face from all men. No one can see Him before the transformation that will take place with Jesus Christ.

The apostle Paul tells us what will happen at the second coming Jesus, he said: "For this corruptible must put on incorruption, and this mortal must put on immortality": [1 Corinthians 15:53].

All people who want to dwell in the New Jerusalem must have a life of transformation, justification and daily sanctification, because no sinner can see or be in the presence of the Lord.

God's church

God's church is like a human body that has different members, each member is formed to perfect the whole body. God ordered the high command of that institution to form different departments for the perfection of the church in all its integrity.

Sabbath school

Sabbath school is an institution that is highly valued within the church of God. There all the parishioners receive the formations to lead the people of God in the coming time, the formation is the daily bread that each student needs to grow strong in the work of God.

That school has many teachers who are well prepared spiritually and intellectually to nurture each member according to their needs, as they have studied throughout the week, the teachers come to review and clarify some points were not so clear to the students. All students should participate in the review of the lesson.

At what exact time should school start?

If the church board makes an assembly decision in prayer, and school must start at the exact time according to the church manual, all students should be there by now, whether or not there are students.

The officers must go up at the indicated time, because before the hour, the angels who occupy the Sabbath school are there to welcome all the participants. Since they are not human, time and time are highly respected.

All the people who are working in the God work, even if they don't have wages, God is never going to leave them without reward.

Missionary Work Department

The missionary work department is responsible for putting all the parishioners into work for Christ, officers must use all new strategies to put all members in good spirits in the Lord's work; they should not only go up for up, they should be responsible for the smooth running of that department.

They must form many small groups in all places, God's work began with small groups will end in the same way. For the smooth running of that department, officers must always connect with the Deity. They must be people with good testimonies inside and outside their homes.

Their mandates should be: preaching, baptizing, retaining, and training new believers for heaven with the help of the Holy Spirit. They must have good academic levels because they will have contact with different ranks of society. Their duties are to bring everyone to the feet of Jesus.

All people who are part of the body of Christ must be missionaries, from the first days of baptisms until today, Jesus has not called them, to occupy a place within the church only. Our mission is to multiply the parishes for Christ.

Jesus said, "Go ye therefore, and teach all nations, baptizing them in the name of the Father, and of the Son, and of the Holy Ghost: Teaching them to observe all things whatsoever I have commanded you: and, lo, I am with you always, even unto the end of the world. Amen": [Matthew 28: 19-20].

If a person does not have the gift of preaching, can he do missionary work?

Of course, because not all people have the same gifts. The apostle Paul spoke about that situation in his letter to the Corinthians, he said: «Now there are diversities of gifts, but the same Spirit. And there are differences of administrations, but the same Lord.

And there are diversities of operations, but it is the same God which worketh all in all. But the manifestation of the Spirit is given to every man to profit withal. For to one is given by the Spirit the word of wisdom; to another the word of knowledge by the same Spirit.

To another faith by the same Spirit; to another the gifts of healing by the same Spirit; to another the working of miracles; to another prophecy; to another discerning of spirits; to another divers kinds of tongues; to another the interpretation of tongues: but all these worketh that one and the selfsame Spirit, dividing to every man severally as he will.

For as the body is one, and hath many members, and all the members of that one body, being many, are one body: so also is Christ»: [1 Corinthians 12: 4-12].

Everyone does not have the same gifts, but each can do something or can work in a different way to win people for Christ. If you have not yet found your gift, ask Christ in prayer; He will show you, because he wants you to participate in the salvation of others. No one should have their crown without even a star.

Why should we preach the gospel of Christ?

Saint Matthew gave the reason why everyone should preach the good news of God, he said: "And this gospel of the kingdom shall be preached in all the world for a witness unto all nations; and then shall the end come": [Matthew 24:14].

Now, all those who feel safe on this earth, should not preach the gospel of Christ, but with or without you the gospel will continue its way, God has thousands of ways to finish his work on earth.

Christians do not preach the gospel to convert others only, preach to them as the testimony, because no one should be guilty of the perdition of others.

Advertising department

Publicity is very important within the church, to make known all the things that will happen inside it and outside it. All the parishioners must know all the developments of that institution; all departments are important within the church. No one can post or announce any information without going through that section first.

All the departments that we have within the church have a group of highly specialized angels to ensure the smooth running of that department. Because it is God himself who is running his church. So no one can be against it. Although there are false leaders who are leading that institution, do not be afraid, because God is very aware of his business.

In the advertising department, you cannot advertise or publish anything is not from that department. All departments or people who want to give an announcement, must deliver it a week before depending on the urgency or the case.

Chapter 27

The church's worship and worship department

All departments are important to God, but the department of praise and worship is much more important than all departments. Praise is the way to express ourselves or raise our prayers to our God.

God wants us to worship Him in the Spirit and in truth, if we have a willing spirit we can worship the Creator according to his will. The psalmist David said: "My soul shall make her boast in the Lord: the humble shall hear thereof, and be glad": [Psalms 34: 2].

The only department that elevates all worshipers to the throne of grace is praise, that's why this department has received all attacks from the enemy. The enemy has created many forms of worship to confuse us with the true one. Within the church of God the enemy is using even the groups of praise leaders not to give worship according to the will of God.

There are two types of praise and worship: before and after sin. On the throne of God there are seven heavenly choir groups give glory to God at every moment, especially on his holy day. But three other groups mentioned by their names in the bible.

Who are the seraphim?

Seraphim are, according to Christian theology, the first of the nine choirs or type of "blessed spirits" of Christian angelology. They belong to the highest order in the highest hierarchy. They surround the throne of God and are in constant praise singing to the honor of the Deity.

They are superior to the cherubims as they are much closer to the throne of God. They have greater command and degrees than the others. They never stop saying holy, holy to Jehovah of armies.

How do seraphim worship and praise Jehovah in heaven?

Prophet Isaiah said in his letter: «In the year that king Uzziah died I saw also the Lord sitting upon a throne, high and lifted up, and his train filled the temple. Above it stood the seraphims: each one had six wings; with twain he covered his face, and with twain he covered his feet, and with twain he did fly.

And one cried unto another, and said, Holy, holy, holy, is the Lord of hosts: the whole earth is full of his glory. And the posts of the door moved at the voice of him that cried, and the house was filled with smoke.

Then said I, Woe is me! for I am undone; because I am a man of unclean lips, and I dwell in the midst of a people of unclean lips: for mine eyes have seen the King, the Lord of hosts.

Then flew one of the seraphims unto me, having a live coal in his hand, which he had taken with the tongs from off the altar: And he laid it upon my mouth, and said, Lo, this hath touched thy lips; and thine iniquity is taken away, and thy sin purged»: [Isaiah 6: 1-7].

John said: "And the four beasts had each of them six wings about him; and they were full of eyes within: and they rest not day and night, saying, Holy, holy, holy, Lord God Almighty, which was, and is, and is to come": [Revelation 4: 8].

They hold a great reverence when they are before God, because they clearly know that they are not before any one, but before the King of kings and Lord of lords; they worship him with all respect and humiliation. With that great reverence they never stop saying holy, holy, holy it is Jehovah of armies.

Because of that great reverence, they never look the Creator in the eye, they always cover their heads and cover their eyes with their two wings to worship the "GREAT I AM". Their skirts cover all their bodies before Jehovah in worship.

Who are the cherubims?

In Christian angelology, a cherubim is a type of angel, the second of the nine angelic choirs. They are considered as the guardians of the glory of God. Its name means "the next" or "the second".

They are perfect beings who have lower degrees than the seraphim, they are before the throne of God to worship him in all integrity. They have been specially created to praise and worship Jehovah.

What does the Bible say about cherubims?

The author said: "So the people sent to Shiloh, that they might bring from thence the ark of the covenant of the Lord of hosts, which dwelleth between the cherubims: and the two sons of Eli, Hophni and Phinehas, were there with the ark of the covenant of God": [Samuel 4: 4].

He said: " And David arose, and went with all the people that were with him from Baale of Judah, to bring up from thence the ark of God, whose name is called by the name of the Lord of hosts that dwelleth between the cherubims": [2 Samuel 6: 2].

Prophet Isaiah said: "O Lord of hosts, God of Israel, that dwellest between the cherubims, thou art the God, even thou alone, of all the kingdoms of the earth: thou hast made heaven and earth": [Isaiah 37:16].

The psalmist David said: "Give ear, O Shepherd of Israel, thou that leadest Joseph like a flock; thou that dwellest between the cherubims, shine forth": [Psalms 80: 1].

John said: "And before the throne there was a sea of glass like unto crystal: and in the midst of the throne, and round about the throne, were four beasts full of eyes before and behind": [Revelation 4: 6].

Although God dwells in their midst, his commands are: to praise and worship the Creator in all its fullness. They are two categories of angels who have great command and a great privilege to be before God day and night to worship him.

What office did Satan have in heaven before his fall?

Prophet Ezekiel very well describes the position of that rebel on Jehovah's holy mountain before he was fallen, he said: «Thou hast been in Eden the garden of God; every precious stone was thy covering, the sardius, topaz, and the diamond, the beryl, the onyx, and the jasper, the sapphire, the emerald, and the carbuncle, and gold: the workmanship of thy tabrets and of thy pipes was prepared in thee in the day that thou wast created.

Thou art the anointed cherub that covereth; and I have set thee so: thou wast upon the holy mountain of God; thou hast walked up and down in the midst of the stones of fire. Thou wast perfect in thy ways from the day that thou wast created, till iniquity was found in thee.

By the multitude of thy merchandise they have filled the midst of thee with violence, and thou hast sinned: therefore I will cast thee as profane out of the mountain of God: and I will destroy thee, O covering cherub, from the midst of the stones of fire.

Thine heart was lifted up because of thy beauty, thou hast corrupted thy wisdom by reason of thy brightness: I will cast thee to the ground, I will lay thee before kings, that they may behold thee». [Ezekiel 28: 13-17].

The great enemy was a protective angel on the mount of God, he was a protective cherub, he knows a lot about praise and worship. He knows all the tricks to deceive humanity with false praise and adoration. Like the king of darkness, he accepts worship because he wants to be like God. In praise and worship you must be very wise and careful so that you do not praise yourself in vain.

You have to seek God's help so that he can teach you how you should give worthy praise and worship according to his will.

How should true worshipers worship and praise the Creator on his holy day, and what should they do to offer a worthy worship according to the will of God?

The day God wants them to worship is the seventh, true worshipers know what clothes, suits, perfumes, shoes to wear in the presence of the Lord; you see in many verses the forms of praise and adoration that living beings raise to God in heaven; the obeisances, respects and humiliations they have when they are worshiping and praising the Creator.

You must copy over them if you want God to accept your prayers.

What kinds of praise and worship are you offering to God? What clothes do you have when you are worshiping the one who deserves all the glory, the honor for ever and ever? Did you go to have a personal encounter with God or with your friends? Is it that you are the true worshipers or the false ones? Who are you and what do you look for within the place of praise?

If you do not want to worship and praise the Creator, He has thousands of thousands of angels who are praising and worshiping Him according to his will.

Who are the beneficiaries of praise and worship, God or us? The real secret of praise and worship is: God's direct response to his servants in the midst of worship and praise. If you want to receive all the heavenly blessings, praise and adore the one who deserves all the glory, praise, honor, with all his body, soul and spirit.

The times of praise and worship

Angels are faithful in the times of praise and worship, when the praise group begins to worship, God sends cherubims and seraphims for one purpose to prepare and verify the place where his presence will be in the Spirit within the church.

If we are not in good formal condition when we are offering praise to the Creator, the angels will be saddened, because they have never accustomed to that style of praise with informal and disrespectful views we are offering to God.

His works are: preparing the ground that our hearts are to give or offer worthy adoration according to his divine will, it is a very solemn moment for heaven and earth when those two main moments arrive: praise and adoration.

At this time we must not think about anything else, we must hold our minds and spirits in that worthy worship, without concentration no one can give or offer a worthy worship according to the will of the Lord.

Divine worship

The earthly sanctuary, which is the temple of God, has three places: the conference room, the holy and the most holy. Each has its importance within the church, the conference room is the room where all worshipers kneel to worship their Creator, all worshipers have to fully respect that place, because when God is inside his holy temple, all his glory fills that place.

How should true worshipers dress when offering worship to Jehovah?

They must dress very modestly with a willing heart so that God can receive their adorations and their prayers. Because the temple of God is not a place of fun where individuals can go to recreate, it is a place where sinners come to have a personal encounter with God. They must have all the respect for this place.

The holy place is the prelude to the most holy place, that place is available especially for the Sabbath school department, missionary work and the praise department. In that place all the services of the week take place; all shows and concerts are also held.

The most holy place within the temple of God, is a place especially to execute the divine worship, where the presence of God is in spirit, all the people who are going to participate in this worship must be well represented, their clothing must be acceptable before the heaven and the great assembly; all must confess their sins before going up to the most holy place which is the pulpit where God will speak to his people through the preacher.

The cult must be very solemn. You must have two services at the same time, one for adults and the other for children, if it is not possible, all parents must have their children by their side, very calm, only authorized officers who must circulate when necessary, All participants must go to the bathroom first before the officers go up to the Holy of Holies.

At the entrance, the assembly in general, large as well as small, should stand up to give the entrance and welcome to the officers who are going to carry out that sublime and solemn worship.

Before the arrival of God to receive that cult, He sends seraphim and cherubs with the mission of preparing the ground and the place where he will be in spirit. They will check if the worshipers are in a good condition to receive the presence of God before their arrival. The messenger's mission is to call him with a circumstance prayer, no one should start worship without his call through a circumstance prayer first.

Since he is a God of order, he wants all worshipers to have order in the way they are offering worship.

What does God ask of all worshipers when his presence is in his holy temple?

The prophet Habakkuk gave a good initiative of how all worshipers should behave in the presence of God, he said: "But the Lord is in his holy temple: let all the earth keep silence before him": [Habakkuk 2:20].

This message is not written for the people of Israel only, but for all Christians in this century. God does not change, He is the same as yesterday, today and forever. All the earth must be silent in his presence.

The prophet was saying we cannot change the temple of God in a municipal market or in a boat, or in place of entertainment; it is a place where his presence is in the spirit. We must show all reverence before Him.

Not only did Habakkuk clarify about the reverence within the temple, the prophet Zacharias gives an explanation similar to his, he said: "Be silent, O all flesh, before the Lord: for he is raised up out of his holy habitation": [Zechariah 2:13].

Silence: Silence is the total absence of sound. It also means abstaining from speaking, in the field of human communication, bone State in which there is no noise or no voice is heard, "close your mouth."

The two messengers are not just saying what is incumbent on the followers of God, all those who have moral reasons must remain silent in his presence.

If there is any presentation of the children, everyone should stay in the holy place to do that ceremony, the minister should go down to that place to present the children at the feet of Jesus. Parents, believers or not, must respect the dress code when presenting children. At the end of the presentation, all participants must wait for the end of the service before leaving.

In the execution of the worship, the exposition or the sermon of the preacher should not exceed 40 minutes, because there are people who have suffered some illnesses and need to leave in time to take their medicines, or eat something, although when we are in the presence of God.

We should not be in a hurry or time, because king David said in his exposition: "I was glad when they said unto me, Let us go into the house of the Lord": [Psalms 122: 1].

Everyone should feel happy and joyful about spending a lot at Jehovah's feet. David gave another explanation of his joy when he is before the Creator, he said: "For a day in thy courts is better than a thousand. I had rather be a doorkeeper in the house of my God, than to dwell in the tents of wickedness": [Psalms 84:10].

The psalmist was expressing his joy and gladness when he is at the feet of his Savior. No one should be in a hurry to leave the holy place. The psalmist knew the presence of God is everywhere, but for him, the temple is the most correct place to be in communion with his Creator. All those who are in a hurry to get away from the temple without any reason, it is because they had no encounter with the Master.

The apostle John, who changes into the apostle of love, gave a good explanation for all those who do not want to spend much time at the feet of Jesus, he said: "But the hour cometh, and now is, when the true worshippers shall worship the Father in spirit and in truth: for the Father seeketh such to worship him.

God is a Spirit: and they that worship him must worship him in spirit and in truth": [John 4: 23-24].

Why should we worship the Creator?

John said: "And I saw another angel fly in the midst of heaven, having the everlasting gospel to preach unto them that dwell on the earth, and to every nation, and kindred, and tongue, and people, Saying with a loud voice, fear God, and give glory to him; for the hour of his judgment is come: and worship him that made heaven, and earth, and the sea, and the fountains of waters": [Revelation 14: 6-7].

God does not want anyone to worship him for fear of punishment, fear destroys love completely, but fear of Jehovah is respect for him, we do things for love not for fear. All humanity has been specially created to worship the Creator, no one can worship other gods, only the one who made heaven and earth with his knowledge.

Because there we find refuge, healing, the hope of eternal life, but as a human, the preacher must take precaution with his long sermons, so that nobody gets bored. Also no one should leave without the completion of the sermon. All participants must receive the final blessing. Then he can fire each parishioner in the name of the Lord.

All worshipers must feel the presence of God in their hearts, no one should return in the same way that he had come from the church. At the end of the worship they must feel a transformation, a peace, they must feel a great relief from their problems. For that to happen, you must have a willing heart, you must offer worship with all the conditions that the Creator asks for.

If you feel the same as you were in the beginning, you should do a self-analysis of your own life: what was you doing that prevented God from accepting or hearing your prayer and worship. Because the church is like a hospital, no sick person should go home without healing.

Music and rhythms

What do some professionals say about music?

Review by Andrea Imaginario, specialist in Arts, Comparative Literature and History, the author begins her presentation with a question: "What is music?". She explains it like this: "The ordered combination of rhythm, melody and harmony that is pleasing to the ears is known as music. Due to its immaterial nature, music is considered a temporal or time art, just like literature.

In the restrictive sense, music is the art of coordinating and transmitting sound, harmonious and aesthetically valid effects, which are generated through the voice or musical instruments.

Music is an artistic and cultural manifestation of peoples, so that it acquires various forms, aesthetic values and functions according to their context. At the same time, it is one of the means by which an individual expresses his feelings.

The person who puts music into practice, or plays it by means of an instrument, is called a musician. As such, the word can be used metaphorically. For example, it can be used in colloquial phrases such as: "Go somewhere else with that music", which means that the person vehemently dismisses someone who has disturbed them.

"What you say is music to my ears", which means that the person listens to a news item that is pleasant to hear".

She illustrates her exhibition with many with music from around the world, too, with an explanation of the way she learned in college.

But I can define music this way too. It is something that can lift us up before the throne of God. God Himself has created music. Music is the art of combining sounds in a temporal sequence according to the laws of harmony, melody and rhythm.

Also, it is a set of successive sounds combined according to this art, which generally produce an aesthetic or expressive effect and are pleasing to the ear.

What is the melody?

The researchers say: It is a succession of sounds that is perceived as a single entity. It unfolds in a linear sequence, that is, over time, and has its own identity and meaning within a particular sound environment.

In other words, an ordered and coherent linear succession of musical sounds of different heights that form a structured unit with a musical sense, independent of the accompaniment. The constituent elements of music are rhythm, melody and harmony:

"I like the melody of this song, but the lyrics are too simple." A succession of sounds that, due to their way of combining, is musical or pleasant to hear. «From there you can only hear the dull melody of the wind among the myrtle trees; in the distance you could hear the melody of birdsong".

Who invented music?

According to science and history, written in stone and unequivocal, the music was "discovered" by Pythagoras.

He was the first man who in his countless moments of leisure when he had nothing better to do than look at the sky and burn his eyes with the sun, he thought of the wind, the birds, he did not brush his teeth, he needed going to the bathroom, and again he thought about the wind and the sounds produced by it, and studied it.

He discovered the chords that were produced in it, so it could be said that he was the one who discovered the music. The story is also not very clear in explaining the true function of Pythagoras. Of course, he discovered the laws of music, but it already existed. Someone had already created it; someone made music and dancing to their rhythm.

Who invented music according to the bible?

The apostle of love gave a great explanation about who invented music and why he did it, he said: «And they sung a new song, saying, Thou art worthy to take the book, and to open the seals thereof: for thou wast slain, and hast redeemed us to God by thy blood out of every kindred, and tongue, and people, and nation; and hast made us unto our God kings and priests: and we shall reign on the earth.

And I beheld, and I heard the voice of many angels round about the throne and the beasts and the elders: and the number of them was ten thousand times ten thousand, and thousands of thousands.

Saying with a loud voice, Worthy is the Lamb that was slain to receive power, and riches, and wisdom, and strength, and honour, and glory, and blessing. And every creature which is in heaven, and on the earth, and under the earth, and such as are in the sea, and all that are in them, heard I saying.

Blessing, and honour, and glory, and power, be unto him that sitteth upon the throne, and unto the Lamb for ever and ever»: [Revelation 5: 9-13].

John said: «And the four beasts had each of them six wings about him; and they were full of eyes within: and they rest not day and night, saying, Holy, holy, holy, Lord God Almighty, which was, and is, and is to come. And when those beasts give glory and honour and thanks to him that sat on the throne, who liveth for ever and ever». [Revelation 4: 8-9].

It is impossible for science to explain the whole truth about music. Literary people can teach music, inventing instruments according to their knowledge, as they do not know the kingdom of the universe or its existence, so it is impossible for them to know who invented the music.

The prophet Zephaniah said: "The Lord thy God in the midst of thee is mighty; he will save, he will rejoice over thee with joy; he will rest in his love, he will joy over thee with singing»: [Zephaniah 3:17].

All who breathe must worship the Creator with new songs. We must always have a victory song on our lips.

Singing means praying twice, that is why we must rejoice with songs and psalms, birds never cease to praise their creator with their trills because they have recognized and obeying all heavenly rules, if we want to enter the kingdom of heaven we must obey the Creator without any excuse.

Who is worthy to receive all the praise and adoration?

God showed John in a vision of who among all living beings can receive all the glories and all the praises, John said: "And hast made us unto our God kings and priests: and we shall reign on the earth.

And I beheld, and I heard the voice of many angels round about the throne and the beasts and the elders: and the number of them was ten thousand times ten thousand, and thousands of thousands": [Revelation 5: 11 -12].

No one, on earth or in the clouds, nor in the heavens, has the right to receive that immense privilege, only he who overcame death and Satan on the cross of Calvary: "Christ Jesus."

John saw another great event that is happening in his presence in heaven, he said: "And every creature which is in heaven, and on the earth, and under the earth, and such as are in the sea, and all that are in them, heard I saying, Blessing, and honour, and glory, and power, be unto him that sitteth upon the throne, and unto the Lamb for ever and eve": [Revelation 5:13].

For that reason, heaven is partying and rejoicing to worship the Lamb of God who removed the sin of the world with his death. Therefore, all heaven is celebrating this great victory over the great accuser and deceiver who is called Satan, the devil.

In John's great vision, God allowed him to see how living beings worship the Creator, he said: «And when those beasts give glory and honour and thanks to him that sat on the throne, who liveth for ever and ever, the four and twenty elders fall down before him that sat on the throne.

And worship him that liveth for ever and ever, and cast their crowns before the throne, saying, thou art worthy, O Lord, to receive glory and honour and power: for thou hast created all things, and for thy pleasure they are and were created». [Revelation 4: 9-11]

And we humans, how should we dress to praise and worship the GREAT I AM?

The apostle Paul said: «Speaking among you with psalms, with hymns and spiritual songs, singing and praising the Lord in your hearts; always giving thanks to God and Father for everything, in the name of our Lord Jesus Christ»: [Ephesians 5: 19-20].

God does not accept all kinds of music even if his name is mentioned, in order for God to accept these sound offerings, all worshipers must respect the criteria that he has established. We must worship him with thanksgiving and worthy and respectful praise; We must dress in presentable and pleasing clothing in the presence of the Lamb.

We cannot neglect ourselves and, for the pleasure of that world, offer a worship service in our own way, God will never receive that worship.

Nor does the lamb receive all kinds of praises, letters or harmonies. The melodies should only please the Creator, we cannot offer a praise with Christian lyrics in worldly rhythms. God never accepts that praise. Satan is looking for a way to filter everything, so that God does not accept our praises.

The great problem of the enemy is only about praise and worship, for that reason, he has lost all the privileges he had in heaven, because he wanted to be worshiped too. All worshipers must verify the way they are worshiping God, because we can think that it is the Lamb that we are worshiping, and in truth, it is the enemy.

The Lamb himself has expressed it in the letter of Saint Matthew, he said: «Not every one that saith unto me, Lord, Lord, shall enter into the kingdom of heaven; but he that doeth the will of my Father which is in heaven.

Many will say to me in that day, Lord, Lord, have we not prophesied in thy name? and in thy name have cast out devils? and in thy name done many wonderful works? And then will I profess unto them, I never knew you: depart from me, ye that work iniquity». [Matthew 7: 21-23].

Not all artists and worshipers will enter the kingdom of heaven, because the vast majority are representatives of satan.

Chapter 28

Vices in the home

Vices are the best tools the enemy uses to destroy anyone. Even the homes of great religious leaders are no exception. The enemy's plan is: find where the couple is weakest to attack.

It only takes a little bit of carelessness to put in a drop of its venom, enough to spread throughout the victim's physical and spiritual system.

Satan wants to dwell within homes to educate children according to his will; That enemy has control even over some Christian homes and the children of the great religious leaders, because many of them do not live on what they preach, there are many who are theologians who are not called.

When they have neglected the presence of God in their homes, the enemy finds the empty ground where he can enter, make and break in this family. Many leaders are less spiritual than their church parishioners; others, more womanizing and vain than unconfessed.

Why has church membership fallen so far into sin?

There are two main factors that can cause this great oversight. First the psalmist gave an explanation of why that always happens in the minds of almost all people, he said: "Behold, I was formed in iniquity, and my mother conceived me in sin": [Psalms 51: 5].

It is because of the sinful nature of man.

The second place is because Christians have more attacks from enemies than worldly ones.

Who is the intellectual author of the fall of the Christians?

The apostle Paul explained why we fall so much into sin, he said: "For we wrestle not against flesh and blood, but against principalities, against powers, against the rulers of the darkness of this world, against spiritual wickedness in high places": [Ephesians 6:12].

Although we are bombarded by all the attacks of the enemy, he cannot force us to sin if we don't want to. We have a big problem that is shaking us, which is flesh. Anyone can fall into the lusts of the flesh, into their inexhaustible need for sensual pleasure and survival, for how many crimes have not been committed motivated by a stomach?

What must they do to resist the lusts of the flesh?

The author of that chapter in the Bible clearly explained what we must do if we want to have victory over sin and vice, he said: «For the rest, my brothers, strengthen yourselves in the Lord, and in the power of his strength. Put on all the armor of God, so that you can stand firm against the snares of the devil.

Therefore, take all the armor of God, so that you can resist in the bad day, and having finished everything, be firm.

"Stand firm therefore, girded on your loins with truth, and clothed in the breastplate of righteousness, and shod your feet with the readiness of the gospel of peace. Above all, take the shield of faith, with which you can extinguish all the fiery darts of the evil one.

And take the helmet of salvation, and the sword of the Spirit, which is the word of God; praying at all times with all prayer and supplication in the Spirit, and watching in it with all perseverance and supplication for all the saints; and for me, so that when I open my mouth I will be given a word to boldly reveal the mystery of the gospel.

These are the criteria we must have to fight the enemy, with our strength we cannot, but with the help of the Holy Spirit, we will be more than conquerors. Sometimes when we fall into the unfortunate mistakes, we excuse ourselves with a why, there is always a why.

Sometimes we fall into vices and sins of curiosity. It is the nature of almost all women: "curiosity." They always want to see, they want to know; out of curiosity Lot's wife became a pillar of salt, out of the same curiosity Eve was tempted in the Garden of Eden. Curiosity always discovers secrets that on many occasions should have been hidden.

Vices come in all forms, the worst vices are like carapaths, they are very difficult viruses to overcome, nobody can leave them by their own strength, the products that feed them are pleasures, tastes and appetites... Only the Holy Spirit who can make that change.

Without your help, it may be left for a moment, but in the end, they will regain lost ground.

Why do people fall into vices without leaving?

Many people who fall into vices because they want to have money lightly, without trying or sweating. The impudences are deadly viruses that are against moral, family, professional and intellectual developments and growths.

They are germs that are against the education and training of children who are the future leaders of the church of God and the government.

Family and intellectual education are two things inevitable and irreplaceable for all children, all parents must do everything possible to give these two educations to their children, children must make all parents the priority, they returned triple to their parents in the future, well-educated children are like money kept in banks.

You want to enjoy a better life in old age, you must sacrifice yourself for the good education of your children.

People who have been affected by these germs, are under the curse of failure, automatically switch to the enemy of prosperity. All the vicious are very pessimistic, their mentality is to prosper without sweating; they want to have wealth through all kinds of vices.

What is vice?

A vice is any word that can also refer to a fault, a defect, an illness or just an evil. Some synonyms for this term are: lack, depravity, excess, bad habit, hobby, deviation. It can also be defined as the habit of doing something wrong or doing something harmful or considered morally reprehensible.

I can say that a form of freedom or unbridled surrender to sexual pleasures. It is an expression that has various uses and meanings. It can treat the defect or the poor quality of things, it is something that affects the mentality of man, that virus works with four elements: the ears, the eyes, the spirit and the hands.

There are many people who have sunk into vices under the influence of others.

When a person hears about a new option, the appetite or taste of trying it is automatically awakened regardless of the consequences, because there is no vice that does not have its consequence, in the negative sense, of course.

How does the human spirit react within a flawed body?

The spirit is the agent that guides and controls the whole body in general. No member of the body can work or function without it, it is the one that files all things in the memory archive, when the body wants to commit an act, it cannot do it by itself: it must make a request to the spirit, to that the eyes and the hands carry it out.

Vices are very difficult to leave when you are practicing them frequently, they become habits and merge with your body. When you reach that level, you are zombies under his control. No professional can do something for you, because they become one with your nature, only the Holy Spirit can make a renewal in your nature, in the blink of an eye, you are reborn again.

If someone cannot change their attitude, it is because they have not yet met the Holy Spirit or they have not accepted the invitation or the call.

Why has humanity dropped so deep into all kinds of addictions?

It is because they allow themselves to be entangled with the nets of the enemy, because all vices are debaucheries, they are contrary to the word of God. When they are practicing a vice they are saying that Satan is right, that he has the truth, and God is a liar.

Why does it cost so much to abandon vices?

Because it is a work of art of Satan, a brilliant creation in accordance with his dark genius. He has legions of demons that are taking care of his parents' business in you, when you are under the domination of the enemy with the use of vices, he blinds you with the sweetness of appetite, no human can resist the pleasures and appetites of vices, Christian or not.

No one should condemn or criticize a vicious or an addict, because he is under the dominion of the enemy, who exposes him to the public for his own pride, to demonstrate that he reigns on earth. If you have been born again in Christ Jesus, you must pray without ceasing for him, until he can have a personal encounter with Jesus.

Vices always attack the family financially, emotionally and physically, almost the vast majority of the vicious are violent with their partner even with their own children. When their mentalities change into addicts, their hearts harden like a stone, they feel no compassion or guilt, their thoughts are the vices at all times.

If they work, before payday arrives, that salary has already been spent. They are always in debt.

When an addict is playing any type of gambling, Satan always puts in his mind, even if he is losing, that he will win, ignoring that all machines and all gambling are cursed. All games of chance have been invented by Satan; those are the kinds of fruit of his science out of grace.

Satan as the king of darkness, always lives with his government in the invisible world, no human can see him in person because they are evil spirits.

Every week his government meets called by its great leader. Its purpose is to design all kinds of games for humans, it is they who decide who can win or not; they have exchanged wealth for blood or their lives. Also, all games of chance are run by a legion of demons specialized in that way of corrupting the soul.

His government is like that of humans; it has all kinds of positions and degrees.

What do professionals say about vices?

Francisco Fourier Drew, director of the dif. State, commented on those great tragedies that are shaking almost 80% of families around the world. He said: "First, the system strengthens family values to prevent domestic violence, since its members are exposed to multiple situations that can put their stability at risk, hence the impetus for these programs that focus on strengthening the presence and value of women.

That is why we work hard to raise awareness, inform and train parents on issues related to family dynamics and their main conflicts, in addition to involving them in the education of their children and sensitizing them to their work as training agents through his testimony and his own training.

Also, the psychologist María de los A. Pérez gave her opinion on that calamity, she said: "Vices can be represented and grouped into a wide variety of classifications, which many of the experts in the different disciplines could point out with great skill and extensive knowledge, but according to the purposes of this course, it is necessary to sinter the topic, pointing out a Simple list of the best known and most damaging vices in recent times.

Listings of the most popular vices:

1. Addiction to alcoholic beverages.

2. Addiction to gambling.

3. Addiction to horse racing betting.

4. Drug addiction.

5. Addiction to criminal and illegal activities.

6. Addiction to video games.

7. Addiction to compulsive shopping.

8. Addiction to pornography.

9. Tobacco addiction.

10. Addiction to chocolate.

11. Cigarette addiction.

12. Addiction to horror movies.

13. Internet addiction.

14. Addiction to sweets.

15. Addiction to soft drinks.

16. Addiction to foods that have been medically prohibited.

17. Addiction to new technologies.

18. Addiction to programs that promote violence, etc.

She continues saying "There are many other personal situations, which could be included in these lists, however these are the most common vices, because they are the ones with the greatest social acceptance, and although people reject these vices, many of them before becoming vices, are very common activities that allow themselves socially.

It is for this reason that many of the people, in most cases, do not realize when it ceases to be a social habit, to become a vicious pattern, it is also for this reason that many people who fall into a vice when they are advised, they go into a process of denial, and they have a hard time understanding that it has already become a disease.

The psychologist is absolutely right to express herself in that way, because there are many people who think only of the major vices that can affect the family, all vices can destroy any family piece by piece, at first you cannot see the damage, it is little by little, the seed grows until it transforms into a large tree.

It is like a person who, affected by a microbe, does not change to a deadly disease at the same moment, it is gradually damaging a part of the body until death.

What does the Bible say about vices?

The Bible is the most complete book of all, as God is the first and the last is equal to his words. The apostle Paul gave us an alert about addicts and vices, said: «Be not deceived: evil communications corrupt good manners»: [Corinthians 15:33].

Because it is bad conversations with wicked people who have exchanged good habits for bad, for the curiosity of trying. Because the vast majority have been tainted by the experiences of others. When we are in a dangerous situation, we must rebuke all false spirits who want to harm us in the name of the Lord.

The servant of God continues to instruct us in the good way, he said: «All things are lawful for me, but not all agree: all things are lawful for me, but I will not get under the power of anything. Food for the belly, and the belly for food; However, God will destroy him and them. But the body is not for fornication, but for the Lord; and the Lord for the body».

All things are authorized to say them, because nobody can put interdiction in the languages of others, but not everything they say is convenient for us, it really is. What suits us are all the things that have come out of Jehovah's lips.

We must know that the people who advise us about illegal things are ambassadors of the diplomatic corps of the enemy, we have to be very careful what we pay attention to.

What should we do when we are faced with vices?

The apostle Paul tells us in his letter what we should do: «No temptation has overtaken you that is not human; but faithful is God, who will not allow you to be tempted more than you can resist, but will also give way together with temptation, so that you can endure.

It is impossible for temptations to come other ways, they are always humans who are well formed or instructed by their great teacher Satan, with their destinies to tempt us until we fall, we must resist in all, if we try to be faithful to God, the Holy Spirit will help us to overcome all temptations».

When you are faced with that great and contagious problem called vices, the only solution is to pray, sometimes you do not have any strength to pray at any time, because the reflection of the enemy with its temptations covers all the good wishes you had to pray.

When you are in this situation, you must shout very loudly, "I rebuke you in the name of the Lord!" If you can't, you must say in your heart: "Jesus save me!" He will come to your aid as quickly as possible.

The apostle Paul warns us of some vices, which affect even the parishioners of God, said: «And manifest are the works of the flesh, which are: adultery, fornication, filth, lust, idolatry, witchcraft, enmities, lawsuits, jealousy, anger, strife, dissent, heresy, envy, murder, drunkenness, orgies, and the like. These; about which I admonish you, as I have already told you before, that those who practice such things will not inherit the kingdom of God».

The great problem of humanity is the pleasure of the flesh, the taste, all kinds of appetites, no one can overcome the pleasures of the flesh without the Holy Spirit, there are many who are very difficult to overcome, even the great preachers have fallen for the pleasure of the flesh, but God always provides the solution.

King Solomon warned about the drinks, he said: "Wine is mocking, cider is rowdy, and anyone who errs by them is not wise."

That curse has left many children without education, without families, orphans, although Christians have overcome these addicts, but there are many who have allowed themselves to be contaminated by adultery and fornication.

Many families have separated because of addictions, because when Satan wants to harm the family, especially children, addiction tastes and appetites occur.

The apostle Paul gave a very clear answer to all married people, he said: "But put ye on the Lord Jesus Christ, and make not provision for the flesh, to fulfil the lusts thereof": [Romans 13:14].

We are living in an area, almost no one wants to dress Lord Jesus outside as inside the church, all have dressed according to their tastes and their carnal desires, no one can identify who are followers of Christ and Baal, all have looked alike, all those who want to go to heaven must be like Christ, everyone can see that great transformation in you.

All those who want to have a different and successful family and life, must make a decision today, they must totally clothe themselves with the Lord Jesus Christ, they must connect every second in the Lord. There is no better joy than when a woman enjoys only one man, and the man of a single woman in love; where one respects the other as the bible asks.

This way your children will have an exemplary life inside and outside the church in the house God.

Chapter 29

The homosexuality

We are living in a changed world in all dimensions, sometimes we are confusing men with women. Everyone is aware of everyone, like jungle animals, because there are many men who have changed their sex for the female and women alike.

Everyone is afraid of falling in love by not knowing if it is a real or transsexual woman or man. Another great masterpiece of Satan.

The gifts

The apostle Paul explained to us why Jesus chose some members of the church as doctors, he said: «Now there are diversities of gifts, but the same Spirit. And there are differences of administrations, but the same Lord. And there are diversities of operations, but it is the same God which worketh all in all.

But the manifestation of the Spirit is given to every man to profit withal. For to one is given by the Spirit the word of wisdom; to another the word of knowledge by the same Spirit; to another faith by the same Spirit; to another the gifts of healing by the same Spirit»: [1 Corinthians 12: 4-9].

Jesus has given the gift of medicine for the benefit of humanity, not to do the work of Satan. Jesus gave that gift especially to perfect God's work, not to corrupt it.

What do some doctors do with their gifts?

They have used them against the will of God for money, they say God had made a mistake in the creation of man, they think they are much smarter than the Creator, with the advice of the enemy in their hearts.

They have invented the reassignment surgery gender, genital reconstruction surgery and genital reassignment surgery, among other medical terms, such as: "feminizing genitoplasty", or "penectomy", "orchiectomy" and "vaginoplasty".

They have made a serious mistake in their lives, a great sin with that action. But before the door of grace closes, they have a chance to be saved if they convert and confess their sins before God.

What do Europeans say about homosexuality?

Jens Spahn of the CDU, a European-level legislation, explained his understanding of that situation, they said: "This means that there are big differences between EU countries when it comes to issues of taxes, inheritance rights or adoptions for gay marriages.

If Brussels forced measures for an opening in this sense, perhaps it would remain in the form of a law, but society would not fully accept it, "said Jens Spahn, MP for the German conservative CDU party, in an interview with Deutsche Welle.

Spahn promotes an increase of rights for homosexuals, but for him, a general regulation across the Union would be fatal. Such a measure would lead to increased protests and rejection.

One of the fundamental principles of the European Union is the free choice of the country of residence for European citizens. Evelyne Paradis criticizes the limited freedom of movement of gay marriages within Europe.

For example, if a gay marriage from the Netherlands, where they enjoy the same rights and obligations as any heterosexual marriage, were to move to Romania, it would no longer be recognized as a marriage, and therefore the couple would not receive the same concessions as a marriage between people of different sex.

"This constitutes visible discrimination, an attack on the rights of a citizen of the European Union," says Paradis. However, he is optimistic: in his opinion, it is only a matter of time before all the countries of the Union are prepared to fight against discrimination against homosexuals throughout Europe.

What does the European Union say about homosexuality?

Valentina T. Sánchez commented on the subject on the page [France 24.com] she said: "In accordance with the decision of the Court of Justice of the European Union, the countries of the bloc must grant the right of residence to the spouses of homosexual couples, even if the nations do not recognize such unions."

Advertisements

The Court of Justice of the European Union determined that the Member States must grant the right of residence to the homosexual spouse of a national of any community country.

That is why the members of the bloc that only recognize marriage as the union between man and woman, will have to grant the right of residence to the same-sex spouses of their citizens, even if they do not legalize homosexual marriage.

The court ruling indicates that "the freedom of residence of a citizen of the European Union cannot be hindered by denying their spouse of the same sex the granting of a derived right of residence in their territory".

The decision comes after the Romanian Relu Adrian Coman and the American Robert Clabourn, who married in Brussels, filed an appeal after asking the Romanian authorities for the right of residence, which was denied to Clabourn for not considering him "spouse."

However, the judgment establishes that "the European Union respects the national identity of the Member States, inherent in their fundamental political and constitutional structures"; and adds: that each nation of the bloc "has the freedom to institutionalize or not homosexual marriage."

What does the United States of America say about homosexuality?

They say: "Same-sex marriage in the United States, also known as gay or gay marriage, has been recognized by the federal government and all states since June 26, 2015, following the ruling in the Obergefell case against Hodges of the Supreme Court of the States, which declared that all States have an obligation to grant marriage licenses to same-sex couples under the Fourteenth Amendment to the United States Constitution.

Before the sentence, equal marriage was already recognized by 37 states and the federal capital.

Previously, on June 26, 2013, the United States Supreme Court repealed the Defense of Marriage Act and Proposition 8 that prohibited same-sex marriages, making it legal in the state of California.

Although previously same-sex marriages had been legalized in California between June 16, 2008 and November 4, 2008, after which Proposition 8 was passed, prohibiting these marriages; Despite that, the proposition maintains the recognition of the unions made.

In all States, legalization has been achieved through judicial sentences, through legislation, and through referendums. As of May 2013, nine states prohibited same-sex marriage through statutes, and another thirty through the constitution of their States.

The social movement to obtain the rights and responsibilities of marriage in the United States for same-sex couples began in the early 1970s. The issue became prominent in American politics in the 1990s, especially once Congress passed the Defense of Marriage Act in 1996.

During the first decade of the 21st century, public opinion for legalization grew considerably, and current polls show that most Americans support same-sex marriage.

What do Latin American countries say about homosexuality?

Taking Wikipedia as a source, we consulted its entry on the subject in relation to Latin American countries: "In Latin America, the laws that affect lesbian, gay, bisexual, and transgender (LGBT) people, vary considerably by country or territory.

The treatment of homosexuality is very uneven in the region, and although machismo and homophobia still prevail in some countries, there are other laws where there have been numerous advances, some of which are among the most progressive and tolerant in the world.

There is a great difference between Latin American penal codes and that of the countries of the Caribbean region. While homosexuality is decriminalized throughout Latin America, in several of the small Caribbean states it is still illegal and condemned with various prison terms.

In some countries there is discrimination that the age of sexual consent is different for homosexuals and the rest of the population, as in the Bahamas, Chile, Paraguay and Suriname. Along with this, several countries have adopted legislation to specifically condemn discrimination and assault suffered on the grounds of sexual orientation and gender identity.

On the other hand, when it comes to civil codes, although projects have been presented in several countries, few states have yet passed laws that allow civil unions and same-sex marriage. In Chile they have legally recognized civil unions, granting rights similar to those of marriage.

Likewise, homosexual marriage is legal in Ecuador, and homosexual adoption in some states of Mexico, and throughout Argentina, Brazil, Colombia, and Uruguay. Costa Rica and the Cayman Islands offer some rights of coexistence for same-sex couples, without being legally registered as a union.

Costa Rica will legalize same-sex marriage and homo-parental adoption throughout its territory by May 2020, following a binding IACHR ruling in 2018.

What does the bible say about homosexuality?

God sent a discipline or rule to all human beings, on the sexual relationship of humanity through his servant Moses, and it was as follows: "And if a man lie with his daughter in law, both of them shall surely be put to death: they have wrought confusion; their blood shall be upon them»: [Leviticus 20:12].

"If a man goes to bed with a man as if with a woman, both of them have committed an abomination; they will be put to death; their blood is on them": [Leviticus 20:13 Kadosh Bible].

This last version is much clearer in english, but both have used the same expression «abomination». All those who have known the nakedness of a person of the same sex, must be condemned to death, because God has not created any man to know the other as a woman, God has never created any relationship of the same sex, they are two different sexes that can cohabit intimately.

Why has God used the expression "abomination" about homosexuality?

It is a strong rejection and condemnation of something that causes revulsion. It has three key words that are: rejection, condemnation, and revulsion. That crime is very disgusting and nauseating to Jehovah, the abomination has received three sentences before Jehovah's eyes, that's why Jehovah ordered that all those who have practiced that crime should receive the death penalty.

The great architect of the universe did not create two Adam or two Eve in the Garden of Eden, God created a man and a woman with a mandate to be productive on the face of the earth. Its mandate is to multiply, bear fruit and fill the earth with its offspring.

For what reason did God completely destroy the cities of Sodom and Gomorrah?

God revealed Moses because he eradicated those two cities from the face of the earth, he said: «And he pressed upon them greatly; and they turned in unto him, and entered into his house; and he made them a feast, and did bake unleavened bread, and they did eat.

But before they lay down, the men of the city, even the men of Sodom, compassed the house round, both old and young, all the people from every quarter: And they called unto Lot, and said unto him, Where are the men which came in to thee this night? bring them out unto us, that we may know them»: [Genesis 19: 3-5].

Not only were they wicked, they wanted to know sexually even the angels that God had sent to destroy those two cities. The corruptions, the iniquities, the evils, the crimes, the immoralities, arrive until before the throne of God. They were so wicked that even the angels of destruction wanted to satisfy their sexual pleasures.

God destroyed those two cities for homosexuality, where men were meeting other men, women as women, humans with animals. God made the decision to remove them completely, to the root. There is a limit where man can get, God had to make a decision.

Prophet Ezekiel said: «Behold, this was the iniquity of thy sister Sodom, pride, fulness of bread, and abundance of idleness was in her and in her daughters, neither did she strengthen the hand of the poor and needy. And they were haughty, and committed abomination before me: therefore I took them away as I saw good»: [Ezekiel 16: 49-50].

Transsexuality is also abominable in the eyes of God, anyone who has committed such deadly sins in the eyes of God should die, Jehovah of armies said. Because man was not created to change his sex, nor to know different types of sexes. All those who have practiced these vices should receive the death penalty according to the bible.

Prostitution is a sin before God and humanity. God has created women especially to please her husband, not to please others, nor can her body be sold like a supermarket commodity. Because God gave a warning in the seventh commandment to all human flesh, dijo: "Thou shall not commit adultery": [Exodus 20:14].

Neither for pleasure nor for sale, only his own spouse who can meet you or discover your nakedness, nobody else.

Zoophilia

What do professionals say about zoophilia?

Oscar Castillero Mimenza, Barcelona Psychologist and editor specialized in Clinical Psychology, commented on the following in psychology and mind page, about that infrahuman instinct incubated as a larva in the human mind: «Passion, flame, desire, attraction... these words refer to the experience of sensuality and sexuality.

This experience or its absence is a very important aspect of the human being. Even at an academic level, authors such as Sigmund Freud have investigated the importance of libido as one of the fundamental elements (in his case the most important) of the psyche and human behavior.

Human sexuality is broad and complex, with great diversity in the type of stimuli that provoke the desire of individuals.

We may like one person or another, awaken the desire for certain characteristics that others dislike, or it may even motivate us to try to maintain relationships in different ways than we normally use.

Regardless of this, as a general rule, the object of desire or what we are attracted to is a human being with sufficient capacity and physical and mental maturity to establish relationships. However, there are people whose experience of sexuality includes an object of atypical desire, in some cases even illegal and harmful to themselves or others.

Within this group we can find people who maintain carnal relationships with living beings of other animal species other than humans: people who practice zoophilia.

What causes zoophilic behavior?

Psychologist Mimenza adds about zoophilic behavior, he said: "Although its exact prevalence is not known (those who have a paraphilia do not usually admit it), this disorder, classified as unspecified paraphilia, is not frequent in the general population.

The mechanism that causes a human being to establish in beings of other species his object of sexual desire, is not yet known.

As with the rest of paraphilias, it has been proposed that it may be due to a chance association between sexual and animal arousal. This association would be the result of chance or the sublimation of sexual affective needs, and in the face of repeated practice it could become a disorder and a fixation on the other being, which would culminate in identifying it as an object of desire.

The practices of zoophilias usually occur in isolated and difficult to access areas, generally in rural areas. In this type of environment, human contact can be very limited, while access to livestock and other animals is relatively simple. This is one of the common characteristics among people with zoophilia: loneliness and isolation.

Another common characteristic in these subjects that could help explain the problem is the presence of a low level of social skills, which cause a high level of frustration and which in some people may cause the need to vent unsatisfied desire and mood discomfort.

If you add to all this the emotional union that exists between a pet or farm animal and its owner or the person who takes care of them, the person may feel a special connection that can lead to a sexual desire principle, and even humanize the animal. This theory would be supported in this case.

In addition, many individuals with this problem indicate that animals give them a higher level of affection and loyalty than other people. Apart from this, some cultures and beliefs may facilitate the presence of this disorder, and in certain mental disorders behaviors of this type may appear secondary.

What does the Bible say about zoophilia?

The creator gave a great warning about that great crime where humanity made its own decision or choice to come in the sexual relationship with animals, Moses said: "And if a man lie with a beast, he shall surely be put to death: and ye shall slay the beast.

And if a woman approach unto any beast, and lie down thereto, thou shalt kill the woman, and the beast: they shall surely be put to death; their blood shall be upon them": [Leviticus 20: 15-16].

The Kadosh bible has explained zoophilia more clearly than the King James Version. His version proposes it as follows: "If a man has sex with an animal, he will be put to death, and the animal will be killed. If a woman approaches an animal, and is related, her blood will be on them": [Leviticus 20: 15-16].

This intimacy can cause many diseases, because when human ejaculation mixes with that of the animal, it cannot become a baby or an animal, it automatically transforms into some deadly viruses. For that reason, there are so many diseases that are tearing humanity apart.

Although they want to put animals in men's places, that will never happen, because man has morals, feelings and thoughts, animals have instincts, they react by their instincts, nobody can fall low enough to be equal to or worse than animals. They are two totally different creatures, each one has its kingdom.

After all these strange things that are happening in the world, it could be said that there is no solution for the human race, because men have gone too far in the eyes of God.

Man, who has been created in the image of God, reaches this low level, worse than animals. As Far as God destroyed Sodom and Gomorrah, it is shortly before the aberrations of this century.

Has everyone lost faith in the human race?

Of course not, there is still hope for all those who confess and accept Christ Jesus as their only personal savior. Jesus gave you and me advice, he said: «I counsel thee to buy of me gold tried in the fire, that thou mayest be rich; and white raiment, that thou mayest be clothed, and that the shame of thy nakedness do not appear; and anoint thine eyes with eyesalve, that thou mayest see.

As many as I love, I rebuke and chasten: be zealous therefore, and repent. Behold, I stand at the door, and knock: if any man hear my voice, and open the door, I will come in to him, and will sup with him, and he with me»: [Revelation 3: 18-20].

Why has God not destroyed all the people who are practicing these crimes?

By the blood of Jesus Christ. Jesus bought and paid us with his own life and blood on Calvary's cross. For that reason, the great buyer is calling all those people who have made any mistake, before the door of grace closes. Why did he say if someone hears my voice? Because he knows very clearly, humanity is very ungrateful, he always wants to be with the wrong person who is harming him.

Although man falls so low before Jehovah's eyes, he has another chance to be saved, Jesus never stopped calling man with the voice of the Holy Spirit and conscience. He is doing that work until the last minute of the closing of the door of grace. The big problem is that nobody knows when death will knock on your door with an accident or illness.

The blood of Jesus has the power to cleanse even the most sadistic crimes, zoophilia, homosexuality and lesbianism, the Holy Spirit has the power to be reborn again. But for that to happen, they must listen to and heed the call of the Holy Spirit.

There are two things that can happen when Jesus is playing:

1.- Vices do not allow us to listen to the voice of the good Master.

2.- The conformist does not allow us to open our hearts to Christ. Jesus respects the decision of each one, he cannot enter by force, if we do not want to open it. Never forget we only have one chance today, because nobody knows tomorrow.

Chapter 30

Assaults and abuse in the home

What is aggression?

It is an action whose objective is to cause physical or mental harm. Aggression can be normal and is only an indicator of an underlying illness when feelings become excessive and absorbing and interfere with daily life.

Also Violent action carried out by a person with the intention of causing harm to another. You can define it as an action that is contrary to the physical integrity of a person.

Turning again to the expert in clinical psychology, Oscar Castillero Mimenza, who lists eighteen types of assaults.

The types of attacks according to their nature

There are multiple ways to classify the different types of assaults that exist. One of the most common is the one that takes into account the nature of the aggression. In turn, these can be classified into two large groups, although in general the categories are not totally mutually exclusive.

1.1. Direct assault

Direct aggression is called any type of aggression that is carried out perceptibly for the person attacked, whether it is on a physical or psychological level. This includes both the direct exercise of the aggression and the threat of carrying it out, requiring at least an aggressor and assaulted in said relationship. The assaulted is fully capable of identifying his attacker. From adolescence, it tends to be more frequent in males.

1.2. Physical aggression

Any act that involves the voluntary and intentional causation of direct damage generated through any physical means and with the capacity to generate bodily harm to the person attacked. The injuries caused can be temporary or permanent and appear both in the short and long term, with consequences that can even be fatal.

Physical aggression tends to be more associated with the male sex.

1.3. Verbal/psychological assault

It is understood as such any set of acts and actions that, although they do not generate harm on a physical level, they do cause or seek to cause some type of mental or emotional harm to the person suffering from the aggression. Includes insults, humiliations and devaluations.

In this sense, this type of direct violence is usually more divided between the sexes. Statistically, it is one of the most practiced by women.

1.4. Sexual assault

Type of assault in which the attacking party forces or coerces the attacked party to maintain some type of sexual contact (whether or not there is penetration) or deprive them of the freedom to decide. Includes both rapes such as fingering, pushing or removing the condom without consent/knowledge of the fact.

Although female cases have increased in recent years, most sex offenders are male.

1.5. Indirect assault

Indirect aggression is understood as any act of aggression that is carried out indirectly, causing damages to the attacked anonymously (although he may recognize the aggressor). This type of attack is spreading more and more, and it is the most frequent in women from adolescence, both academically and at work.

It includes the spread of rumors and slanders, anonymous or publication of websites and demeaning and ridiculing messages.

1.6. Relational aggression

Indirect form of aggression based on the social exclusion of the attacked person, or on the accusation of damage to his reputation through slander. It is usually verbal or psychological.

1.7. Cyber aggression

Although it can be included in some of the previous groups (both indirect and direct), cyber aggression has as its main distinguishing feature the fact that information and communication technologies are used for it.

Through it we can find attacks on social networks, impersonations, coercion, account theft, defamatory publications, non-consensual recordings (including that of possible assaults carried out with the victim), etc.

1.8. Property assault

This type of aggression is based on the destruction or damage to the possessions of the attacked person. Its subtraction or usurpation can also be observed. It may or may not be aimed at generating damage to the attacked subject, especially if said possessions are of high emotional value or obtaining them has been a great effort.

In reality, it can be both indirect and direct (since the destruction can take place covertly or not).

1.9. Symbolic aggression

Type of indirect aggression characterized by the fact that the attack is not carried out directly on the victim, but on elements that symbolize aspects related to him or her such as religion, politics, sexual orientation or nationality.

2. Types of attacks according to their objective

In addition to the main aggressions mentioned above, we can also find other types of aggression depending on the objective they pursue.

2.1. Hostile aggression

This type of aggression refers to all that action aimed mainly at inflicting some type of damage on a person, so that damage is the main objective of the aggressor.

2.2. Instrumental assault

On this occasion, the aggressive act is not intended to cause harm to the person attacked, not being the suffering or discomfort of the other what is intended, but what motivates the attack is obtaining some kind of profit or benefit from said attack.

An example may be economic gain, social approval, or the acquisition of a position of domination and power.

2.3. Induced assault

It is a type of aggressive act in which the aggressor acts moved by other people or by factors such as fear or the attempt to escape from a highly threatening situation.

3. Types of aggression depending on the victim

Different types of aggression can also be observed depending on who the person is who is targeting the act of violence.

3.1. Self-inflicted assault

As such, any act of aggression in which the person who is the victim of the same is the one who causes the aggression. In other words, it is an attack on oneself that can be motivated by many causes. It can include self-harm caused by people with different pathologies or suicide.

3.2. Interpersonal aggression

It is the most classic and well-known type of aggression, in which one person inflicts damages on another voluntarily.

3.3. Collective assault

Type of aggression characterized by being carried out in an intergroup way, attacking one group against another. The objective of the aggression can be variable, in many cases with hatred, stigmatization and attempts to eliminate the other group. In this type of aggression we could include events as serious as genocides.

4. Types of aggression according to the context in which it occurs

Another possible classification of assaults may come from the context in which they occur. In this sense, we can find among others with the following:

4.1. Intra-family and partner aggression

This type of interpersonal aggression can be separated from the rest, due to the fact that it has the characteristic of occurring within the same family or between people who in principle maintain an emotional bond.

Intra-family violence can take many forms, being mainly of a direct type, whether at the level of physical, psychological or even sexual aggression.

4.2. Aggression in the workplace

All that act of aggression produced in the context of work. We can include in this the presence of physical, verbal or even sexual assaults between employees with the same rank or those that take advantage of the difference in rank and position within the company.

4.3. Aggression at school

On this occasion we refer to acts of aggression carried out in the academic environment between students or between students and teachers. A very popular modality among adolescents is "bullying".

The psychologist Mimenza gave a good explanation about all the attacks that a person can receive at home, in the church or on the street. The victim cannot go without the complaint with the authorized persons, all the aggressors must be punished according to the law.

We are all human and nobody has the right to attack anyone, everyone has the right, there are three more frequent assaults within marriages: verbal, physical and sexual.

There are many women who incite their spouses to mistreat her with these three types of assaults when they are intimate, since sadomasochism is an aberrant form of pleasure through pain. The emotion of sexuality does not go that far.

Sex is an act that humans must do very gently and with great delicacy, with many sensations, so that the two can enjoy that sweet moment very richly.

But it is the moment that will ask for the intensity. No one should use aggression in sexual intercourse, not even animals use aggression when they are copulating.

What does the bible say about assaults?

God has used many authors of the bible to treat and solve that great virus that is attacking the homes of Christians, that problem affected most of the first believers and continued to make its way to this day. Each one saw the problem of aggression or violence in a different way.

The apostle James said: "Wherefore, my beloved brethren, let every man be swift to hear, slow to speak, slow to wrath: For the wrath of man worketh not the righteousness of God": [James 1: 19-20].

The followers of God must be very quiet, they must take the time to speak, they must analyze everything they are going to say so as not to aggravate the situation, if possible they must leave for a moment, until the other half it returns to normal, if the two are in an uncontrollable situation, their reaction must be silence.

All men should know that the nature of women is to talk a lot. We must reduce our anger to zero in order to control any situation.

The apostle Paul gave a good initiative on the aggressions, he said: "Let all bitterness, and wrath, and anger, and clamour, and evil speaking, be put away from you, with all malice: And be ye kind one to another, tenderhearted, forgiving one another, even as God for Christ's sake hath forgiven you": [Ephesians 4: 31-32].

In order for us to have that quality as a wise and intelligent man, we must walk far from the fruits of aggression. Because no home can be sustained by verbal or physical aggression. No man has ever married a slave, or an animal, even animals have rights in this life, no one has the right to mistreat them under any conditions.

Before generating aggression, you should think about the wedding vow that we made and signed before the pastor, where we must love and care for each other at all times.

The wise Solomon talks about family assault too, he said: "He that is slow to anger is better than the mighty; and he that ruleth his spirit than he that taketh a city": [Proverbs 16:32]. "He that is slow to wrath is of great understanding: but he that is hasty of spirit exalteth folly": [Proverbs 14:29].

"The discretion of a man deferreth his anger; and it is his glory to pass over a transgression": [Proverbs 19:11]. «A soft answer turneth away wrath: but grievous words stir up anger»: [Proverbs 15: 1].

It is the qualities of the man within the home that allows the couple to be out of all aggressions, although sometimes women provoke it. There are many men who physically attack their partners in self-defense, but they must not do so, they must remain silent to avoid such a situation.

Married people should know that they are two sexes and two different temperaments. Neither one should try to understand the other, because that will never happen, the two should try to love each other without malice. All gentlemen should know that ladies have been specially created to be loved and protected from their husband.

Every married and future married person must learn this by heart, fall in love with a body, marry a temperament, no one can change the temperament of others, if you want to be happy, accustomed to what you have chosen.

The man as head of the house must try to maintain good communication, friendship between the two, if he wants to have a successful family.

The apostle Paul made it very clear about this great phenomenon that is affecting almost all families.

He said: «Mortify therefore your members which are upon the earth; fornication, uncleanness, inordinate affection, evil concupiscence, and covetousness, which is idolatry: For which things' sake the wrath of God cometh on the children of disobedience: In the which ye also walked some time, when ye lived in them.

But now ye also put off all these; anger, wrath, malice, blasphemy, filthy communication out of your mouth. Lie not one to another, seeing that ye have put off the old man with his deeds; and have put on the new man, which is renewed in knowledge after the image of him that created him»: [Colossians 3: 5-10].

The apostle Paul as a faithful servant of God was in favor of the family, although you have never married, because he clearly knew that without a unity family, it is impossible to acquire a good formation. God is totally in favor of the institution of marriage, because it is the nest where individuals take all the good formations.

For that reason, the enemy is strongly attacking this institution so that no child can take a dignified, solid and strong formation to attack all the plots of life.

All assaults come from the passions together with the bad desires that produce anger, anger, annoyance, anger, displeasure and blasphemy: all these fruits are fed within the individual's heart daily, producing dishonest words and actions. There are two hierarchical visions that produce this great onslaught on the individual, and they are: superiority and inferiority.

Each member of the family must be against these two expressions that are contaminating almost all the roots of the home. Both are contrary to love, peace and happiness. Superiority and inferiority are the two words that can lead every household to ultimate failure.

But if the average equality, a good understanding can be reached between the two, when there is union between all the members of the family, there will never be a failure in any way.

Chapter 31

The couple's separation and divorce

Divorce is a demonic tool that the enemy has found very useful in destroying any family. The hand that signs it is always Satan's. The divorce has begun since before the courtship, that expression comes from the unequal relationship and the unequal yoke, two factors that are against the good progress of that institution.

Divorce is the dissolution of marriage, while, in a broad sense, it refers to the process that is intended to end a conjugal union; it is a legal dissolution of a marriage, at the request of one or both spouses, when the causes provided by law occur. It can also be said that it is a separation of things or people that are or should be united or related.

What do professionals say about divorce?

Marcel Gratacós comments on the page [lifeder.com], about the factors that cause this virus in the family. He said there are ten factors that produce this phenomenon: "The most common causes of divorce are lack of commitment, over-arguing, unrealistic expectations, lack of equality in the relationship, abuse, financial problems, or lack of problem-solving skills.

Divorce is a growing phenomenon that is increasingly present in our society. In fact, in recent years there has been both a gradual decrease in marriages and an increase in divorces.

Divorce Concept. Couple Having Trouble In Their Marriage.Different, is a study that shows how separations and divorces have increased by around 25% during the last five years. Likewise, the data provided from the United States show how between 40 and 60% of marriages end in divorce.

These data show how romantic relationships are highly complex. Likewise, it becomes clear that it is becoming increasingly difficult to maintain marriages and avoid divorces. Why does this happen? What is the reason for this trend that has been experienced in recent years? What factors cause the separations?

All of these questions are becoming highly relevant in the study of marital relationships. For this reason, we are finding more and more research and more data that try to answer the reasons for separation.

The ten most common causes in divorce

1.- Lack of commitment

Lack of commitment is the factor that has been most prevalent between divorces and separations. Specifically, a recent study conducted in Utah city showed that 73% of people who had divorced pointed to lack of commitment as the leading cause.

If we analyze the characteristics of couple relationships and marriages, it is evident that commitment is an indispensable aspect. Without the will to commit, it is highly difficult to maintain any type of relationship, much less a conjugal one.

Thus, it is observed how many couples decide to get married without being sufficiently committed. This fact translates practically automatically into divorce in subsequent years. Today there is a high consensus in cataloging the lack of commitment as the main cause of divorce. In this way, it is shown that attitudes are more relevant than isolated behaviors in maintaining a marriage.

2.- Excessive discussions

The second cause that has been associated with marital breakdowns is over-arguing. The data indicates that this factor is notably lower than the lack of commitment but higher than the rest. Specifically, the study discussed above revealed how 56% of divorce cases argue over-arguing as a cause of separation.

Likewise, Dr. William H. Doherty comments that when arguments prevail in a marital relationship, the probabilities of divorce increase very high. If we analyze this factor, we can see how excessive arguments can be more of a symptom than a cause in itself. That is, the fact that a marriage is constantly arguing may be a sign that something is wrong. In fact, many experts carry out this type of interpretation on this factor.

In this way, the excess of discussions can reveal other types of problems such as lack of coordination, poor communication, inability to solve problems or different interests within the couple. However, it is clear that discussions are one of the most delicate aspects within marriage. This does not mean that for a marriage to work you should never argue. Discussions are considered normal and necessary in many cases.

However, they must be productive and controlled. When the couple loses control of the arguments, the probability of divorce becomes very high.

3.- Infidelity

This is probably the factor that people most relate to divorces and separations. For many people these behaviors are the most inadmissible within the couple and those that can more easily motivate a breakup.

However, despite the fact that this view is widely spread in today's society, the data shows how, in practice, infidelity falls to the third position in the list of causes of divorce. Most studies indicate that this factor motivates between 50 and 55% of all divorce cases. Thus, despite not being the main cause, its incidence is highly relevant.

However, the study of this cause presents a series of discrepancies. First of all, a study showed that 90% of the American population affirmed that infidelity is a morally inadmissible act. Thus, the attitude of society about this phenomenon seems to be quite clear.

Likewise, as already mentioned, infidelity can cause more than half of divorces. However, only 2% of the American population claimed to have been unfaithful to their partner. This fact shows that infidelity is more individual behavior than that of a couple, so it is subject to highly uncontrollable variables.

4.- Getting married too young

Today there is a high consensus that marriage is a complex type of relationship. In this sense, getting married too young has been shown to be a risk factor for divorce. The data shows that 46% of the separations indicate this fact as one of the main causes. Thus, marriages that take place at an early age are more likely to fail.

The fact that getting married too young is one of the main causes of divorce lies in the conditions on which the relationship is established. In this way, couples who are not well established and consolidated before marriage may not be sufficiently prepared for marriage.

Many experts relate this factor to the level of commitment and attitudes towards marriage. Marriages "hasty" or performed early in the relationship may have fewer options for developing a satisfactory commitment.

Similarly, young people would be more likely not to have the personal maturity necessary to assume the marriage and be consistent in their relationship.

5.- Unrealistic expectations

Marriage represents a remarkable change in people's lives, since it implies a change in lifestyle. In this way, just as happens with any vital change, personal expectations about the new situation are highly relevant. In order to adapt well to a new situation, it is necessary that what is expected be related to what is witnessed.

Otherwise, more adaptive effort and a change in expectations will be necessary. When this does not happen, it is often very difficult to accept and be comfortable with the change that has occurred. This situation is clearly reflected in divorces, which is why having unrealistic expectations is postulated as a major cause of divorce.

In the Utah study it was noted that 45% of divorce cases postulated this factor as an important cause of separation.

Thus, having idyllic and excessively utopian expectations about the future within the marriage can call into question the relationship. In these cases, if the spouses fail to adapt their expectations to their behavior and the functioning of the couple, the marriage may fail.

6.- Lack of equality in the relationship

The establishment of roles and roles is one of the main factors that determines the quality of personal relationships. In the case of couples and, above all, marriages, this element must have certain characteristics.

Regardless of many other variables that may be important in each case, equality is usually a common element in most marriages. Establishing an unequal marriage, in which one of the spouses has a more important role than the other in the relationship, is usually a negative factor.

The conception of marriage has changed markedly in recent years. Relationships in which one of the members assumes a dominant role and the other a submissive role constitutes a currently little approved model. This fact is evidenced in the data on the causes of divorce.

In 44% of cases, the lack of equality in the relationship is postulated as the cause of the separation.

7.-Inability to resolve conflicts

Believing that for a relationship to work, there must be zero conflicts is often a misperception. The study of personal relationships has shown that the appearance of conflicts between two or more individuals is a practically inevitable fact. Being able to agree on everything is an idyllic but often unattainable situation.

In this sense, the ability to resolve conflicts as a couple stands as a factor almost as important as managing to avoid discrepancies.

Thus, the key to every couple is to develop basic rules so that each member of the couple feels respected and listened to. In many cases, this can be accomplished through the relationship's own mechanisms. However, in cases where this does not happen, it is important to incorporate a third element.

Couples therapy can be a very useful tool to learn to resolve conflicts and develop the necessary skills to manage complicated situations. If these problems are not remedied, the discussions may gradually increase and the risk of separation may increase.

8.- Abuse

Abuse in marriage requires special consideration. In this sense, there are behaviors that are clearly outside the moral limits of marriage. All people have the right to be physically, emotionally and sexually safe within marriage and any other type of personal relationship. This fact includes both adults and children, and both spouses and children.

It is not the objective of this article to examine the characteristics of this type of behavior but to highlight its relationship with divorces.

Unfortunately, abuse is a relatively common phenomenon in marriages today. This is shown by the data that shows that 29% of divorces could be caused by this factor. These data shown by the Utah national study are too high and expose a clear social problem and a major difficulty of current marital relations.

9.- Lack of individual identity

The intimacy and proximity of marital relationships can cause a loss of individual identity. In this way, the depersonalized connection in the couple can cause the development of a common identity that destroys the identity of each individual.

This fact can occur to a greater or lesser extent and can affect the relationship to different degrees.

However, in some cases the loss of individual identity can have a negative impact on the couple and cause conflicts. So sometimes this factor can increase the probability of divorce. On the other side of the coin, we find another situation that can also negatively affect marriage. This situation deals with the development of important discrepancies in the priorities and individual interests of each of the spouses.

In these cases, having very distant needs and preferences can break the stability of the relationship and call it into question. In fact, many couples therapists emphasize the importance of maintaining common attitudes and priorities for the proper functioning of marital relationships.

10.- Economic problems

It is not usual for marriages to fail due to lack of money or financial difficulties. However, the lack of compatibility between spouses in the financial field is usually a much more important problem. In this sense, a marriage in which the members present opposite levels of life, can present greater difficulties to function properly.

In fact, if a marriage with these characteristics fails to properly manage their differences, over time the conflict can reach such heights that divorce seems to be the most logical solution.

What do American psychologists say about divorce?

Drake Baer, from Thrive Global, publishes on November 20, 2017 on the page [expansion.mx] about the divorce. According to the psychologist there are five factors that can cause this problem.

Like divorces themselves, divorce rates are a difficult subject to study. Questions abound: do we really want divorce rates to drop? Is it true that about half of all marriages in the United States end in divorce? Why are so many baby boomers suddenly deciding to end their relationship?

There are also questions about the factors that predict a divorce, a complex line of research that Justin Lehmiller, associate professor at Ball State University in the United States, recently analyzed on his blog Sex & Psychology. Although there is little literature on many of the aspects, some have emerged in various studies.

Age does matter. Couples who take longer to marry often have longer relationships. The younger the members are when they marry, the greater the risk that they will divorce later. It is interesting that the same thing happens with couples who decide to live together when they are very young (teenagers, for example).

Advertising

Demographic aspects also matter. According to data from the Centers for Disease Control and Prevention, both educational level and religion are powerful indicators of the durability of relationships.

Women with a bachelor's degree have a 78% chance that their marriage will last twenty years, compared to 41% of women who studied high school alone. In the case of men, this proportion is 65 and 57%, respectively.

Furthermore, the duration of the relationships of people who consider themselves religious is longer in a similar proportion.

A personality trait makes things particularly difficult: neurosis (or emotional instability) is a personality trait that indicates how sensitive you are to what you perceive as threatening and how likely you are to become obsessed with it. It has to do with anxiety and depression disorders and, as Lehmiller indicates, has been repeatedly shown to predict divorce.

Infidelity definitely doesn't help. This is not exactly surprising. When people cheat on their partner, as documented in a 17-year longitudinal study, involving almost 1,500 people, infidelity causes less marital happiness, as well as a greater feeling of "proclivity for divorce" and a higher incidence of separations.

It is important to note that these are all correlations, even in cases of infidelity. These studies cannot definitively indicate what causes a divorce. This can be known with more specific research.

Over the past forty years, John Gottman, pioneer of relationship research and author of the book "The Seven Principles to Make Marriage Work" (among many other books on the subject), has unraveled the mysteries of what it makes a relationship work or not.

Number one killer, as stated in the lab and in the therapist's office, is contempt, things that indicate that you dislike your partner and that are super toxic for a relationship, such as hostile humor, nicknames, and expressions of annoyance.

But there are still hopes: if you want your relationship to last, from being kind to your partner. It's that simple.

In this, the opinions of professionals in the United States are similar to those of their colleagues in Europe. All professionals around the world almost have the same opinion. But the majority of American citizens are divorced. Also divorce is much easier in the USA. They fall in love for any reason, marry and divorce without reason.

The failure of children does not depend on the parents, also the civil law professionals are guilty, because they do not see or think of any child, only in their money, in their interest.

What does the Bible say about the disunities of the mundanes?

The apostle Paul said: "But if the unbelieving depart, let him depart. A brother or a sister is not under bondage in such cases: but God hath called us to peace": [1 Corinthians 7:15].

As unbelievers, they can do their will, since they do not know God or his principles, they can receive divorce letters at any time. They can get married and divorced and, although that institution was blessed by God, He does not recognize all kinds of marriages. Furthermore, they have their own gods and lifestyle, so it stands to reason that they act accordingly.

Divorce within the people of God

The prophet Jeremiah said: «The Lord said also unto me in the days of Josiah the king, Hast thou seen that which backsliding Israel hath done? she is gone up upon every high mountain and under every green tree, and there hath played the harlot.

And I said after she had done all these things, Turn thou unto me. But she returned not. And her treacherous sister Judah saw it. And I saw, when for all the causes whereby backsliding Israel committed adultery I had put her away, and given her a bill of divorce; yet her treacherous sister Judah feared not, but went and played the harlot also.

And it came to pass through the lightness of her whoredom, that she defiled the land, and committed adultery with stones and with stocks»: [Jeremiah 3: 6-9].

Jesus answered the Pharisees about divorce as follows, he said: And he answered and said unto them, Have ye not read, that he which made them at the beginning made them male and female, and said, for this cause shall a man leave father and mother, and shall cleave to his wife: and they twain shall be one flesh? Wherefore they are no more twain, but one flesh.

What therefore God hath joined together, let not man put asunder. They say unto him, Why did Moses then command to give a writing of divorcement, and to put her away? He saith unto them, Moses because of the hardness of your hearts suffered you to put away your wives: but from the beginning it was not so.

And I say unto you, Whosoever shall put away his wife, except it be for fornication, and shall marry another, committeth adultery: and whoso marrieth her which is put away doth commit adultery: [Matthew 19: 4-9].

For one reason heaven allowed married people to disown their partners: fornication and adultery, because married people never wanted to have a single partner. To stop this situation within the people of God, Moses had to make that great decision to separate or disunite them, although it is not God's will.

"And Jesus answered and said unto them, For the hardness of your heart he wrote you this precept": [Mark 10: 5].

This commandment was not written for couples who respect their relationships, who are faithful at all times, this law was written especially for all those who like infidelity and who like to cheat on their partners, all those who respect their partners, They are free from the Curse of Divorce.

What does Jesus think about divorce in the Christian family?

He answering said to them: "Have you not read that he who made them in the beginning made them male and female, and said: "For this reason a man will leave his father and mother and be united to his wife, and the two will become one flesh? So they are no longer two, but one flesh; therefore what God has joined together, let not man separate": [Matthew 5: 4-6].

Jesus asked two questions to married Jews about disunity, he continues to ask the same questions to married people of this century. Every future divorce must think very carefully about Jesus' response before carrying out the disunity.

If the couple formed a single flesh within the marriage, there should be no separation between the two, a body separated in half cannot continue living, it automatically becomes death, all believers who have disunited with a divorce letter, have emotionally and morally dead.

All married people must fight day and night to save their marriage, because they will not be the only ones destroyed, but also their children. Divorce is a curse to the entire human race.

What does the bible say about bigamy?

"Whosoever putteth away his wife, and marrieth another, committeth adultery: and whosoever marrieth her that is put away from her husband committeth adultery": [Luke 16:18].

All people who have divorced and remarried to someone else are in adultery, because God does not know two marriages. All those who want to free themselves from the curse of divorce, should take enough time to get to know their partner well before joining in marriage.

Nor does God bless all kinds of marriages, they must meet the criteria of the bible before receiving the blessing of heaven in the sacred vows, so there are no longer two, but one being. Therefore, what God has joined, let no one separate. So they are no longer two, but one flesh.

Can a divorced person remarry?

There was a similar problem to our present time with the Romans, they wanted to give divorce letters to their partners. God had to intervene through the apostle Paul to give a solution to this problem. It is the same thing that is happening in our current membership: they are marrying like unbelievers, and in the same way they are divorcing.

We do not have an apostle Paul to intervene, sometimes the shepherds are more corrupt than their subjects, the only solution is the intervention of the Holy Spirit and the deep study of the Holy Bible.

The apostle Paul said: «For the woman which hath an husband is bound by the law to her husband so long as he liveth; but if the husband be dead, she is loosed from the law of her husband.

So then if, while her husband liveth, she be married to another man, she shall be called an adulteress: but if her husband be dead, she is free from that law; so that she is no adulteress, though she be married to another man». [Romans 7: 2-3].

There is only one way the individual can marry for a second and up to four times, if the married are dead, while they are alive, it cannot be disunited for any reason, because they have been united for life.

What does the apostle Paul say about bigamy?

Paul said: "And unto the married I command, yet not I, but the Lord, Let not the wife depart from her husband: But and if she depart, let her remain unmarried or be reconciled to her husband: and let not the husband put away his wife.

But to the rest speak I, not the Lord: If any brother hath a wife that believeth not, and she be pleased to dwell with him, let him not put her away": [1 Corinthians 7: 10-12].

Paul received a very clear message from the Lord for Christians who are married on different occasions. As the Bible says only for the reason of adultery they can give a divorce letter, but they must remain unmarried, and if for any reason they cannot continue with loneliness, they must reconcile again with their partners.

Nowhere in the Bible do we find that after divorce we can remarry if the couples are alive. All Christians who have married multiple times while their exes are alive are in adultery before God, and if they are in sin, they can never be part of the kingdom of heaven.

The divorce

Can earthly law disunite or divorce Jesus' disciples except through adultery or fornication? in no way, because Jesus said clearly in the Gospel of Mark: "And the two shall become one flesh'; so then they are no longer two, but one flesh. Therefore what God has joined together, let not man separate.": [Mark 10: 8-9].

If they have really been married by the Lord, no man can disunite them in any way, they can be divorced by humanity, but they are married before God. Marrying again means that you have two husbands or wives before the eyes of God.

The divorce letter

Can married believers give divorce letters to their husbands according to the bible? In no way. God says, again through the mouth of the apostle Paul, that they must be together until death: "The wife is bound by the law as long as her husband liveth; but if her husband be dead, she is at liberty to be married to whom she will; only in the Lord": [1 Corinthians 7:39].

The evangelist Marcos said: "And if a woman shall put away her husband, and be married to another, she committeth adultery". [Mark 10:12].

Similarly, no Christian woman should give her husband a divorce letter to remarry another man, as long as the repudiation is alive, if she is dead, she is free to marry again, if she did, she should be left alone, and if you can't bear it. Loneliness must return to her husband again.

The apostle pablo said: "And unto the married I command, yet not I, but the Lord, Let not the wife depart from her husband: But and if she depart, let her remain unmarried or be reconciled to her husband: and let not the husband put away his wife": [1 Corinthians 7:10-11].

There are many people who have taken the marriage union by a game, until there is a business marriage. Marriage is an institution blessed by God. No one can take that act lightly. No human can separate what God has united.

Can religious believers who have given a divorce letter and remarried to someone else hold a position in God's church? Never ever!, because they are in sin; Because the Bible says that all those divorced who have remarried with other people are in adultery, no adulterer will enter the kingdom of heaven if he has not repented.

There are high-ranking leaders within the church who have been divorced and remarried as a joke. Everyone should be removed as leaders. For that reason, no one should marry by emotion, without consulting God before that choice.

All those who have taken their own risks of taking that great responsibility on their own without God's will will end in failure for their entire lives.

What do the great researchers say about the cause of the divorce?

There is a group of researchers at the University of WTAH (USA) that has dedicated itself to deeply investigating that great calamity that is shaking the entire world. Its leader is sociologist Nick Wolfinger. After that great study, they found that the main cause of that problem is immaturity.

At the end of the investigation, the psychologist Nick published his results on the university page: "The ideal age to get married is between 28 and 32 years old."

At that age, both have the maturity and the economy to maintain any relationship, although there are people of that age who still think like minors, but it is not as frequent. According to the conclusions of this study, couples who marry in that age range divorce less than those who do so at other ages.

The author of the study, supported by statistics collected in the United States and data grouped into two stages - from 2006 to 2010 and 2011 to 2013 - compared the former with the latter.

The results showed that between 28 and 32 years of age there was a lower divorce rate, but that divorces increased for each year that moved further away from this last figure. That is, with 42 years there are more possibilities of divorce than with 35 years.

It seems that the idea was correct, because all those people who have married at a very young age, have a 70% chance of divorcing, because their minds are still enjoying pleasures in all categories, their minds scream to the four winds "we are young, we have to enjoy our time!", because immaturity is incapable of making commitments due to its own biological stage.

There are also many people who are professionals at a very young age, but a good economy combined with immaturity are insufficient to assume responsibilities.

Many think that it is good to have their children at an early age, but the reality is that they end up forming single-parent homes, living with men or women who become stepparents and stepmothers with the risks that this implies in terms of threat of sexual abuse or mistreatment for their children, or close to their parents.

Some conclusions of the study

If these data are confirmed, what are the causes? The author of the study states that it is highly likely that from 28 to 32 years of age is the ideal age "because at that age individuals have already reached a certain degree of maturity" both professionally and economically.

Although the Bible gives us the conditions to support a family to success, we must keep these factors in mind, so that the little ones can grow up strong, healthy and with a future ahead.

Actually, when a person takes his own responsibility to marry at that age, he is mature enough, emotional, sentimental, moral and spiritual, he already knows what he wants, where he wants to go. At that age, you may have enough resources to bring that relationship to a good position, although there are people at those ages who are more unsure than the younger ones.

I can say that scholars are absolutely right: getting married at an early age can cause immaturity, inexperience, problems in the economy, insecurity, disappointment with the very institution of marriage and not wanting to struggle more with that in the future, etc.

It is true that young people appear with a high degree of responsibility and commitment, but that is only the exception to the rule. And God is the rule, not his exception.

So, to avoid all those inconveniences, you should marry at a mature age, without excuses, so that you can face all the responsibilities of a good husband.

Chapter 32

The role of grandparents in the discipline and correction of grandchildren

Many couples think that the good education and training received from their parents will be transferred by default to their children.

They are very wrong, they are different times, the stage of parents who can give good guidance to their children, the stage of grandparents with principles, has been replaced by one of spoiled parents and grandparents.

Although birth parents should ideally be the best breeders. But the physical condition that a child can bear has nothing to do with an evolutionary vision of how to raise them.

Due to a lack of guidance and professionalism, the biological parents make incorrect decisions and leave the children in the hands of the grandparents to take care of them and educate them, because they have to go to find the daily food, precisely they are the mothers who have to support the children, sometimes parents too.

There are two things that can happen with grandparents.

On the one hand, because of their love for grandchildren, they will never educate their own children as equals. Second, it does not have the strength or the initiative to deal with the energy of the new generations.

They are the poor and unemployed grandparents who have time to care for the grandchildren, but all professional parents who work the same as their children will not have it. Neither friends or siblings can educate them. In this new time, they have searched for a wrong but equally necessary new strategy: paying a caregiver.

These spend more with them, establishing a closer bond than that of the parents.

We are so concerned with work that we neglect the teaching of the little ones. Do we know how the workers are taking care of them? The bad expressions you are listening to daily? The bad practices you are seeing daily? It is normal, everyone has to work, but the education of children is our priority too.

All those who take their own responsibilities to have children, have to take their own responsibilities for their education and teaching as well.

Children will have mirrors of the people who keep and care for them. What mirror do you want to be for your child? It is you who will choose what your children will be tomorrow.

Parenting Grandparents To Grandchildren

What do psychologists say about raising grandparents to grandchildren?

The vast majority of grandparents have spoiled their grandchildren, not because they are bad, but because of their love for them. Many grandparents take care of grandchildren while their children work.

Values are another thing, because although there are perennial principles of behavior and social, grandparents are not updated in the uses and changes of modern times, in which many of their customs are obsolete.

Because of that problem, they will not be able to educate the grandchildren, as they have educated their own children; for love they allow everything and consent to all the things they do, without having a proper correction.

Luciano Montero, director of psychology, expressed on the page [serpadres.es], he said: "Grandparents often make the mistake of being too permissive with grandchildren to earn their love, because they think that" to educate them, there are their parents."

Counterproductive attitude

1.- The problem is in the education and discipline that the parents try to instill in the children, it can come down because of an attitude of grandparents too tolerant of any whim of the little one.

Montero continues saying: "The child may feel confused if the grandparents disavow the parents, when they receive contradictory messages: from their parents and from their grandparents, with whom they spend many hours a day."

2.- If grandparents pamper their grandchild too much, it is best to talk to them alone, without the child in front of them. The author goes on to say: "In the conversation with the grandparents, first of all, we should commend their work and their effort to care for the grandson, and then diplomatically clarify the things they have failed at."

3.- Then, very tactfully, we can ask for help to unify the criteria when educating the child.

4.- It is convenient to explain how they should do things when they are with the grandson or the granddaughter by means of an example.

5.- A solution must be found that satisfies both parties so that the conflict does not occur again. If the grandparents do not follow the pact perfectly, there is no need to be overwhelmed either. Children distinguish who is who the family is, and know what is allowed with the grandmother may not be with the mother.

From my point of view, I think Montero is absolutely right. When grandparents are too permissive with children, they lose control of correcting them, when they are doing the wrong things, when they are not in the right lanes.

Their minds are being modified with everything they file in their memories, so that they are cunningly using the nobility of their grandparents to do whatever they want.

Excessive love and indulgence will prevent grandparents from taking control of that situation. They do not listen or pay attention to the old people, because they have no fear for them, when the grandparents speak they never listen to them or they ignore their mandates, they will live under the banner of their own decisions, that is until the parents return from work in the afternoon.

But fathers and mothers, be careful not to get lost in the fringe of television and laptop.

Psychologist Carla Pino reviewed about raising grandparents to grandchildren, she said thus: "It is the fault of the parents to let the education of our children get out of our hands, and fall on the grandparents, in this case the grandmother carries the whole load (she is a father, she is a mother and she is a grandmother).

Of course, if the grandmother lives in the same house, the situation is complex, because there is no complete freedom to make decisions about our children.

Psychologist Ana Paula Magosso Cavaggioni also commented on grandparents: "Parents have to be in the role of parents. From the moment they occupy that position, the grandparents will be able to occupy the one that corresponds to them, which is the place of grandparents.

In many cases, children stay with grandparents while parents work, making it difficult to identify the border of responsibilities.

Of course, spending a lot of time with children implies that grandparents are responsible for some activities with them. However, it is necessary that the parents decide what will be in charge of the grandparents and talk to them to find out if they agree.

The power to spoil

Ana Paula explains that parents must set rules and limits. Grandparents and other relatives do not have the power to spoil a child. Their relationship is not one of father and mother.

What can hurt the little ones is that the parents have not been able to establish clear rules and limits for the children at home, since, in this way, they will not have a firm reference to what is expected of them.

The starting point is the home itself. "Education and limits are given by parents in the family, at home," says psychologist Ana Paula. Also psychologist Ana Roselia Romero Valdez, explains very well on the same topic of parenting dynamics between grandparents, parents and grandchildren:

It is true that in these times parents must work countless hours to maintain the home. Having help in childcare is a huge relief, and if that help comes from our parents it's even better.

But what happens when grandparents give you everything they ask for? Do they give you all the toys they want? What if the parents have given him a punishment, he gets it up or they buy too many goodies?, because they don't know how to say no. That disavows parents before their children; grandparents do not put norms or rules... and so, an endless number of complaints that we sometimes hear parents say about these grandparents».

All the psychologists gave good explanations about the grandchildren's spoiling by grandparents while their children work.

Grandparents often make the mistake of being too permissive with grandchildren to earn their love; attitude that also has to do with their need for affection in their senile stage, since they find old age companions in the grandchildren, almost as if they were pets. They spend more time having fun with them than correcting them.

Cecilia Zinicola gave her opinion on July 26, 2017 on the page [es.aletias.org], about the bad parenting of the grandchildren. She said: "There is a famous saying that says" in the grandmother's house, every day is Sunday. "They can give you all tastes without having to suffer the consequences.

Is it an inalienable right of grandparents to spoil their grandchildren? To some extent yes. They have fulfilled their obligations and have now earned the comfortable job of "spoiling". The important thing is to have sensible and clear guidelines that everyone agrees to respect.

Why do grandchildren like to be with grandparents more than with their own parents?

If grandparents don't see their grandchildren much, they should definitely have more freedom to "spoil." There are cases in which grandparents live far away or for different reasons cannot meet regularly with their grandchildren, limiting their encounters to two or three times a year, at parties or on special occasions.

They cannot spoil, but parents should give them every opportunity to try. If you miss a nap or time to go to bed when your grandparents are visiting for a day or two, or if you are treated like royalty - more than your parents would like - you should let children enjoy special treatment from grandparents. Children will soon return to their normal routine after the visit.

As for the grandparents who live nearby, the situation could be more difficult, but even so, the children quickly learn that the rules change according to the territory: they can spread all the food on the table in the grandmother's house, but not in yours. So grandparents always have some freedom of action in some areas.

Grandparents can spoil (yes, spoil) their grandchildren with a little more of everything: love, time, material objects. But not to the point that this dedication regularly violates parental rules.

Certain rules that grandparents must abide by

Since parents are the ones who live with their children all day, it is they who must decide the rules on the most important questions. And grandparents, whether they are far or near, must abide by those rules even if they don't necessarily agree.

Bedtime, sugar consumption, junk food in the diet, how much television time are they allowed to watch... If parents want to stick to each of their rules, they should allow grandparents to negotiate some concessions for Occasionally.

But if grandparents overstep the bounds of what is fair for them to do, if they openly ignore or violate all the rules parents conscientiously set, it is time to speak out. With love and discretion, parents can explain to them how much they want them to spend time with their children, but how, by violating agreed rules, they can confuse them, alternate their schedules and family balance.

The psychologist Cecilia is absolutely right, so much love that grandparents have for their grandchildren, all the rules of parents are broken to their children, no father can discipline any grandchild in front of them.

Children always have their grandparents as shelter, the grandparents feel unworthy and very uncomfortable when the parents are disciplining the children. Sometimes they argue hard with parents about their grandchildren.

Grandmothers over forty to fifty years old would prefer to lose their own husbands and not their grandchildren, as they offer more. It is a fresh and life-filled experience, so grandchildren are your priorities. It is very difficult.

No one can understand the love of grandparents towards their grandchildren, sometimes they are very strong with their own children, they are much weaker with their grandchildren, it is something that is very great and very deep, which is inevitable for them.

Traditionally it is considered that a mother's love for her children is something very great, and if there is another love that can be compared to the mother's love as a human, it is the love of the grandmother.

But the love of God has no comparison, if a father wants to break all the rules inside his house, he leaves the grandfather or grandmother to live in the same house with the grandchildren. If so, you have to get used to the tricks and overprotections. And of course: to spoiling.

Chapter 33

The children's thanks to the parents

What is gratitude in reality?

It is an action of gratitude towards others that all human beings should have, it is a feeling of esteem and recognition that a person has towards someone who has done him a favor or rendered a service, for which he wishes to reciprocate.

It can be defined like this: gratitude is the feeling of gratitude that is normally experienced as a consequence of having received from someone something that was expected or needed, of having been helped in some difficult circumstance, among other situations.

Why should all children thank their parents?

Javiera Spröhnle exposed on March 15, 2017 on the page [upsocl.com], about the thanks to the parents. She said there are eight reasons why we should thank our parents. He started his exposition like this: "Thank you parents for" ruining our lives ", because if not, our lives would be ruined."

And continues:"I am only a few months away from becoming independent from my parents and I have had some crazy weeks. On the one hand, I am extremely excited to start building my own home, but on the other hand, I am deeply saddened to know that I will no longer see my parents every morning when I get up and every time the day ends.

"It is very nostalgic, but it has also been a nice process to reflect on many things, including everything my parents have done for me all these years (and they will surely continue to do so even if we are a little further away).

Things that sometimes, on a day-to-day basis - and especially in adolescence - I did not always value. Therefore, in this note I will repeat a thousand times: thank you mom and dad!

1.- For supporting jobs that you did not like

I know that many times you fell into jobs that did not make you happy and surely there was more than one morning on the way to the office you thought "I should look for something I like." I know that if I had been twenty years old and the only mouth you had to have fed had been yours, you would have done it right away.

I know that many times you endure nine or ten hours a day, doing something that did not fill you, in order to get home, look me in the eye and know that I was absolutely missing nothing.

2.- For your advice, even when I don't hear you

How many times have you not said to one of your parents "you don't understand me", or have you blamed them for "making your life impossible"? We forget that what we are going through, they already lived it. That his advice comes from experience and with the deepest love and concern.

We forget that even when we were punished or scolded, it was because they wanted the best for us. Thank you parents for "ruining our lives", because if not, our lives would be ruined.

3.- For never forgetting any detail

Thank you mom and dad because they never forgot anything they said or did. From the simplest, such as commenting on the desire that you had to eat a dish and that the next day there would be "magically" that for dinner, to the most complex as the dream of a trip that with a lot of effort made it come true. I had a hard time noticing, but in reality the "fairy godmothers" do exist and are disguised as parents.

4.- For loving me, just as I am

I think I can make an infinite list of mistakes that I have made in life — well, like everyone else — that an endless number of people have never forgiven me and for which more than a "poster" I have earned for life.

But with my parents, it doesn't matter how many times I'm wrong, they never stopped seeing me with that confident look, they never stopped believing in me and what I would become. Even when I doubted me, they never did.

5.- For being strong, when I was bad

You know If you ever think that you are suffering to the bone for something, your parents are probably suffering worse. They can live with their problems, but when they see us badly, they just feel like taking away all that pain and living it for us. There is nothing they want more in the world than to look happy and sometimes we don't even notice it.

6.- For accompanying me in all my triumphs

Even in the smallest, our parents celebrate them as the achievement of the year. They are proud, they tell everyone and even their hearts inflate more than ourselves. Thank you!

7.- For worrying that every moment of my life is perfect

Birthdays, Christmases, holidays, absolutely everything is magical when it is with you. They take care of every detail and I can always say that I keep the most beautiful memories of my childhood. Sometimes I would like to reproduce those moments a thousand times.

8.- In short, thank you for making me so happy...

Now I have to leave, I will have my own house, my own bills to pay, my own responsibilities, even someday I will have my own children and I sincerely hope to become at least half of how good my parents were with me. Because at his side, I have been SO happy.

In Javiera's exposition, she has highlighted, very gratefully, all the efforts of her parents and, although I do not know her Christian faith, it is evident that she has fulfilled the fifth commandment of God that says: "Honor your father and mother, so that your days may be prolonged in the land that Jehovah your God gives you": [Exodus 20:12].

Many parents have suffered hardships, sufferings, disappointments and humiliations as responsible parents; who have endured everything to ensure a good education for their children and security for their health and physical well-being.

Tomorrow, if the children return evil for good, if they do not ignore and dismiss the sacrifices of their parents, even if they have great wealth, it will never prosper for a long time, because the Bible never lies. Although there are many wicked, irresponsible parents, children should be grateful even if only for the life they were given, no one has wealth or money to pay for life.

The thanks to the mother

It is something that has no comparison, the love or the feeling of a mother for her son, although she does not have the fortune to educate him as it should be, only nine months in the womb is enough for the son to thank her for life.

The so many bad nights, the inconvenience, the bad state, so much pain that she spent with you in her belly, being able to get rid of that yoke by aborting you, however, she endured everything so that you could be what you are today. Before trying to hit or mistreat your mother, you should take a little time and think about her role in your life.

No one should worship a human being, because only God deserves all the adorations, the honor for ever and ever; When the Bible says honor your father and mother, it does not mean that children should adore them, it is saying that they should respect them and obey their orders.

That said, if a human being made of clay deserves worship, that is the mother. Of course, the primary responsibility for having a child is hers, since no child asks to come into the world, least of all in very poor conditions. But the truth is that the mother otherwise fulfills a biological need designed by God himself. So he had no other.

Most of the parents who have received good treatment and respect in front of their children, are those who have good economies, businessmen, professionals.

Children do not respect them only as their parents, also for wealth, with all the pride in the world they present to all their friends as their parents, as they admire their achievements and the way they have succeeded in life. They are their models.

But if they don't have anything, not even a family name, they will harbor the frustration of being the children of losers. That they only had children by chance, not because they were prepared or because they deserved it. Although they love them, they will never see him as role models.

They will even fear to bequeath their genes to their future offspring... And a long etcetera of bitterness.

Many are the men and women who have succeeded in the world, who are ashamed to present their parents, neither on television nor in the networks, not even in a social activity. They are bad grateful people who do not know or value the efforts of their parents that allowed them to become what they are.

That in case they have made such efforts, because, otherwise, well: each one reaps what he sows.

If the parents are very old and can no longer work, if the children do not have enough time to support them, they must not leave them alone or abandoned, they must pay a person to give all the necessary care, they must visit them frequently, they must always call them on the phone, the children must change as supervisors to go see how the employee is taking care of their old men.

What does the bible say about thanksgiving?

We must be grateful for everything, we cannot be ungrateful or ungrateful like fools, because it is the fools who, with their foolishness and irrational pride, who do not recognize the efforts of others in their favor Dr. Luke has explained that scene very clearly so that everyone can understand it.

He transcribed the words of the great Master thus: «And it came to pass, as he went to Jerusalem, that he passed through the midst of Samaria and Galilee. And as he entered into a certain village, there met him ten men that were lepers, which stood afar off: And they lifted up their voices, and said, Jesus, Master, have mercy on us.

And when he saw them, he said unto them, Go shew yourselves unto the priests. And it came to pass, that, as they went, they were cleansed. And one of them, when he saw that he was healed, turned back, and with a loud voice glorified God, and fell down on his face at his feet, giving him thanks: and he was a Samaritan.

And Jesus answering said, Were there not ten cleansed? but where are the nine? There are not found that returned to give glory to God, save this stranger. And he said unto him, Arise, go thy way: thy faith hath made thee whole»: [Luke 17: 11-19].

That story resembles that of a stepfather or stepmother who has raised their children together with a stepchild, and sometimes legitimate children are ungrateful to their parents: it is the stepson who has known all the sacrifices in his favor, because he clearly knows that he is not a legitimate child.

Why only the foreigner returned to thank the Master?

That fact indicates very clearly to us that foreigners are more grateful than citizens themselves, and although Jesus said that, gratitude has nothing to do with nationality.

It is an act of courtesy, you must learn it in the first school that is the home, for that reason, all parents must teach their children to thank for everything, when they grew up, they will make that law in their mind and conduct.

Not only did he heal him from his illness, Jesus saved him too, he received great blessings. The ungrateful can never fully prosper, they will always lack something. The big problem of them is their pride in too much, they feel too big to thank.

Since Jesus is a God of love, he has a very special message for all the proud, he said: «I know your works, that you are neither cold nor hot. I wish you were hot or cold! But since you are lukewarm, and neither cold nor hot, I will vomit you out of my mouth.

Because you say: I am rich, and I have become rich, and I have no need of anything; and you don't know that you are a hapless, miserable, poor, blind and naked person. Therefore, I advise you to buy gold refined in fire from me, so that you may be rich, and white garments to clothe yourself, and that the shame of your nakedness should not be discovered.

And anoint your eyes with eye drops so that you can see. I rebuke and punish all I love; be zealous therefore, and repent». [Revelation 3: 15-19].

Jesus is saying that he knows that you are proud and evil; that you can never humbly acknowledge the person who did you a good or a favor, I wish you were grateful!

You think that you have everything, that you do not need anyone, but it does not cross your mind that you are alive only because of that breath God gives you, and that at any moment it can extinguish it, because you are nothing and nobody without Jesus.

Jesus' advice is that if you want to be a person of great value, you must buy it from the Holy Spirit so that it can make a total change in your life.

Psychologist Arturo Torres listed seven characteristics of a grateful person:

1.- They thank us in a strategic way

It is clear that, if we think about it, any pro-social behavior can be seen as a strategy to obtain benefits in return. However, in practice, when we do things that benefit others, we don't usually stop to think about how that will benefit us. This is another key that helps to identify grateful people: they give thanks spontaneously, instinctively, without that being due to a calculation of costs or benefits.

2.- They show appreciation to everyone

For grateful people, showing gratitude is one more element that comes into play frequently in personal relationships. For this reason, they do so regardless of the degree of friendship or the intensity of the emotional bond that unites that person.

This is especially important in adulthood, a vital stage in which the number of close friends is relatively small, and therefore most of the people with whom you interact are relatively unknown.

Basically, this characteristic is related to the previous one, since the cases in which gratitude is expressed towards people with whom you do not have much contact, most likely, the opportunity does not appear that they can return the kind gesture.

3.- They use creativity to show gratitude

Grateful people are grateful in every way that thanks can be given; they are not limited to a single category of "material gifts" or "thank you notes." Any context, with any type of resource, it is possible to reveal what is valued and appreciated what someone has done for us, and putting a little imagination, the idea of what to do to express it appears easily.

4.- They adapt their message to the person to whom they direct it

Something to keep in mind when expressing gratitude is the knowledge you have about the tastes and personality of the person to whom the message is addressed. After all, if you want to convey a feeling of well-being, it makes sense to maximize this effect by adapting the way you say thank you.

5.- They don't always wait for celebrations

Why be constrained by the calendar when giving thanks? There are no reasons to stop being grateful people during the days that go from one celebration to the next. Beyond birthdays and Christmas, there are many other times when you can give gifts or make dedications. The message is even more powerful precisely when any day comes.

6.- They are fair in their personal relationships

Just because you are grateful people does not mean that you have a natural tendency towards candor or altruism, but it does mean that you tend to offer fair treatment to everyone.

Beyond the image that is offered to others when it comes to speaking or the ease of making friends and liking others, who is grateful integrates this fact in his way of seeing human relationships, and these are governed by the idea that justice is important.

7.- Make sure that the other person understands the message

It is no use giving thanks if the person to whom this symbolic action is directed does not interpret this sign of gratitude as such. It is not a question of gaining positive points in front of her, but the important thing is that she is aware that she has given someone reasons to thank, which says a lot in her favor.

Professionals, like the Bible, are in favor of gratitude, the parents' job is to help you be what you are today, tomorrow it will be your turn with them: "Then said Jesus unto him, Put up again thy sword into his place: for all they that take the sword shall perish with the sword": [Matthew 26:52].

Jesus again repeats the same warning: "He that leadeth into captivity shall go into captivity: he that killeth with the sword must be killed with the sword. Here is the patience and the faith of the saints": [Revelation 13:10].

All the bad decisions that you have made, you must pay on earth before dying, your mistake will be from generation to generation, it is the norm of life. If you sow the air you must reap the storm. If you want to be successful in everything, you must love your neighbor as yourself.

Chapter 34

About me

My name is Jacquelin Xavier. I was born in a small town called Dilaire! very close to the Haitian city of Ouanaminthe, located at the height of the province of Dajabón, Dominican Republic.

My parents' story

My dad was born into a military family. His father was a colonel in the Haitian armed forces at the time. His parents were preparing him to be a military, just like his younger brothers, but he took the path of teaching. Over time, he was appointed as the director of a public school in that town.

He had loves with an illiterate woman of that time who became my beloved mother. His illiteracy was due to the educational neglect of that time, especially towards women.

They never cared about the education of the females. As chauvinists, they thought that the work destination of women was housework. Females were not the same value as males.

After a long time of waiting, he became committed to her. By the date of the marriage, she was five months pregnant. Two months before the wedding, that gentleman committed a devastating crime that separated the family: he raped my mother's first cousin.

The girl's dad found him in the act. A single path opened to a bloodless and disgraceful future: to marry them as soon as possible. At that time my mom had three big problems:

1.- The house where that new marriage would live, was built with my mom's money, because that man did not have enough money to build a house.

2.- Not only were they cousins, they were best friends.

3.- she was a maiden and a virgin, it was with that man who lost his virginity, she also loved him very much. Therefore he felt helpless, with much indignation, bitterness, incapacity. She is alive because God had to enter that situation and because of the presence of the good doctors of that time.

After that painful test for her and the family, he took advantage of their vulnerability to continue having more children with both of them, putting them in a situation of extreme embarrassment and humiliation, unbearable, especially since they were two illiterates.

Since he knew very well that there was love between the two, he sexually exploited them in the best patriarchal and alpha male style and, it must be pointed out: cowardly.

He had my mom as a prostitute. Every time she gave birth to a baby, at two-year intervals, he brought the boy to the cousin. He had three women with twenty-one children in the same locality: they all died, only five of us remained.

My birth

I have not come from a close family, like that of many children. My birth to this day is a long story, and I know that there are many children who are going through many critical situations in this world because of the fault of a father or a mother.

I do not write this book so that no one decides to take revenge, I am witnessing my story for all those who are descending into their own hells, and learn to love and forgive the guilty, because through the study of the Bible, I see things very different, and although it sounds implausible, I never hated my father, I always loved him.

It seems that something similar happened in Ephesians. The apostle Paul revealed where the problem arose; a knowledge that was convenient for me, and it will help you who are going through the same situation. He said: «For we wrestle not against flesh and blood, but against principalities, against powers, against the rulers of the darkness of this world, against spiritual wickedness in high places.

Wherefore take unto you the whole armour of God, that ye may be able to withstand in the evil day, and having done all, to stand. Stand therefore, having your loins girt about with truth, and having on the breastplate of righteousness;

And your feet shod with the preparation of the gospel of peace; above all, taking the shield of faith, wherewith ye shall be able to quench all the fiery darts of the wicked.

And take the helmet of salvation, and the sword of the Spirit, which is the word of God: Praying always with all prayer and supplication in the Spirit, and watching thereunto with all perseverance and supplication for all saints». [Ephesians 6: 12-18].

So, all the evils of my father were the works of the enemy of which he was a simple medium. So I have never condemned him in any way, on the contrary: I love him very much.

My mother was in the middle of a storm with no exit for many years, because she couldn't cope with my dad's lifestyle, although everything was difficult for her, in the midst of suffering, she found a solution to completely end that bitter relationship; one that from the very beginning was demeaning.

One Tuesday at noon, my grandmother went to the supermarket, her youngest children — her little brothers — were playing on the patio with the doors open. At the time, my future mother was in a deep sleep, my future father took advantage of that carelessness to meet her again, without her consent. The result of that rape was me. As you can see, there was nothing noble in my gestation and birth.

She was trapped in any way with that man, so that she could get out of that hell, she had to marry another man without wanting, without feeling any passion and love for him. However, he knew that my mother was not in love, that she was with him out of obligation, but he treated her very well, and me too.

But in truth, I did not feel well with him or his children, because the part of my dad that is in me, claimed his presence. So I left my stepfather's house to go to my grandmother's house where I could see my dad and my brothers frequently.

The following year, I had to leave my grandmother's house to join my royal family, within which I felt good and comfortable. I was not welcome by my stepmother, because she did not treat me the same as her own children. For me it was nothing, because I felt good with the whole family.

My dad's vices

My dad was the biggest gambler in the region, he was not only a womanizer, he did not respect anyone's wife, he slept with the wives of all his friends; He had different addictions: alcoholism and gambling like the great player he was. He never worried about the education of his children, all his money was for his vices. His passions were foreign women, alcohol and gambling.

He had three main days to practice his addictions: Wednesdays, Saturdays and Sundays. He always came home drunk, but he never hit us under the influence of alcohol.

Sometimes he peed on his pants. Until today, he has not attempted to abandon his customs, since they are already part of his nature: they define him as a human being.

My growth

At my early age, God put me on his path, although I came from a vicious and corrupt family — I have the blood of a womanizer because it is a genetic inheritance — God fought hard with me so that I could be in the Seventh-day Adventist church until today.

God has strong control over me; Every time I want to shake my wings to reclaim my father's blood as a womanizer, God commands me "stop! You have not been born by chance, since before I was born I know you and I claim you to be my servant".

All my male siblings have taken my father's inheritance: many children with different mothers. But until now, God is in control of my life. My whole family is Roman Catholic, I am the only person who is a Christian, for me it is a great blessing.

My education

I had to leave my town and my family very young to go to the capital, Port-au-Prince, to the home of my mom's family without knowing her physically, in order to look for what I had not found in my dad's house, which it was a better education.

As a youngster I worked very hard in discriminatory and humiliating conditions, but shielded behind a positive mindset and unafraid of life's challenges. All in order to become a good professional like every human being worthy of being considered as such.

I always did it with the help of God, who never failed me and gave me the lights to get the necessary money, not only to finish my secondary studies, but also the university ones. With my own effort; without the help of any human agent but of divinity.

In the midst of suffering, I armed myself with three psalms: 91, 23, and 27. They strengthened my purpose to be great in life, without giving back to Satan or his human representatives who always intervened in my way; turned into an eagle that flew above all the storms unleashed by human pettiness; knowing that there was no Canaan without a desert.

After the turbulence the clouds of the purest white appear against the background of the bluest sky; that without the test of pain one does not reach success... What on the other side of the descent into hell that we all must do in imitation of Christ, awaits us a life of achievements and useful to the plan of God!

No one has been born in this world to be suffered, all children need a decent home or family, where they can receive a good family and intellectual formation to face life in the future. They are tomorrow.

All those children who are going through a situation similar to the one I went through, must seek the presence of God, because it is the only solution and the path that can lead them to a better tomorrow.

What should you do in that situation?

Never give up on your fight. You must fight to the death, if you have to die you must die fighting, nobody can win without fighting. Jesus always leads those who are fighting, not the cowards.

The good fighter does not think about his nationality, his rank or his color. He always has in his mind that everyone is equal. In the fight there are many people who will remind you of your past, or your offspring, to get discouraged.

Never twist your arm, you must continue fighting with more force, the victory does not depend on how you arrived, you won or the amount of time, the most important thing is the arrival.

I repeat by way of clarification.

As a family victim, I do not write this book so that no one has the pretext of taking revenge on the family that was lucky. On the contrary, as a victim and a servant of God, I want to see a different world where all children can be born and raised in a nest that fills their lives with love and peace. Therefore, we must make a difference starting today.

My behavior towards my father

From an early age, my mom told me about her past with my dad. As an illiterate woman, she was not explaining that bitter story to me to hate my father, just so I could know her story. Thus, as a person who has been educated without the help of a father, I have never hated my father in any way.

In fact, I love him very much, and I must confess that I do not have enough gold or diamonds to pay him for giving me life. At least he educated me until the eighth grade, a base without which I could not have embarked on my path throughout life.

My recommendation: all children should be very grateful to their parents, even if they have never done anything for their life except give it to them. And that life that came from them is priceless.

I hope all those people who are reading this book can put all these tips into practice so that we can have an exemplary family where children can find good training for a better tomorrow.

The grace of the Lord Jesus Christ, and the love of God, and the communion of the Holy Spirit be with all readers of this book today and always. Amen. Maranatha!

Made in the USA
Columbia, SC
29 September 2020